Mastering Micross CRM 2016

An advanced guide for effective Dynamics CRM
customization and development

Deepesh Somani

BIRMINGHAM - MUMBAI

Mastering Microsoft Dynamics CRM 2016

First published: November 2017

Production reference: 1271117

Published by Packt Publishing Ltd.
Livery Place
35 Livery Street
Birmingham
B3 2PB, UK.
ISBN 978-1-78646-661-7

www.packtpub.com

Credits

Author
Deepesh Somani

Reviewer
Nishant Rana

Commissioning Editor
Amarabha Banerjee

Acquisition Editor
Chaitanya Nair

Content Development Editor
Vikas Tiwari

Technical Editor
Jijo Maliyekal

Copy Editor
Muktikant Garimella

Project Coordinator
Vaidehi Sawant

Proofreader
Safis Editing

Indexer
Francy Puthiry

Graphics
Tom Scaria

Production Coordinator
Arvindkumar Gupta

About the Author

Deepesh Somani currently works as a Microsoft Dynamics 365 lead architect, a corporate trainer, and an author. He has been Microsoft's Most Valuable Professional awardee for 3 consecutive years, making his way into the top 90 CRM professionals in the world. He is currently working in an IT start-up called Dynamisity Private Limited, based out of Ahmedabad, India.

With his fervor for the technology and constant adherence, Deepesh has been an active contributor to the global technical community and has been honored as a key contributor on leader boards from time to time.

His blog (https://dynamicsofdynamicscrm.com/) has more than 270,000 hits and 500+ followers from 150 countries worldwide. It was recognized as one of the top 100 CRM blogs worldwide by Feedspot in 2017. He developed 14 free tools with 7000+ downloads, and a Dynamics app with around 1000+ downloads and a 4.4 rating.

Deepesh has extensive experience working in different domains, such as banking, public sector, telecommunication, and retail, to name a few, with teams from different parts of the world and with renowned multinational companies such as Microsoft, Infosys, and SanDisk.

As a passionate explorer, he enjoys travelling, interacting with people of various ethnicities, trying different foods, and dancing.

Acknowledgment

I would like to thank all the people who helped me during the journey of writing this book, which has involved passing through severe health conditions. A special note of thanks to my wife, Yamini, without whose support this book would not have been possible. I dedicate this book to my parents. I would also like to thank the professional and extensive support offered by the team at Packt, including Chaitanya Nair, Anurag Ghogre, Vikas Tiwari, Vaidehi Sawant, Jijo Maliyekal, and Muktikant Garimella. A big thanks to Nishant Rana, who reviewed this book extensively.

Sincere thanks to Simaranjit Singh Bhalla, for the code contributions. He helped me when I was struggling with my health and was bed ridden for 3 months. I cannot thank him enough for this. I've known him for 8 years now; he is a Dynamics 365 consultant working in SMS management and technology in Sydney, Australia. His expertise lies in requirements gathering, creating technical design documents, providing project estimates, and handling technical development tasks of a team. He has extensive experience in Microsoft technology stack. He has executed multiple successful engagements in Dynamics CRM, .Net, SSIS, and SSRS. His forte is in Dynamics CRM, wherein he has been working since CRM 4.0. He also maintains a technical blog on Dynamics 365.
He is a good friend and a great human being.

Last but not least, thanks Microsoft and the Microsoft community for letting me have the experiences to author this book. Happy CRMing as usual!

About the Reviewer

Nishant Rana is a Microsoft MVP – Business Solutions (Dynamics 365) with over 10 years of experience in Microsoft Dynamics CRM, Microsoft SharePoint, and other Microsoft .NET technologies. He is a Microsoft Certified Professional in Microsoft Dynamics CRM, SharePoint, and Microsoft .NET. He has been the technical reviewer of books on Microsoft Dynamics CRM, such as *Microsoft Dynamics CRM 2015 Application Design, CRM 2013 Quick Start, Microsoft Dynamics 2011 Application Design*, and *Microsoft Dynamics 2011 Reporting*. He is an avid blogger and likes to learn, help, share, and contribute to the Dynamics CRM community. Nishant is also the author of *Nishant Rana's Weblog*, a technical blog on Microsoft .NET technologies, which has more than 2.5 million hits and 1,000 followers. This blog has also been recognized as one of the top 35 blogs on Microsoft Dynamics CRM and was also one of the top 100 CRM blogs and websites for small and large businesses by Feedspot. You can follow Nishant on Twitter via his handle, `@nishantranaCRM`.

I would like to thank Packt and the author for giving me the opportunity to technically review this book. This is my fourth book with Packt as a technical reviewer. The experience has been wonderful. Looking forward to further collaboration.

www.PacktPub.com

For support files and downloads related to your book, please visit www.PacktPub.com.

Did you know that Packt offers eBook versions of every book published, with PDF and ePub files available? You can upgrade to the eBook version at www.PacktPub.com and as a print book customer, you are entitled to a discount on the eBook copy. Get in touch with us at service@packtpub.com for more details.

At www.PacktPub.com, you can also read a collection of free technical articles, sign up for a range of free newsletters and receive exclusive discounts and offers on Packt books and eBooks.

https://www.packtpub.com/mapt

Get the most in-demand software skills with Mapt. Mapt gives you full access to all Packt books and video courses, as well as industry-leading tools to help you plan your personal development and advance your career.

Why subscribe?

- Fully searchable across every book published by Packt
- Copy and paste, print, and bookmark content
- On demand and accessible via a web browser

Customer Feedback

Thanks for purchasing this Packt book. At Packt, quality is at the heart of our editorial process. To help us improve, please leave us an honest review on this book's Amazon page at https://www.amazon.com/dp/1786466619.

If you'd like to join our team of regular reviewers, you can e-mail us at customerreviews@packtpub.com. We award our regular reviewers with free eBooks and videos in exchange for their valuable feedback. Help us be relentless in improving our products!

Table of Contents

Preface

Microsoft Dynamics CRM is the most trusted name in enterprise-level customer relationship management. The latest version of Microsoft Dynamics CRM comes with the important addition of some exciting features guaranteed to make your life easier with Dynamics CRM.

This book provides a comprehensive coverage of Dynamics CRM 2016 and helps you make your tasks much simpler while elevating you to the level of an expert.

The book starts with a brief overview of the functional features and then introduces the latest features of Dynamics CRM 2016. You will learn to create Word and Excel templates using CRM data, which will enable you to provide customized data analysis for your organization. You will understand how to utilize Dynamics CRM as an XRM framework. You will gain a deep understanding about client-side scripting in Dynamics CRM and learn to create client-side applications using JavaScript and Web API. Extending your CRM applications is described, along with introducing visual control frameworks for Dynamics CRM 2016 mobile and tablet applications. The book then moves on to introducing Business Process Flows, Business Rules, and their enhancements. By the end of this book, you will have mastered Dynamics CRM 2016 features through real-world scenarios.

What this book covers

Chapter 1, *History of Dynamics CRM*, covers the history of Microsoft Dynamics CRM and gives an overview of the functional entities of Dynamics CRM 2016, including the Sales, Service, and Marketing modules.

Chapter 2, *Working with Sales*, covers the Dynamics CRM Sales module, which supports the typical sales cycle followed in any organization. It automates the entire process, starting with the acquisition of a new Lead until its logical conclusion, in the form of either a lost or won opportunity. The Sales module in Dynamics CRM helps organizations provide effective selling capabilities. It helps the organization to track the sales activities and see their sales pipeline.

Chapter 3, *Working with Services*, explores the Service module in Dynamics CRM, which helps organizations provide effective service capabilities by automating the entire process of providing a resolution to the problems of the customer, aiding the customer by means of Knowledge base, and so on.

Chapter 4, *Working with Marketing*, gives an in-depth understanding of the Marketing module of Dynamics CRM, which helps the organization by creating leads that can then be targeted by the Sales module.

Chapter 5, *Working with the XRM Framework*, explains the XRM framework, which defines a strategic approach to customize the out-of-box features available in Dynamics CRM to make sure that it implements all the business aspects of a system.

Chapter 6, *Analytics with CRM*, focuses on introducing and using advanced analytical features available in Dynamics CRM 2016. The chapter covers some features available within the Dynamics CRM 2016 product offering, provides ways to enhance the analytics experience using other Microsoft product offerings, and explains how this can be interconnected with Dynamics CRM 2016.

Chapter 7, *Workflow Development with Dynamics CRM*, covers workflows, which are the handlers for the events fired by Dynamics CRM. You can either utilize workflows using a native drag-and-drop interface, or extend the standard behavior of Dynamics CRM using customizations with custom code written in the .NET framework.

Chapter 8, *Client-Side Scripting*, focuses on introducing and using client-side enhancements available with Dynamics CRM 2016. The chapter covers some client-side script functions with examples and also discusses the Web API in the later part, which is a new way of querying CRM data directly from JavaScript.

Chapter 9, *Enhancements for Mobile*, extensively covers the newly introduced mobile and tablet capabilities of Dynamics CRM 2016.

Chapter 10, *Plugin Development with Dynamics CRM*, explains plugins, which are the handlers for events fired by Dynamics CRM.

Chapter 11, *Business Process Flows and Business Rules*, takes you through various scenarios that will explain Business Process Flows and Business Rules in detail.

Chapter 12, *New Features in CRM 2016*, focuses on covering some small but awesome features that have been left uncovered in the rest of the scenarios presented in this book. It also covers some of the features already discussed in the book again for a quick reference and every such feature is explained by means of a business scenario.

What you need for this book

You will need Visual Studio 2015 for development tools and the Dynamics CRM 2016 online or on-premise edition for the CRM tools.

Refer to the following link to check the platforms compatible with Microsoft Dynamics CRM 2016:

```
https://support.microsoft.com/en-in/help/3124955/compatibility-with-microsoft-dynamics-crm-2016
```

Refer to the following link for a list of supported web browsers and mobile devices:

```
https://technet.microsoft.com/en-us/library/dn531055.aspx
```

Who this book is for

This book is for those with Dynamics CRM knowledge who want to utilize the latest features available with Dynamics CRM 2016 and Update 1. Extensive Dynamics CRM development experience would be beneficial.

Conventions

In this book, you will find a number of text styles that distinguish between different kinds of information. Here are some examples of these styles and an explanation of their meaning.

Code words in text, database table names, folder names, filenames, file extensions, pathnames, dummy URLs, user input, and Twitter handles are shown as follows: "We can include other contexts through the use of the `include` directive."

```
using Microsoft.Xrm.Sdk.Query;

namespace SamplePluginProject
{
  public class PreCreateUpdateAccountSamplePlugin : IPlugin
  {
    public void Execute(IServiceProvider serviceProvider)
    {
    }
  }
}
```

When we wish to draw your attention to a particular part of a code block, the relevant lines or items are set in bold:

```
using Microsoft.Xrm.Sdk.Query;

namespace SamplePluginProject
{
   public class PreCreateUpdateAccountSamplePlugin : IPlugin
   {
     public void Execute(IServiceProvider serviceProvider)
     {
     }
   }
}
```

New terms and **important words** are shown in bold. Words that you see on the screen, for example, in menus or dialog boxes, appear in the text like this: "In order to download new modules, we will go to **Files** | **Settings** | **Project Name** | **Project Interpreter**."

Warnings or important notes appear like this.

Tips and tricks appear like this.

Reader feedback

Feedback from our readers is always welcome. Let us know what you think about this book-what you liked or disliked. Reader feedback is important for us as it helps us develop titles that you will really get the most out of. To send us general feedback, simply email feedback@packtpub.com, and mention the book's title in the subject of your message. If there is a topic that you have expertise in and you are interested in either writing or contributing to a book, see our author guide at www.packtpub.com/authors.

Customer support

Now that you are the proud owner of a Packt book, we have a number of things to help you to get the most from your purchase.

Downloading the example code

You can download the example code files for this book from your account at `http://www.packtpub.com`. If you purchased this book elsewhere, you can visit `http://www.packtpub.com/support` and register to have the files emailed directly to you. You can download the code files by following these steps:

1. Log in or register to our website using your email address and password.
2. Hover the mouse pointer on the **SUPPORT** tab at the top.
3. Click on **Code Downloads & Errata**.
4. Enter the name of the book in the **Search** box.
5. Select the book for which you're looking to download the code files.
6. Choose from the drop-down menu where you purchased this book from.
7. Click on **Code Download**.

Once the file is downloaded, please make sure that you unzip or extract the folder using the latest version of:

- WinRAR / 7-Zip for Windows
- Zipeg / iZip / UnRarX for Mac
- 7-Zip / PeaZip for Linux

The code bundle for the book is also hosted on GitHub at `https://github.com/PacktPublishing/Mastering-Microsoft-Dynamics-CRM-2016`. We also have other code bundles from our rich catalog of books and videos available at `https://github.com/PacktPublishing/`. Check them out!

Errata

Although we have taken every care to ensure the accuracy of our content, mistakes do happen. If you find a mistake in one of our books-maybe a mistake in the text or the code-we would be grateful if you could report this to us. By doing so, you can save other readers from frustration and help us improve subsequent versions of this book. If you find any errata, please report them by visiting http://www.packtpub.com/submit-errata, selecting your book, clicking on the **Errata Submission Form** link, and entering the details of your errata. Once your errata are verified, your submission will be accepted and the errata will be uploaded to our website or added to any list of existing errata under the Errata section of that title. To view the previously submitted errata, go to https://www.packtpub.com/books/content/support and enter the name of the book in the search field. The required information will appear under the **Errata** section.

Piracy

Piracy of copyrighted material on the internet is an ongoing problem across all media. At Packt, we take the protection of our copyright and licenses very seriously. If you come across any illegal copies of our works in any form on the internet, please provide us with the location address or website name immediately so that we can pursue a remedy. Please contact us at copyright@packtpub.com with a link to the suspected pirated material. We appreciate your help in protecting our authors and our ability to bring you valuable content.

Questions

If you have a problem with any aspect of this book, you can contact us at questions@packtpub.com, and we will do our best to address the problem.

1
History of Dynamics CRM

Microsoft Dynamics CRM was first introduced in 2003 as Microsoft CRM 1.0. It had far fewer functionalities, which focused on the Sales and Service modules. Organizations faced some difficulties as the customization capabilities were limited and the business process were harder to map with the processes in the system. This product targeted the organizations working with relationship management.

After this version, Microsoft launched Dynamics 3.0 in 2005 instead of 2.0. The UI was enhanced and the Marketing module was introduced with this version. The customization capabilities were also increased. The XRM platform was used to create and enhance applications on Dynamics CRM. Due to this, some more features, such as integration with Outlook 2007, integration with Microsoft SQL, and reporting services were possible.

In December 2007, Microsoft introduced Dynamics 4.0, also called *Titan*. There were no major changes made with the GUI, but many platform changes were made. CRM Online was introduced in North America, which provided customers with the option of hosting the CRM on cloud. It also had improved security features, data importing functionalities, mail merge, and support for operating systems such as Windows 2008 and SQL 2008. This version provided options for selecting multiple currencies and choice of base languages. Plugins and workflows were introduced with this version, which increased the capabilities of the platform.

Microsoft released a beta version, Microsoft Dynamics 2011, in February 2010. The full release was released in February 2011. Features such as charts and dashboards were introduced with this version, which allowed the users to visualize the data in a pictorial format. It provided a 360-degree view of customer profile, which enhanced productivity. Solutions were also introduced in this version.

With the release of Microsoft Dynamics 2013, it was possible to run Microsoft Dynamics CRM on any browser from a tablet device powered by Windows 8 or iOS and any smartphones running Windows Phone 8, Android, or IOS. The popups were also reduced, which was a significant change. Business rules and real-time workflows were introduced in Microsoft Dynamics 2013. This reduced the need to embed code in plugins, thus reducing the customization effort required on the platform.

With the release of Microsoft Dynamics by Microsoft in September 2014, more features, such as Rollup and Calculated fields, one-note integration, themes, pause and resume SLAs, and so on, were introduced. Business rules were enhanced more, and it was now possible to embed more complex logic in the conditions. Business Process Flows didn't have in-built features, which prevented the movement of stage if some of the mandatory steps were not completed.

In November 2015, Microsoft Dynamics 2016 was released with features such as Word and Excel templates. With this version, it was possible to integrate CRM with other products such as SharePoint, Azure, and Power BI, which provided better cross-selling.

Microsoft Dynamics CRM 2016 overview

Now that we've gone through the history of Microsoft Dynamics CRM and how it evolved during the years, let's get an overview of Microsoft Dynamics CRM 2016.

Sales module

The Sales module in Dynamics CRM takes care of the entire sales process and the activities involved in sales. The Sales module has entities such as **Contacts**, **Accounts**, **Leads**, and **Opportunity**. These entities are used to store the information required in the sales process:

- **Account**: Account stores the information related to your customers, which can be a company or an organization. It can also contain records of stakeholders, vendors, business partners, or other organizations you interact with.
- **Contact**: This stores the information related to the people or individuals that are generally your customers or contacts of customers. Contacts are mostly related to a customer. Sometimes, a contact is not linked to any customer. In such cases, they are not related to any account.

- **Lead**: Leads are the potential customers generated from multiple sources, such as entering them manually, from company website, mails, or from other social media. If the lead is qualified, then they are converted to an opportunity.
- **Opportunity**: When your customer responds or shows some interest, then your **Lead** is converted to an **Opportunity**. An **Opportunity** can be *won* or *lost*.

Sales life cycle

Generally, the sales life cycle starts with **Lead** generation. A lead is your potential customer. When an individual or a company shows any interest in your product/service and provides some details for further communication, then it is considered a lead:

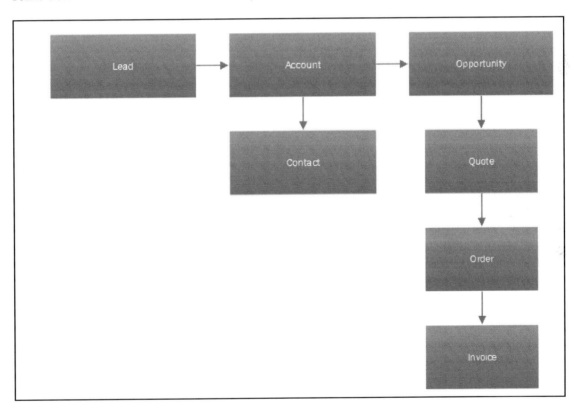

The salesperson either manually enters the details of the lead into the CRM or captures the details through mails, websites, phone calls, campaigns, and so on. It requires a lead name (first name and last name) and a topic that describes the lead.

After lead creation, the salesperson does multiple activities to convert it to a customer. This can be done in form of appointments, phone calls, and emails to gather more information about the customer. If the customer gives a positive response, then **Lead** is qualified to an **Opportunity**. A contact and an account record is created after lead qualification. If the lead is disqualified, the sales process ends.

Once the lead is qualified, the salesperson gives quotes to the customer. Quotes can be revised multiple times until the customer agrees. Once the customer agrees with the quote, the opportunity is won; otherwise, the opportunity is lost and the sales process ends.

After winning an opportunity, an order is placed and an invoice is created after the order is delivered to the customer.

Marketing

The marketing module of Dynamics CRM is designed to track all the marketing activities. It mainly consists of **Marketing Lists** and **Campaigns**. This module helps in analyzing the marketing efforts, which can be tracked back in the future. The Marketing module keeps track of all the marketing expenses and tracks the **Return on Investments(ROI)** gained from the marketing efforts.

Marketing life cycle

The marketing life cycle starts with creating **Marketing Lists** and distributing **Campaign** to **Marketing List**. **Marketing List** is made up of records in accounts, contacts, and leads. One can market new products to the existing customers or contacts and other references:

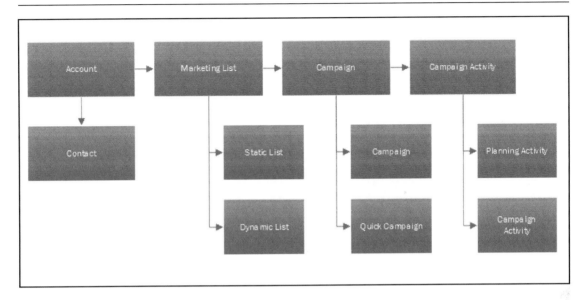

The responses from the campaigns are recorded and new leads are generated. After lead generation, marketing executives can pitch your product or service to those leads.

Marketing list

Marketing in Dynamics CRM generally starts with having marketing lists on place. A marketing list is a collection of accounts, contacts, and leads. Marketing lists are created to distribute a campaign.

Marketing lists can be static or dynamic:

- **Static list**: In a static marketing list, members are added manually.
- **Dynamic list**: In a dynamic marketing List, members in the list are added using an advanced find. When a new record is created that meets the criteria in the query, then it is also added to the marketing list.

Campaigns

Campaigns are a part of the Marketing module in CRM. Campaigns are conducted for the promotion of products/services provided by the business. It is a coordinated series of steps that includes the promotion of your products/services, which will eventually increase your sell. It is a way of reaching out to customers, building your brand, introducing your product in the market, and having a positive impact on the customers and leads.

Microsoft Dynamics 365 makes things easier as it provides you end-to-end help, from planning different activities to accounting your **Return on Investment (ROI)** from each campaign.

Working with Campaigns in Dynamics 365

The Marketing module in Dynamics 365 has Campaigns and Quick Campaigns. Before starting with a Campaign, you need to have your marketing lists in place. A marketing list is made up of leads, accounts, and contacts. So, your campaign will be distributed through marketing lists.

After that, you need to plan your campaign. Planning activities help you with organizing and executing your campaign. CRM has different planning activities that will assist you in planning a campaign.

Planning activities

Dynamics CRM helps you with the following planning activities:

- Organizing a meeting with key stakeholders for a marketing project
- Preparing promotional materials for a campaign
- Creating marketing lists for a target audience

Now let's talk about campaign activities. While conducting a campaign, you need to perform different activities. In Dynamics 365, campaign activities are distributed into emails, phone calls, appointments, and letters. It is a way of reaching your customers. They are distributed to the members, that is, the accounts, contacts, and leads in marketing lists. You cannot distribute your campaign without having a marketing list associated.

You can also track your financial costs such as allocated budget, miscellaneous costs, and expected revenue.

The response to a campaign

Response is nothing but interest, in the context of marketing. After organizing a campaign, the responses to the campaign are collected and recorded. The records for responses can be created manually. You can also generate responses through email tracking. These responses generate leads to sell your product.

Quick Campaigns

When you want to complete a campaign in a short duration, you can choose Quick Campaigns. They are a simplified version of campaigns, wherein only a single activity is included. You do not track the entire campaign in this case.

Campaigns versus Quick Campaigns

A quick campaign is nothing but distributing a single activity to marketing lists, that is, a distributed list of accounts, contacts, and leads. The duration of a Quick Campaign is short and fast. It does not have any built-in metrics.

Whereas, campaigns are of longer duration. Multiple activities are involved throughout a campaign. You can associate target products, price lists, and sales literature with a campaign. It supports planning and has built-in metrics.

Service

The Service module of Microsoft Dynamics CRM helps you in tracking all the activities performed to provide customer service in your organization. The entities that store the data and information related to services are Case, Knowledge Base, and Contracts.

Once the customer becomes a part of the system, your organization needs to provide support for the product or service you sold. Therefore, the customer may make a phone call to raise an issue regarding the product. The customer service agents will come forward and help the customer with resolving the case. The Service module of Microsoft Dynamics CRM supports the tasks that are necessary for service management.

Service life cycle

The Service life cycle starts with case creation. The case is assigned to a customer service representative and the activities are tracked by CRM until the case is resolved:

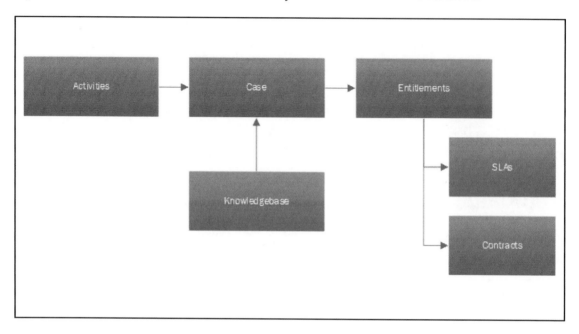

Activities

Activities help you in keeping track of the interactions made with the customers for resolving a case. To resolve a case, a customer service representative may perform multiple activities to converse with the customer. In Microsoft Dynamics CRM, the service activities are categorized into the following:

- Phone call
- Task
- Email
- Appointments

You can convert an email or a phone call to a case.

Case

The Case entity, which is also called ticket in Microsoft Dynamics CRM, pertains to the issues and problems of customers. Therefore, whenever a customer raises an issue, the customer service agent will record it in the form of a case. These cases are routed to service agents in a queue. A case is tracked until it gets resolved.

Before assigning the case, you need to check the customer's entitlements. Through entitlements, it can be known whether the customer is eligible for a service.

You can also check if there is an existing case in the system; it can then be reopened.

Entitlements

Entitlements are the terms and conditions of the support to be provided. The customer's support agreement depends on the products and services bought by them. The support level may vary according to the type and cost of the product. Therefore, the information stored in entitlements helps the agent to verify the type and eligibility of service to the customer.

An SLA is associated when an entitlement is added to a case.

SLAs

SLAs are **service level agreements** defined for each customer. They define the **Key Performance Indicators** (**KPIs**) to attain the service level. KPIs help with warnings to provide support in a timely manner.

Microsoft Dynamics CRM helps you create two different types of SLAs: standard and enhanced. Standard SLAs can only be used with the case entity, while enhanced SLAs are supported by multiple entities in CRM. The following are the entities that support enhanced SLAs:

- Account
- Contact
- Order
- Invoice
- Quote
- Opportunity
- Lead

Contracts

Customers can purchase a service with the help of service contracts. Service contracts contain information, such as the price of a service for each product, number of calls or minutes to be spent on a customer issue, and the time duration of the contract.

Knowledge Base

The common problems and issues that occur frequently can be recorded with their solutions in Knowledge Base. Knowledge Base is made up of a library for business information, product guides, data sheets, and other articles with timely and relevant information. This will help the customer service representatives with the required information and help them to resolve issues more efficiently. The articles stored in Knowledge Base are searchable.

The XRM framework

The XRM framework defines a strategic approach to customize the out-of-box features available in Microsoft Dynamics CRM to make sure that it implements all the business aspects of a system. The central idea of the XRM framework is to extend the standard functionalities provided in Microsoft Dynamics CRM to suit any business requirement. Businesses could be of varying types, such as public sector, insurance, banking, retail, telecom, and so on.

Owing to the underlying .NET framework, Microsoft Dynamics CRM 2016 provides a very powerful tool that can be easily extended to map any business requirement that is not provided out of the box.

Using the XRM framework, an organizations can achieve the following:

- **Increased productivity**: Microsoft Dynamics CRM can automate many critical tasks required in any typical organization. This can lead to increased productivity.
- **Quicker development cycle**: As the core product is already built in, less effort is required in customizing it to suit the end client.

Using the XRM framework, we can create and customize the following components:

- **Mapping the entities:** Using entity mapping, you can copy certain values from a record to an associated record. For example, if you create an opportunity from a lead, you can map the existing values from the lead to the opportunity.
- **Creating custom fields:** Microsoft Dynamics CRM allows users to create attributes of different types. In Microsoft Dynamics CRM 2016, an attribute can be of the following data types:
    - **Single line of text**: A string representation.
    - **Option set**: An attribute that can have values among a picklist.
    - **Two options**: An attribute that can have only two possible values.
    - **Image**: An attribute to which we can upload an image.
    - **Whole number**: An attribute that can acquire an integer value.
    - **Floating point number**: An attribute that can assume a float value. It is similar to decimal and is generally used when we are not much concerned with accuracy after the decimal point.
    - **Decimal number**: An attribute that can assume a decimal value.
    - **Currency**: An attribute that can assume a money-related value.
    - **Multiple lines of text**: A multiline string representation, for example, the description of a book.
    - **Date and time**: An attribute that can assume a date-time value, for example the date of a class.
    - **Lookup**: An attribute that links two different entities.
    - **Customer**: An attribute that links the entity to an account or a customer.
- **Defining relationships between entities:** Entity relationships define how two different entities can be related to one another. There are three types of relations possible between entities: 1:N, N:1, and N:N.
- **Forms:** Microsoft Dynamics CRM provides several types of forms that could be utilized for different purposes. The following are the available form types:
    - **Main form**: This is the main web form, which is opened when the user navigates to a record. This form provides the main user interface for interacting with an entity data.
    - **Quick create form**: This form can be configured for data entry by the user.
    - **Quick view form**: This is a form that can be configured on the main forms of entities that exhibit a 1:N relationship with the current entity.

- **Mobile form**: Users browsing the Microsoft Dynamics CRM site form mobile devices fill the mobile form.
- **Views:** The following are the main views that are present for any entity:
    - **Active records**: This view shows the active records of an entity
    - **Inactive records**: This view shows the inactive records of an entity
    - **Associated records view**: This view shows the associated records (N:1 and N:N) of this entity with the other entities
    - **Lookup view**: This view appears on the 1: N control
    - **Advanced find view**: This view allows users to create queries, and save and export the results

Analytics with CRM

Microsoft Dynamics CRM 2016 provides some advanced features that provide ways to enhance the analytics experience using other Microsoft products.

In Microsoft Dynamics CRM 2016, two new features have been introduced to provide standardized documents for analytics. These two features integrate to the Microsoft Office suite of applications. They are described in further detail in the following subsections.

Word templates

Word templates provide means to create reusable templates in Microsoft Word and then save them to Microsoft Dynamics CRM 2016. These Word templates can then be used to generate standardized Word documents based on the CRM data. The following table describes the supported versions of Word that can be used to generate or open a document generated via the Word template feature of Microsoft Dynamics CRM 2016.

Excel templates

Just like Word templates, a user can also generate Excel templates in Microsoft Dynamics CRM. The only main difference between Word and Excel templates is that, while a Word template is for information relevant to one entity record, Excel templates are for information relevant to a set of entity records. We will look through some scenarios in the later chapters in this book, which will give you a comprehensive idea of these features.

Workflow development

Workflows are the handlers for events fired by Microsoft Dynamics CRM. The events that a workflow can support are limited as compared to plugins. Using workflows, we can either utilize workflows using a native drag-and-drop interface, or extend the standard behavior of Microsoft Dynamics CRM using customizations or with custom code written in the .NET framework.

Types of workflows

Workflows can be categorized into the following:

- **Out-of-box workflows:** This type of workflows is provided by default in Microsoft Dynamics CRM out-of-box components. Workflows can be fired on create, update, delete, and on-demand. These workflows can be customized and created without writing code.
- **Custom workflows:** Out-of-box components can be extended and customized by using .NET, and more complex business operations can be done. These workflows are called custom workflows.

A work can be triggered in two ways:

- **Background workflows:** In background workflows, the processing is done asynchronously and are not triggered immediately. This kind of workflows is used when you need to perform some tasks that are not to be triggered urgently or immediately after some operation.
- **Real-time workflows:** These workflows are also known as synchronous workflows. They are triggered immediately as soon as a particular event is occurred.

Workflows and Plugins can both be utilized to accomplish the same functionality, as both essentially run on the server side to do automation or processing. In this book, we will go through some real-time scenarios that will help you in deciding when to use workflows and when to opt for plugins; new features will also be introduced.

Client-side enhancements in Microsoft Dynamics CRM 2016

This section is focused on introducing and using client-side enhancements available with Microsoft Dynamics CRM 2016. Generally, in Dynamics 365 JavaScript is used to perform actions in form scripts, ribbon commands, and in web resources.

Form scripts

JavaScript can be used to handle different form events and perform some actions whenever an event occurs. The advantage of using form scripts is that they don't require any interaction with servers and they are executed on the client side itself. Scripts can be used for the following:

- **Validating data:** We can use JavaScript for validating data entered into the fields. We can check the valid formats for fields, such as email, mobile number, and so on. We can restrict invalid data using this type of validations.
- **Automating tasks:** Using JavaScript, field values can be populated depending on the data filled on the form.
- **Form enhancements:** Using JavaScript, you can customize and control the data that is to be displayed on the form. You can also show or hide some fields on the forms.
- **Ribbon commands:** JavaScript can be used for ribbon commands, such as performing an action on button click, setting some rules for displaying a button, showing dialogs on button click, and so on. You can write JavaScript on a ribbon button, which can then perform an action accordingly. You can even call a function inside a JavaScript web resource.

Web resources

Web resources are the files stored in Microsoft Dynamics CRM. They are JavaScript, HTML, Silverlight, Stylesheets, or image files. You can write JavaScript in JavaScript and HTML web resource. You can also write Web APIs inside a web resource for performing **Create, Read, Update, and Delete (CRUD)** operations with Microsoft Dynamics CRM.

Enhancements for mobile

In this section, you will get a brief overview of the mobile enhancements in Microsoft Dynamics CRM 2016. Microsoft Dynamics CRM 2016 enhances the capability of the sales and service teams at any time by providing enhancements in its mobility features. It provides support for mobility applications across a range of devices, including tablets and phones, and also supports multiple platforms. A few mobile enhancements that we will go through in this book are as follows:

- Mobile and tablet enhancements available with Microsoft Dynamics CRM 2016
- Supported platforms and browsers for mobile and tablet apps
- How to install Microsoft Dynamics CRM 2016 phone app
- How to preview form customization changes in the phone and tablet look-and-feel
- New visual controls available with Microsoft Dynamics CRM 2016
- How to configure calendar and pen control on an Opportunity entity
- Supported languages for Microsoft Dynamics CRM 2016 phone and tablet app

Entity forms for mobile and tablet

Dynamics CRM provides the functionality to configure and preview the forms for mobile and tablet. You can just enable mobile and tablet for an entity and configure it.

The Microsoft Dynamics CRM app for Android

There are new features in the Dynamics CRM app for Android. The Android app provides a feature to store records even in the offline mode and to synchronize them into Dynamics CRM whenever network is available.

Visual controls

Microsoft Dynamics CRM 2016 introduces controls for mobile and tablet applications, which help the users to enter and use CRM apps faster. These controls are designed considering a touch-friendly environment provided by modern smart phones and tablets.

The main advantage of these visual controls is they are very user-friendly and it makes operating easier while using on phones or tablets.

Plugin development

As Microsoft Dynamics CRM continues to evolve, the focus of Microsoft is to try to make the custom coding as less as possible. However, every now and then, there is bound to be some customer requirement that cannot be implemented without any custom coding. That's when plugins come to our rescue.

The main motive and skill that every Dynamics CRM consultant needs to enhance is to analyze the requirements correctly and categorize them categorically in terms of configurations and customizations. Other out-of-box configurations such as workflows and business rules should be explored before we accept the need for writing a custom plugin to meet the desired needs of the customer.

In plugin development, we will go through the following functionalities:

- **Event execution pipeline:** Through the event execution pipeline, one can get an idea about the different stages where plugins can be registered and the types of operations that can be performed using a plugin. Every action in Dynamics CRM results in a call made to the organization web service. The message contains business entity information and core operation information. These messages are passed through a standard execution pipeline or stages where it can be modified by any custom logic written by users. This custom logic is a plugin.
- **Isolation modes:** The plugin isolation mode signifies the level of security restrictions imposed on the plugin execution pipeline. The isolation mode is specified on the assembly level and not on the individual plugin step. When a plugin assembly is registered, it can either be registered in an isolated or sandbox mode, or in no mode. The sandbox is more secure and some actions are restricted.
- **Plugin Development:** Plugins are custom classes that implement the IPlugin interface. The class can be written in any .NET framework-compliant language, such as Microsoft Visual C# or Microsoft Visual Basic .NET.

Business Process Flows and Business Rules

Earlier, developers used JavaScript for any client-side scripting or validation. Business Rules provide a rich interface with which people can configure most of the client-side scripting and validations, which previously required some sort of coding experience.

Business Rules were introduced in Microsoft Dynamics CRM few versions ago with an idea of enabling business analysts and users to configure the Microsoft Dynamics CRM entity forms and perform actions without writing a single line of client-side code. Because of the rich graphical interface provided to the users, it is quite easy to understand and configurable. With the correct usage and implementation of Business Rules, users can reduce the development efforts considerably.

Business Process Flows are a representation of the business processes followed in the associated organizations. They act as a guideline for the end users and help them in following through the business process. They also act as a safeguard in ensuring that all the required steps have been carried out before the user can proceed to the next stage.

This book will give an overview of how Business Process Flows and business processes work, and how they can be helpful for automations in Dynamics CRM. You will learn how to use Business Process Flows to execute the logical steps in your business process. In addition, we will look through how business rules can easily define and set rules for validating data, setting visibility, disabling fields, and so on.

In this book, we will go through the following

- How to create a Business Rule for an entity
- Different components of a Business Rule, that is, scope, condition, and action
- How to set up a business rule having multiple if else conditions
- How to create a business process flow for an entity
- How to add conditions, steps, and conditions to a business process flow
- Abandoning / Switching a business process flow

New features in Microsoft Dynamics CRM 2016

Here's a quick list of the new features in Microsoft Dynamics CRM 2016:

- Customer field type
- Solutions improvements for entity assets
- The feedback and rating functionalities
- The Relevance Search functionality

Now let's look at each of these in brief.

Customer field type

There can be account or contact linked with entities such as opportunities, invoices, orders, and cases. Therefore, the customer field type is a lookup field, which allows you to either link a contact or account field with an entity. This field is includes out of box in entities such as opportunities, invoices, orders, and cases. If you want to link records of account or contact with any other entity, then you can create a custom lookup field of type customer.

Solutions improvements for entity assets

Whenever, one needs to add an existing entity to a solution, one can add only the required assets into the solution. Microsoft Dynamics CRM 2016 provides with the feature where one can select the list of components that are required in the solution. Only the selected components will be a part of your solution. Entity assets can be Forms, Views, Charts, Keys, Relationships, Dashboards, and so on.

Two other configuration options that can be set are:

- **Include entity metadata**: Entity metadata information, such as audit settings, are included
- **Include all assets**: If checked, all the entity assets are included

Feedback and Rating

Microsoft Dynamics CRM 2016 introduced a new entity called Feedback, which lets users provide feedback and rating for a product or a case entity. This will help organizations to track the feedback and ratings for the services provided, which may help improve the quality of products and services.

The Relevance Search functionality

Relevance search is an improved search functionality in Microsoft Dynamics CRM 2016, which uses Azure Search. Using relevance search, you can search through all the fields in all the entities and provide improved results. It is faster and more relevant, as it searches through all the entities.

Summary

In this chapter, we had a brief overview of all the concepts that will be covered in this book. We will cover each and every concept with comprehensive real-time scenarios that will give you a better understanding of the concepts. Hope you have a great time reading through the book!

2
Working with Sales

The main purpose of the Dynamics CRM Sales module is to support a typical sales cycle followed in any organization. It automates the entire process, starting with the acquisition of a new lead until its logical conclusion, in the form of either a lost or won opportunity.

The Sales module in Dynamics CRM helps organizations provide effective selling capabilities. It helps the organization track the sales activities and see their sales pipeline.

Some examples of sales are as follows:

- Creating a lead for potential sales in an organization
- Adding notes and activities to the lead while trying to sell a product or service to the customer
- Qualifying a lead to opportunity
- Generating quotations and orders
- Capturing competitor information

The stages of the sales process

A typical sales process consists of the following stages:

- **Lead generation**: This involves generating potential customers who may be interested in the products that the organization has to offer. Leads may be generated via different means. They could either be generated by the CRM marketing process or by interaction activities such as phone calls, emails, appointments, and so on.

- **Qualify leads**: After the leads are captured, each lead needs to be evaluated to understand their requirements in detail and the related products/services that the organization has to offer. Based upon the interaction with the lead, the lead may be converted into a viable opportunity.

- **Demonstrate value**: After an opportunity is identified, the next step is to identify the resources and the personnel that will pursue the lead prospect. They will try to capture different information, such as prime customer contact details, requirements, and the list of competitors. They may also do a SWOT analysis to compare their product with that of their competitors.

- **Quote creation/negotiation**: Finally, after proper calibration, the organization may share a quote with the client. A quote basically consists of the product information and the associated price, along with other major information. The client may ask for some negotiation, and accept or reject the quote.

- **Closing out the Quote**: When the client finally accepts the Quote, the organization issues an invoice to the client. An invoice is a formal contract consisting of product information, associated cost, and support details. It should be on the same lines as that of the Quote. The buyer must then sign the contract and pay the organization as agreed in the contract. At this stage, the lead is identified as a **won opportunity**.

- **Supporting the customer**: After the lead is converted to a won opportunity, the organization must manage the customer as per the agreement details in the contract. In case the customer requires any support, the organization creates service requests either at the client's onsite location or via call.

Entities in Dynamics CRM

Dynamics CRM provides various revenue management and goal management processes, which can be easily customized to suit the business process of an organization. The following are the entities provided by Dynamics CRM:

- **Lead, Contact, and Account**: These entities are already listed as part of the Marketing module. They represent the same business actors in the Sales module as in the Marketing module.
- **Opportunity**: This represents an interaction with a lead that may be converted into a revenue-generating avenue for the organization.
- **Competitors**: These represent third-party organizations that are competing with the organization for the services required by the customer.
- **Product**: This may represent a resource, service, or item offered by the organization for the services of the client.
- **Product unit**: This represents the possible unit of groups in which the product is available.
- **Price list**: This identifies the price that the organization charges the client for its products. Dynamics CRM allows us to configure different prices for different regions/countries.
- **Currency**: Each price list is associated with the currency of the underlying region/country.
- **Quote**: Dynamics CRM captures the list of product line items, which they offer to the client as a quote. Along with the product information, it also captures the contact details of the prime contact, shipping information, and discount, if any.
- **Invoice**: As in the general sales cycle, when the customer accepts the terms and conditions mentioned in the Quote, the quote is converted into an invoice. It captures the same information as that of the Quote; however, it just acts as a formal contract between the organization and the customer.
- **Goal**: Dynamics CRM allows the organization to capture preset targets in terms of won opportunities, revenue generated, and so on, which a sales representative should adhere to.

The following is a sequence diagram explaining the interaction involved in the Sales lifecycle within Dynamics CRM:

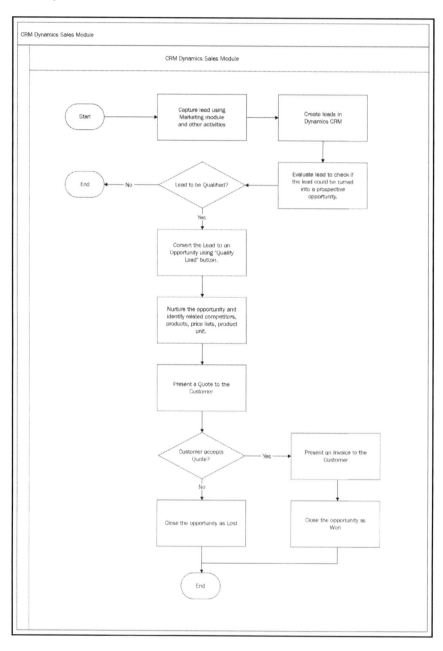

Case studies

In the following section, we will use case studies to go through and understand the Sales module of Dynamics CRM.

Scenario 1

Acme Ltd utilizes Dynamics CRM's out-of-box Sales module capabilities to capture leads from across three global sales offices and process them through lead qualification and the opportunity management lifecycle:

The following are the three global offices:

- New York head office, USA
- London sales office, UK for Europe
- Mumbai sales office, India for Asia

The requirements of Acme Ltd are as follows:

- Central reporting of opportunity management at the New York head office
- Lead capture and qualification based on the location
- Opportunity management

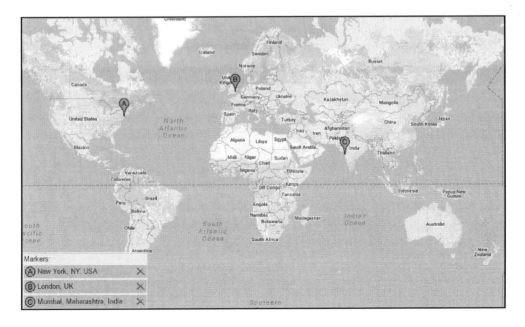

The following steps explain the process adopted by Acme Ltd for capturing leads, filling in the required information in the lead records, and then qualifying a lead to generate opportunities and close them as won or lost:

1. Click on the chevron or arrow to the right of the **Microsoft Dynamics CRM** text to display the navigation menu. Click on the **Sales** CRM Module:

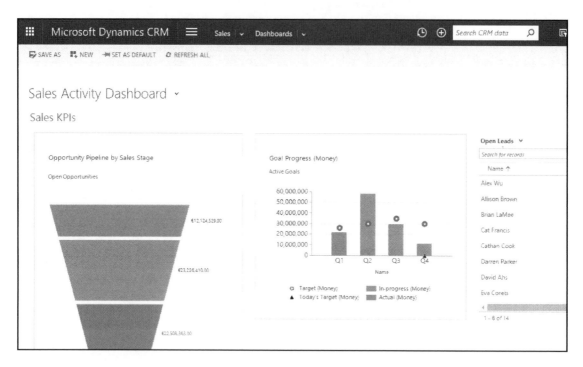

2. Next, click on **Sales** in the top-right corner and, then, click on the **Leads** entity under **Sales**:

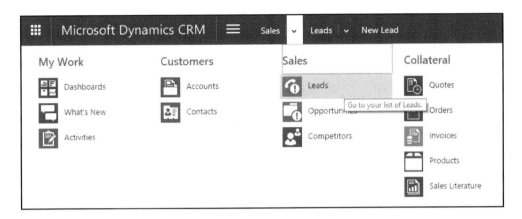

3. The browser will be directed to the **My Open Leads** view on the **Leads** entity. Click **New** in the top-left corner to launch the **New Lead** form:

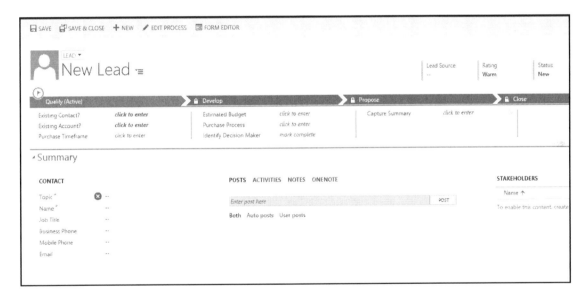

4. The required fields, **Topic**, and **Name**, with the red asterisk showcase fields, need to be entered before the user can save the record:

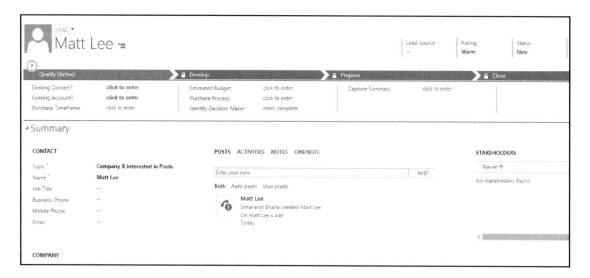

5. Add details for the lead contact and company, and set the **Lead Source** in the header section in the top-right corner of the form:

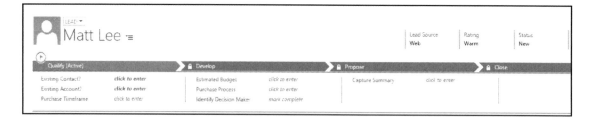

6. These steps are outlined in the **Qualify** stage of the **Lead to Opportunity** business process flow. **Existing Contact?** and **Existing Account?** do not apply, as this lead relates to a new contact and a new account. Fill out the remaining fields as appropriate and click **QUALIFY**:

7. To move the lead to the opportunity stage, select the **Qualify** option from the command bar. Note that when a lead is qualified, an **Opportunity** record is created and the **Lead to Opportunity** business process flow moves to the **Develop (Active)** stage:

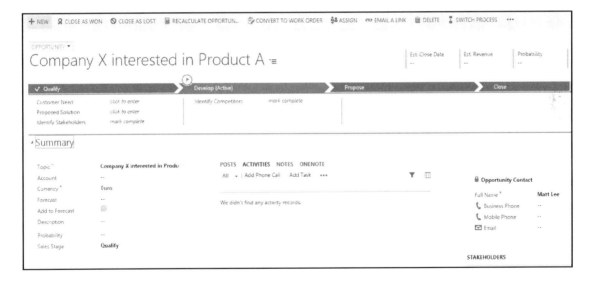

8. In addition, a new **Contact** record is created and populated with the data that was entered in the **Lead Contact** and **Company** sections:

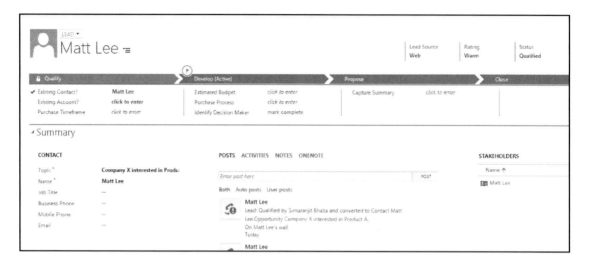

The lead record will now be set to read-only.

9. Navigate back to the opportunity record (by choosing the **Develop** stage); enter a value for the **Est. Close Date** and the **Est. Revenue** in the header section in the top-right corner of the form:

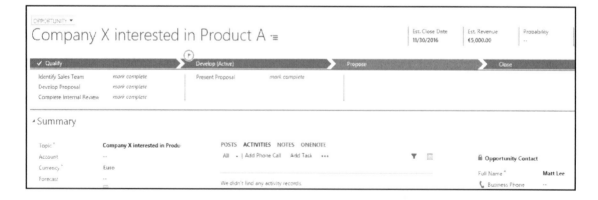

10. Optionally, the users of Acme Ltd may complete the fields in the **Develop (Active)** stage of the **Lead to Opportunity** business process flow. They may enter a description for the **Customer Need** and the **Proposed Solution**. Mark the **Identify Stakeholders** as complete (note that the contact for the opportunity has been automatically set as the stakeholder for this opportunity):

11. Optionally, users may complete the other fields in the **Develop (Active)** stage. To complete the other fields, such as **Identify Competitors**, it is necessary to create a new **Competitor** record. The completion of this data enables the reporting process to track the closed opportunities, as lost by the competitor. Scroll down to the competitor subgrid on the **Opportunity** form and click on the plus icon. Then, click on the lookup icon and, finally, click on the **+New** option to add a new **Competitor** record:

12. This will launch the **Quick Create** form for the **Competitor** entity on the top of the screen. Fill out the required fields and click **Save**:

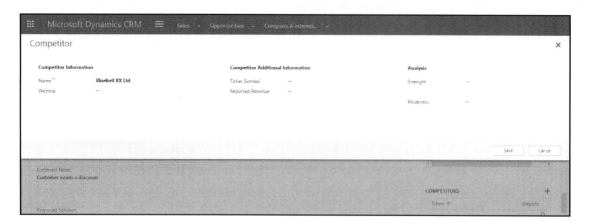

13. The competitor record is added to **Opportunity**. Mark **Identify Competitors** on the process bar as complete and click the **Next Stage** link:

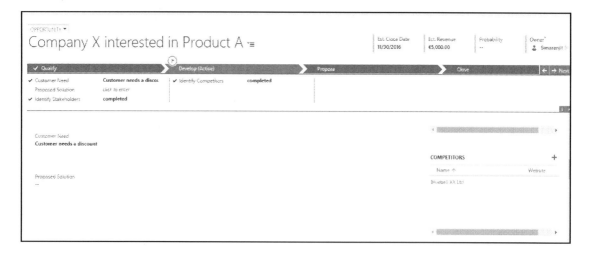

14. The **Opportunity** record now moves to the **Propose (Active)** stage. Proceed to complete the actions in the current stage. Complete the required fields for the **Propose (Active)** stage:

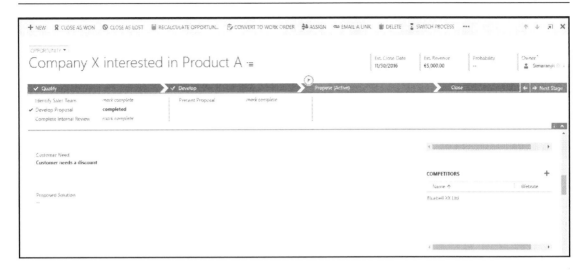

15. The opportunity is closed, dependent on the outcome of the sales activity. Opportunities can be closed as won or as lost from the command bar. In this case, the opportunity is lost by **Acme Ltd** to **Bluebell XX Ltd**, so select **CLOSE AS LOST** from the command bar:

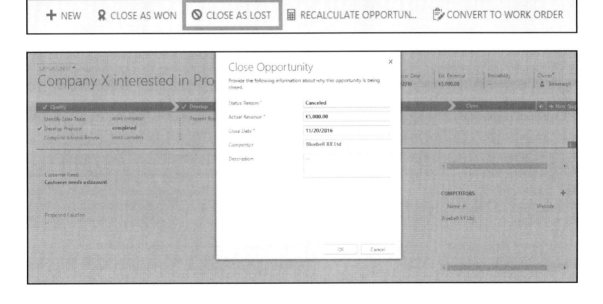

16. The opportunity is now marked as lost and set to read-only:

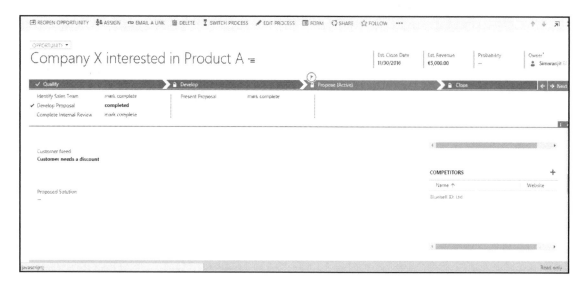

The preceding scenario explains the sales lifecycle from leads to opportunity in a case where **Acme Ltd** lost the opportunity.

Scenario 2

Peter leads the sales team in Contoso, and wishes to go through the goals set for each of the sales members and understand how they are performing against the goals that have been set for them:

1. Create **Goals** for each of the team members:

In Dynamics CRM, we can define goals for each of the sales members. For defining the goals, navigate to **Sales | Goals**

2. For creating goals, we firstly need to define **Goal Metrics**. **Goal Metrics** indicate the criteria against which the goals are being set. Out-of-box, we can configure **Goal Metrics** on three points:

    1. Number of product units.
    2. Revenue earned.
    3. Number of cases.

Check out the following image for better understanding:

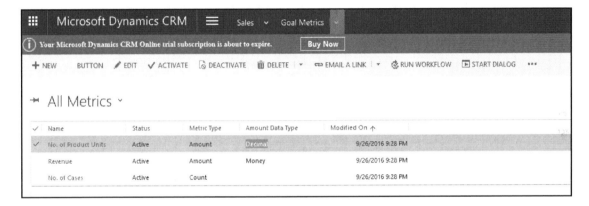

We will just go through one example of **Revenue** to see how it works:

The metrics could be of two types: **Count** and **Amount**. **Count** can be used in metric types such as the number of cases resolved or the number of product units sold, where we are interested in the actual number of items rather than the value in one of their attributes.

The rollup field's grid defines the collection of variables that are used in the calculation of the actual and in-progress fields. In the preceding example of **Revenue Metric**, we use the summation of the actual earned revenue in won opportunities as the actual earned revenue, and we use the summation of the estimated revenue in the in-progress opportunities as the in-progress estimated revenue field.

The following screenshot shows the roll-up query of the actual revenue:

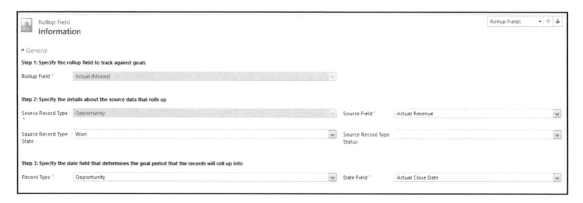

3. After **Goal Metrics** have been defined for each **Sales Member**, we will go ahead and define the goal:

For creating a **New Goal**, click the **New** button. It should open up a form for entering the goal details:

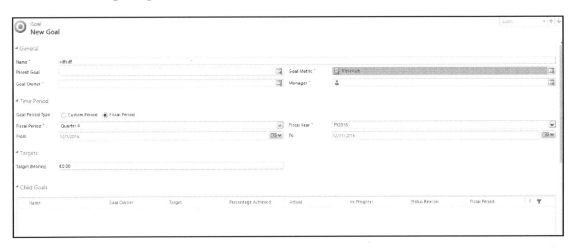

The following are some of the important details for the same:

- **Name**: This is the name of the goal
- **Parent Goal**: This should be filled if there are some parent goals or a goal containing this goal as a child goal
- **Goal Metric**: This is the metric used for creating the goal
- **Goal Owner**: This field should contain the sales member responsible for the goal
- **Manager**: This field should contain the name of the manager of the sales member to whom this goal will be rolled up
- **Fiscal Period**: This is the period for which the goal is defined
- **Fiscal Year**: This is the year for which the goal is defined
- **From**: This is the date from which the goal is defined
- **To**: This is the date to which the goal is defined
- **Target**: This is the target defined in the goal; for the sake of this example, since we are using **Goal Metric** as **Revenue**, the target revenue will be added

This way, we can configure the goals for each of the users. In the previous step, we used **Goal Metric** as the **Revenue**. Therefore, as and when the sales manager closes any **Opportunity** as won, the actual revenue defined in the opportunity will be added to the target that the sales member has already achieved.

4. Let's now talk about the self-evaluation of targets by the sales manager:

Dynamics CRM provides an out-of-box sales member dashboard, which provides several insights to the sales manager as to how the member has performed so far. For navigating the **Sales Manager** dashboard, navigate to **Sales | Dashboards | Sales Activity Dashboard**. The following is a screenshot of the dashboard, along with the information it represents:

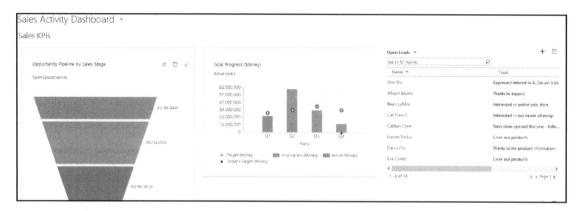

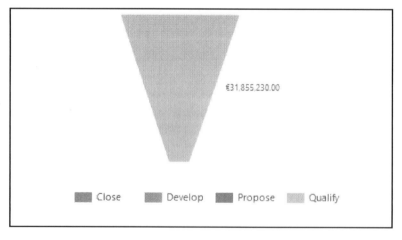

- **Goals Progress**: This is a quarter-based performance of the sales manager against the goals that have been set up. As you can see in the preceding screenshot, the orange bar represents the revenue of opportunities that are in progress, and the blue bar represents the revenue of the won opportunities. The blue and white circles represents the target set.

- **Open Leads**: This represents all the open leads in the system.
- **Opportunities Pipeline by Sales Stage**: Out of the box, a Dynamics CRM opportunity can be in one of the following stages: **Qualify**, **Propose**, **Develop**, and **Close**. The chart shows the distribution of revenue present in these open opportunities in the stage category:

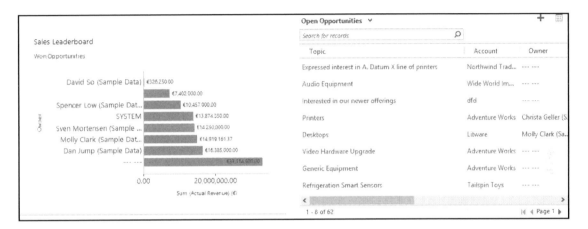

- **Sales Leaderboard**: The chart shows a comparison of how different sales members are performing with respect to each other. The bar represents the sum of all the won opportunities of that sales member.
- **Open Opportunities**: This is a view of all the open opportunities present in the system:

- **My Activities**: This is a list of all the activities owned by the user.

5. **Sales Manager Overview**: As in a real-life scenario, all of the goals individually owned by the sales manager cascade to the sales manager. Dynamics CRM also provides a similar feature in which the goals owned by each user are cascaded to their manager. Once a sales manager logs into the system, he/she can navigate to **Sales | Dashboard | Sales** Management to understand how his/her team is performing. The following screenshot shows the dashboard, along with a summary of what the view represents:

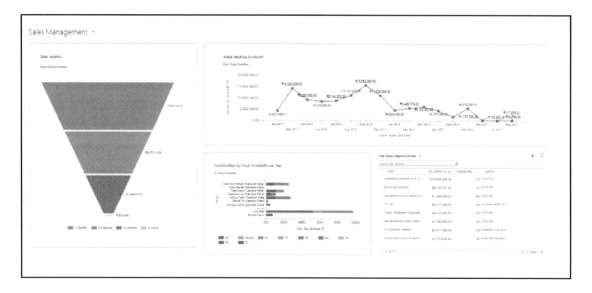

- **Sales Pipeline**: This chart provides a distribution of the revenue present in the open opportunities in terms of their stage category.
- **Actual Revenue by Month**: This is a monthly analysis of the summation of the revenue earned in all the won opportunities.
- **Opportunities by Close Probability per Rep**: This is a revenue comparison of how each sales member is performing. For each sales member, the bar plots the **Actual Revenue** in terms of different opportunity stages.
- **Top Open Opportunities**: These are the top open opportunities in terms of their revenue.

Scenario 3

Acme Ltd has been using Excel files to manage their sales contacts, and they now wish to import their contacts (essential fields) into Dynamics CRM in one go. Dynamics CRM provides out-of-box data import files for this purpose.

1. The following is the Excel file that the Acme Ltd Sales team wants to import into the Dynamics CRM contacts:

First Name	Last Name	Company	Email	Address 1: City	Address1: Region
Martin	Arthur	Litware	MartinArthur.Litware.com	New York	USA
James	Conolly	Adventure Works	JamesConolly.Adventure Works.com	London	UK
Mahesh	Kumar	Northwind Traders	MaheshKumar.Northwind Traders.com	Mumbai	India

The essential fields that Acme Ltd wants to initially import are as follows:

- **First Name**: This is the first name of the contact
- **Last Name**: This is the last name of the contact
- **Company**: This is the company to which the contact belongs
- **Email**: This is the email for communicating with the contact
- **Address 1: City**: This is the city where the contact is based
- **Address1: Region**: This is the country where the contact is based

2. Once the import file is ready, the next step is to start the import process. Navigate to **Sales | Contacts**:

The user has now navigated to the **Contact** grid in Dynamics CRM. There are a lot of buttons available on top of the ribbon, one of which is the **Import Data** button. Click on it to start the import process:

3. Mention the location of the file in the first step:

Note: Only the following file formats are supported: XML Spreadsheet 2003 (.xml), .csv, .txt, .xlsx, and .zip.

4. In the next step, the review summary is presented by Dynamics CRM. Review the details and click **Next** to continue the import process:

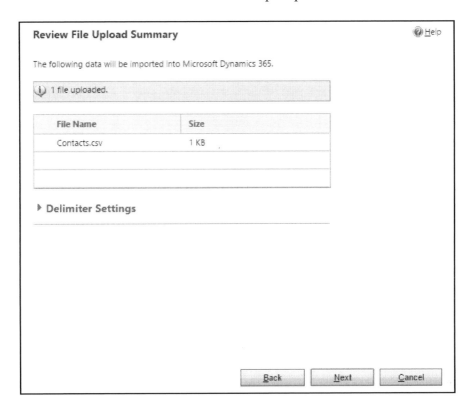

Expanding **Delimiter Settings** will give options to change the delimiter used in your import file:

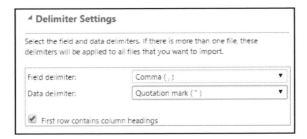

If you do not have **Field delimiter** or **Data delimiter**, you can keep the default settings and continue with the import process.

5. The next step involves the selection of a data map for your import process. The data map is a mapping between the file to be imported and the field name in Dynamics CRM. Data maps can be saved for usage later. For the current import, Select the default option (automatic mapping), and continue the import process by clicking **Next**:

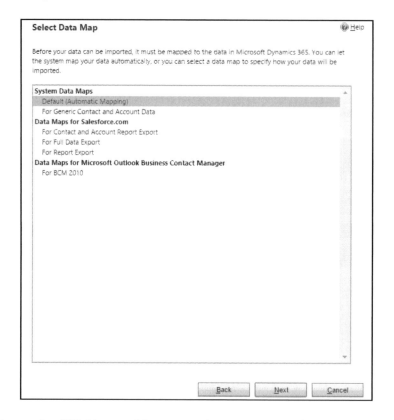

6. If Dynamics CRM is not able to map the entity type, the user needs to map the field type, and click on **Next**:

The data fields need to be mapped to the entity field types in Dynamics CRM. Fields that are not mapped by the system need to be mapped by the user. One of the fields that need to be mapped is **Account Lookup**, as follows:

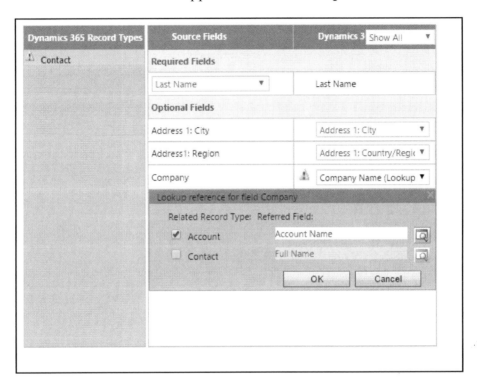

Once all of the fields are mapped, the screen will look like the following:

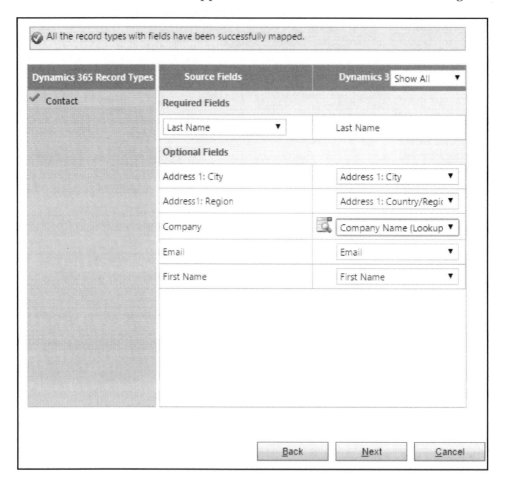

Click on **Next** to continue the data import process:

7. There will be the **Review Data** summary screen, which can be continued by clicking **Next**. Following the **Review Data** summary will be the screen for **Reviewing settings and Import Data**:

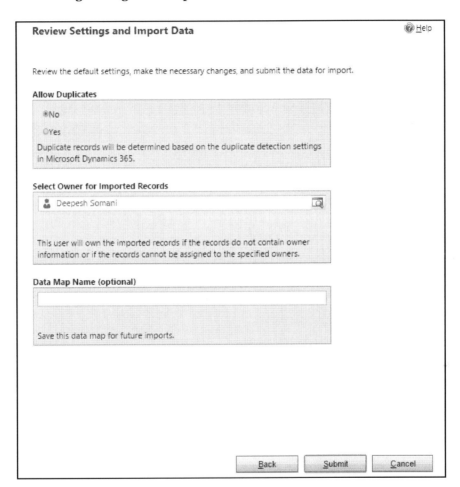

Note: In case you wish to use the data map again for future imports, the **Data Map Name (optional)** field needs to be filled in here. This will avoid the need to map the entity and fields on every import.

Click on **Submit** to submit the data for importing.

8. The data is submitted for import, and you will be presented with the screen to check the status of your data import:

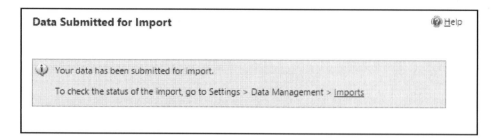

Click on **Imports** to check the details of data import:

All three contacts are now completely imported.

9. Navigating to the contacts grid in Dynamics CRM, you will be able to locate all of the imported contacts:

The preceding scenario explains the process for three contacts. In a real-world scenario, there will be a number of contacts to be imported, in hundreds or thousands, when the data import feature should be used.

Summary

In this chapter, you learned about the Sales module of Dynamics CRM, the entities involved in the Sales module, and the Sales lifecycle in Dynamics CRM. We also looked at some case studies for the Sales module in Dynamics CRM.

In the next chapter, we will cover the Service module of Dynamics CRM and the entities involved in the Service module in Dynamics CRM. We will also look at some case studies for the Service module in Dynamics CRM.

3
Working with Services

In the previous chapter, we covered the Sales module of Dynamics CRM. We focused on entities, processes, and dashboards, which are available for managing the Sales division of any organization, using real-world examples.

The Service module in Dynamics CRM helps organizations provide effective service capabilities. It automates the entire process of providing resolution to the problems of the customer, aiding the customer by means of Knowledge base, and so on.

Some examples of service management are as follows:

- Creating a Case for the resolution of the customer's problem or query
- Adding notes and activities to the Case while creating, tracking, and solving the customer's problem or query
- Creating a Case from Phone support
- Using Knowledge base articles to effectively resolve a case
- Using entitlements and SLAs for efficient service to the customer
- Routing Cases to an appropriate queue

Entities in the Service module

The following are the entities provided by Dynamics CRM for the Service module:

- Case
- Knowledge Base Articles
- Queues
- Service Level Agreements and Entitlements
- Service Calendar

Let's take a look at each of the entities:

- **Case:** This represents a problem reported by a customer and the activities that the customer service representatives use to resolve it. The Case forms the core of service management for Dynamics CRM. Case is sometimes also referred to as an incident, ticket, or issue.
- **Knowledge base**: This provides a process for submitting, approving, and publishing articles about an organization's products and services. It helps the customer service representatives to find information and resolutions about the products and services.
- **Queue:** This provides a process of acting as a hold container for Work items; for example, you can queue the Cases that are to be resolved.
- **Service Level Agreements**: These represent the features of Dynamics CRM that can be used for configuring metrics to attain a service level. A Service-Level Agreement is nothing but the time taken to solve a support request.
- **Entitlements**: Entitlements represent the level of support that is available to and eligible for a customer.
- **Service calendar**: This is a scheduling component in Dynamics CRM, used to view and manage the service activities.

The Interactive Service Hub

The Interactive Service Hub provided by Dynamics CRM is specifically inclined at increasing the efficiency of customer service representatives. It provides redefined forms and key information, bundled in a way that makes it much easier for the Service representatives to perform their duties. Earlier, it used to take a lot of time in loading Forms and Dashboards.

Interactive Service Hub requirements

In the following section, we will go through the requirements of using the Interactive Service Hub with respect to the operating system, browsers, and so on:

- **Operating Systems:** The following are the operating systems that are supported by the Interactive Service Hub:
  - Windows 7
  - Windows 8
  - Windows 8.1
  - Windows 10
  - Windows 10 Anniversary Update
  - macOS
- **Browsers**: The following are the browsers that are supported by the Interactive Service Hub:
  - Microsoft Edge
  - Internet Explorer 10
  - Internet Explorer 11
  - Google Chrome
  - Mozilla Firefox
  - Apple Safari 9
- **Screen Resolution**: The minimum screen resolution required by the Interactive Service Hub is 1024*768
- **Languages**: Right-to-left languages, such as Hebrew and Arabic, are not currently supported

Case studies

In this section, we will look at some case studies, which will represent and give a brief idea of the usage and configuration of Service Hubs:

Scenario 1 - The configuration of the Service Hub

Let's consider a scenario where Contoso corporation wants to use the Interactive Service Hub for Service managements. It helps by filtering and reusing the CRM charts as Interactive Charts. Dashboards can contain records from different Entity views. The following steps need to be performed to configure the usage of the Interactive Service Hub:

1. For configuring the Service Hub, navigate to **Settings** | **Interactive Service Hub**, and click on it:

As you can see in the following image, a new window should open up and automatically start configuring the system:

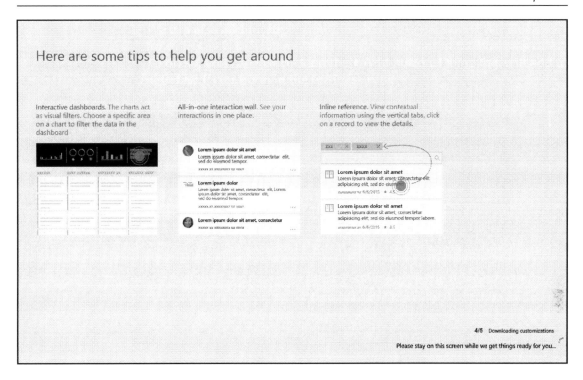

2. Once the customizations are configured, a screen with the following layout should appear:

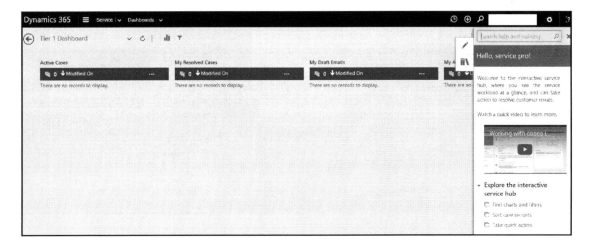

A walkthrough of the Interactive Service Hub

In Dynamics CRM, we can configure the record types that we want to appear in the Interactive Service Hub. By default, the following entities are configured for an interactive experience:

- Account
- Contact
- Case
- Activities, including emails, tasks, appointments, phone calls, and social activities
- Queue items
- Dashboards
- Social profiles

Other records can also be configured in the Interactive Service Hub. To do so, open the solution and navigate to the record that is required to appear in the Service Hub. Now, select the option mentioned in the following screenshot:

The navigation bars in the Service Hub are quite like that of Dynamics CRM, but additional improvements and the faster loading of screens are the benefits over the traditional CRM user interface. The following screenshot shows the UI appearance of **Accounts**:

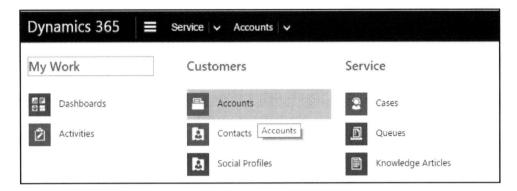

This is how the list of the **Active Accounts** of a user looks like:

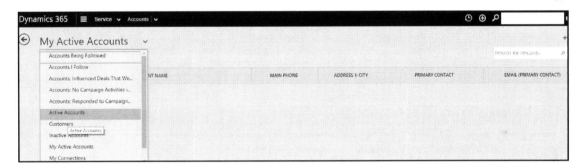

This is how the list of all the **Active Accounts** looks like:

Let's see how to view all of the account records:

1. Click on the record to view more details:

2. To move to the next account record, click on the Next button beside the name of the account:

The TIMELINE tab

The **TIMELINE** tab provides information related to the chronological order in which the related activities are created for an account.

The following are some of the features of the **TIMELINE** section:

- **Searching activities**: The service representative can click the search button to search the activities regarding the account:

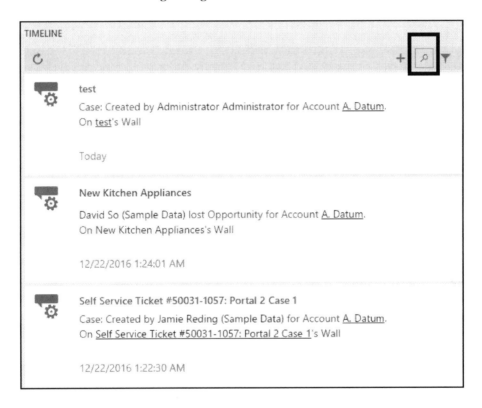

- **Filtering activities by date or type**: The service representative can also filter the activities by date or type, such as **Note**, **Activity**, or **Auto Post**. The following is the screenshot for the same:

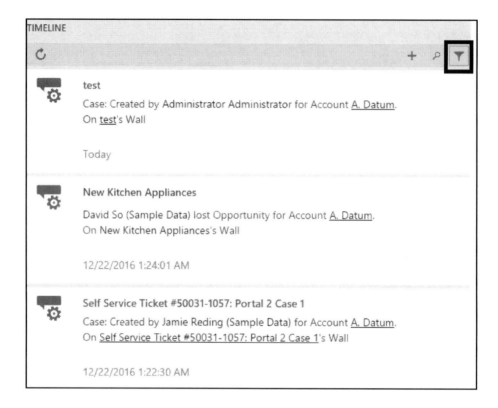

Once the representative clicks the button, a dropdown appears. The user can then select the filtering type in the dropdown:

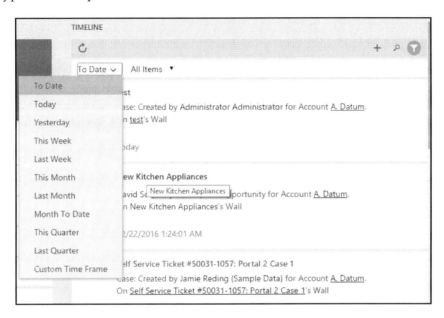

The following image depicts the form for the Interactive Service Hub for the **Account** entity:

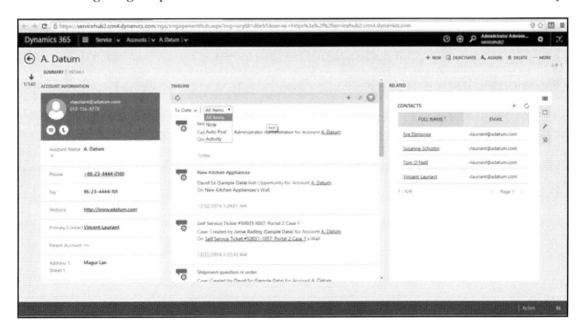

1. The next step is to navigate to any activity. To open the activity, the customer representative can just click on the activity name:

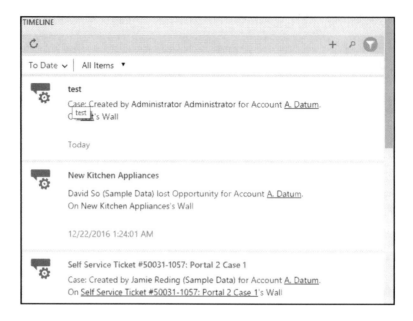

The activity page is opened, as shown in the following image:

The RELATED tab

The **RELATED** tab provides information related to the associated cases, opportunities, contacts, and entitlements. The following image displays the information related to the **CONTACTS** entity:

To create new records of any type, the customer representative can just click on the + button. This will open a new page in which the representative can enter details about the new activity. To open the cases assigned to the customer representative, the user can navigate to **Service | Cases**:

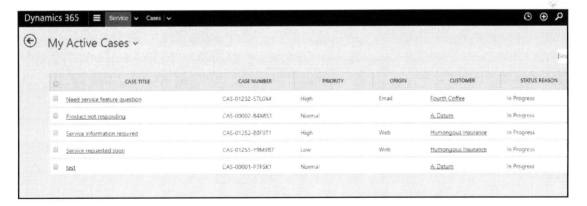

The activities performed in a case

The following screenshot shows some of the key information and activities that a representative can perform on the case:

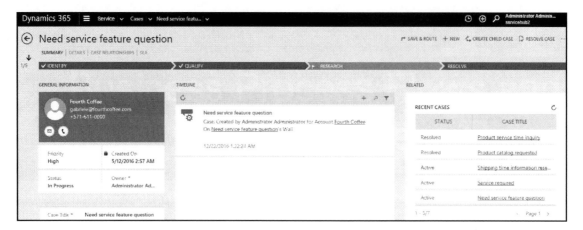

On the related subgrid section, the representative can browse for Knowledge base articles and a list of cases similar to the current case. The criteria for defining similar cases is configured in Dynamics CRM. The following screenshot shows the Knowledge base articles, with respect to the current case:

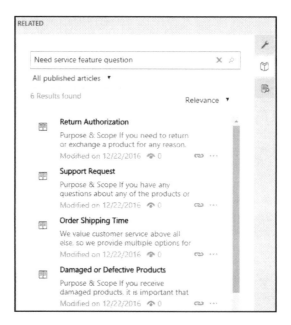

The **DETAILS** section of the case form provides general information about the case. The user can also edit the information by just clicking on the field he/she wants to edit:

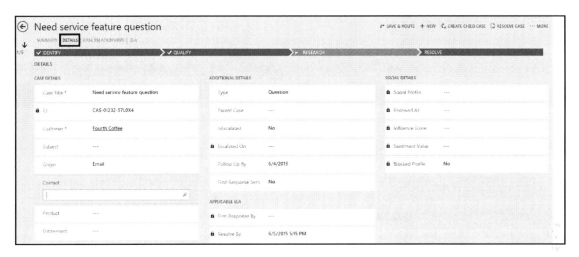

Now, let's have a look at the **CASE RELATIONSHIPS** section. It provides a list of **Merged Cases**, **Child Cases**, and **Associated Knowledge Records**:

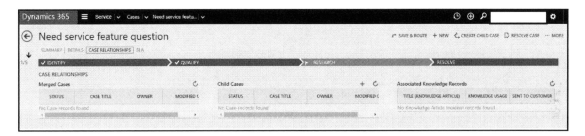

The **Service Level Agreements (SLA)** section provides a list of the associated SLAs with the Case:

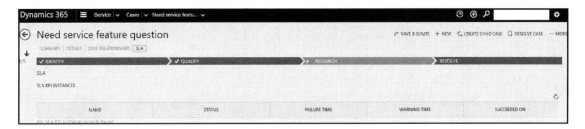

In certain cases, there could be a Business Processes associated with the Case. As illustrated in this example, the Case is going through a business process with Identify, Qualify, Research, and Resolve as the possible stages. A flag indicates the current stage. The customer representative can move to the next stage by clicking the **Next Stage** button. Take a look at the following screenshot:

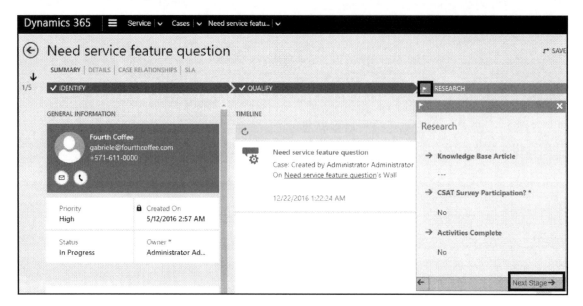

Like in Dynamics CRM, the customer representative can execute various functions, such as resolving the case, converting it to a Knowledge base, and so on.

Scenario 2

Acme Ltd desires to use Dynamics CRM to assist customer representatives in tracking incoming phone calls and creating cases, as necessary, for resolution. The following steps detail the process provided by Dynamics CRM to assist the preceding scenario:

1. Select the **Service** module from the CRM navigation:

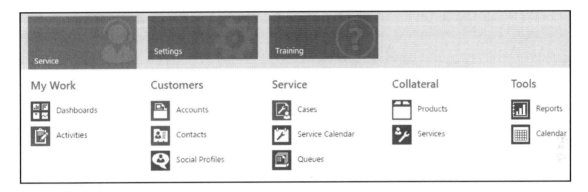

2. Select the **Account** entity on the navigation menu under **Service**, and open the record for **Alpine Ski House** available with the trial data:

3. Navigate to the related activities through the Related record menu on the account record:

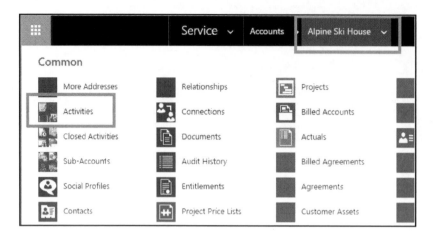

4. The following page will display a list of all the activity records associated with Alpine Ski House:

5. Click on **ADD NEW ACTIVITY** and choose **Phone Call**:

6. A new Phone Call form will pop up with details of the account already populated. Add the relevant fields, such as **Subject**, **Description**, and so on, and then click **Save**:

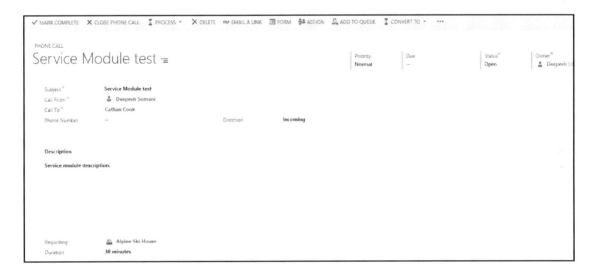

7. To convert the phone call to a case, select the **Convert** button, as shown in the following screenshot:

8. On clicking **Convert**, a case record will be automatically created:

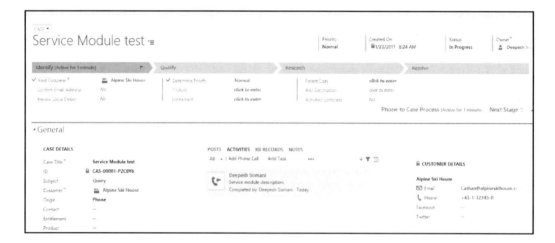

9. A new service case record for the Account is created. Note that the business process bar displays the phone to case process. Also, note that the area shows the phone call record that was used to create the case.

10. Click **Next Stage** to move to the **Qualify** stage. Then, click **Next Stage** again to move to the **Research** stage. Note the **RECENT CASES** step that allows the customer service representative to look up recent cases, as shown in the following screenshot:

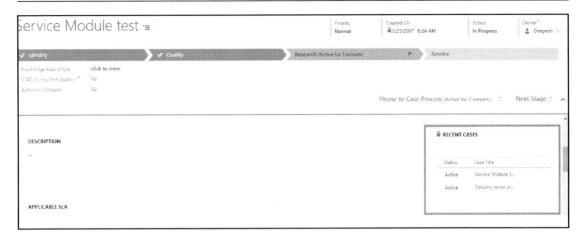

11. Click on **RESOLVE CASE** to resolve the case:

12. Fill in the resolution comments in the **Resolve Case** dialog and click **Resolve**:

13. This brings us to the end of the phone call to case process. As you can see in the following screenshot, you can easily track the phone calls in the **ACTIVITIES** section. Note that the Case record is marked read-only:

Scenario 3

Contoso Ltd. wants to utilize Dynamics CRM 2016 to increase the productivity and efficiency of their customer service managers, and let them have the tracking of service management and case-related activities going on in their system.

Dynamics CRM 2016 provides the Customer Service Manager Dashboard to assist for this purpose. The following steps will guide you through this feature:

1. Navigate to **Service | Dashboards**, and select the **Customer Service Manager Dashboard**:

List of Customer Service Dashboards:

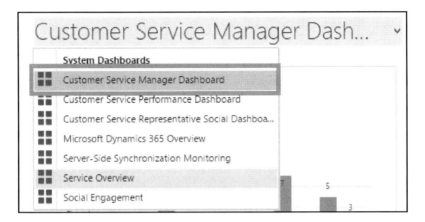

2. The following **Customer Service Manager Dashboard** will be presented to the customer service manager:

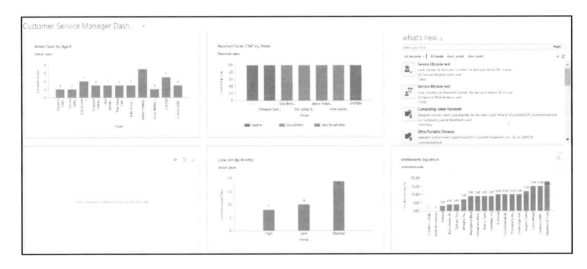

Some of the usual charts and their explanations in the **Customer Service Manager Dashboard** are listed as follows:

- The **Active Cases by Agent** chart shows a list of the active cases per customer service agent. This assists the customer service manager in assigning cases effectively and uniformly:

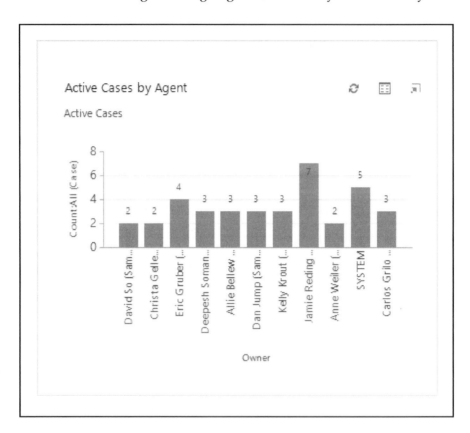

- The **Entitlements Expiration** gives a chart of Entitlements by the customer:

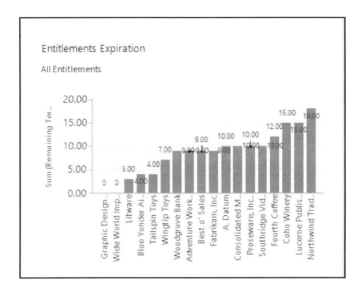

- The **Case Mix (By Priority)** chart gives a view of the number of cases by priority. This assists the customer service manager in assigning the right cases to the customer service agents or representatives:

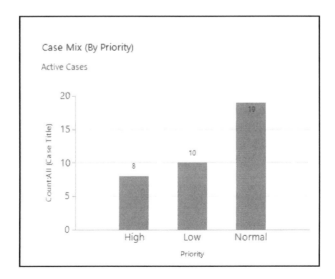

Summary

In this chapter, you saw several examples and entities involved in the Service module for Dynamics CRM 2016. You also learned how to configure the Interactive Service Hub, and how to use and navigate the Interactive Service Hub. You understood how customer service representatives can use Dynamics CRM 2016 to track phone calls, raise a service ticket or case, and then resolve the customer's problem. In addition, we walked through how customer service managers can utilize Dynamics CRM 2016 to serve their customers and assign cases effectively.

In the next chapter, we will cover the Marketing module of Dynamics CRM. We will focus on the entities, processes, and dashboards that are available for managing the Marketing division of any organization by using real-world examples.

4
Working with Marketing

The Marketing module of Dynamics CRM helps the organization by creating leads that can then be targeted by the Sales module. The Marketing module in the CRM helps the marketing team in assigning, scheduling, and tracking the marketing activities. Rich CRM reporting features then help the team in analyzing the performance of marketing campaigns and tracking the progress of the same.

In this chapter, we will understand the following key concepts:

- Entities involved in the Marketing module
- Case studies to understand the Marketing module

Contents of the Marketing module

The marketing module in CRM is mainly made up of the following entities:

- Marketing lists
- Campaigns
- Leads
- Account
- Contacts
- Campaign activities
- Campaign response

Let's discuss the Marketing module in more detail:

- **Marketing list**: This describes the list of leads, accounts, or contacts that we need to target in any campaign. A marketing list can be static or dynamic. In a static marketing list, the user must manually add the records in the list. In a dynamic marketing list, the user can define an advanced find query. The results of the query are then automatically added to the marketing list at run time. This is how a marketing list record looks like:

- **Campaign**: This defines the promotion that a user can run against the marketing lists. For example, a grocery outlet may run a campaign, *Summer Clothing*, on people between the ages of 20 and 25 years.
- **Campaign activities**: These define the list activities that are carried out to convert the lead into a potential business opportunity. Campaign activities could be an email, appointment, meeting, phone call, or even a custom activity.
- **Lead**: This defines a potential customer who could be converted into a potential business opportunity.
- **Account**: This defines a company or a prime who could do business with the organization.
- **Contact**: This defines the person associated with the account doing business with the organization.
- **Campaign response**: This defines the positive or negative outcome of the campaign activity associated with any customer; for example, if you receive an enquiry or if a customer shows interest in your product.

The structure of the Marketing module

The following is a *Visio* diagram explaining the structure of and the interactions involved in the Marketing module:

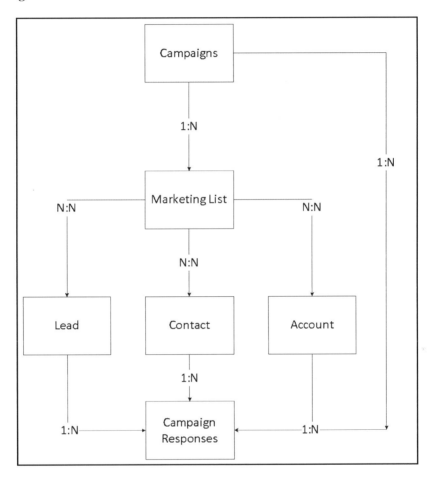

In a nutshell, the Dynamics CRM Marketing module provides solutions so that the Marketing team can assign, schedule, and track their marketing campaigns and measure the campaign performance.

Marketing list

Marketing list defines a collection of contacts, leads, or accounts that can be targeted for a marketing activity. Dynamics CRM provides two types of marketing lists, as follows:

- **Static marketing list**: This is a kind of marketing list that does not get automatically updated. The user must manually add the contacts, leads, or accounts that they want to be targeted in the campaign.
- **Dynamic marketing list**: When a user creates the dynamic marketing list, they just create a query for contacts, leads, or accounts. When records are created/updated based on the criteria defined in the query, the list is automatically updated according to the query. For example, if the query is to select contacts with names starting with *A* and you add more records with names starting with *A*, they will also be added to the marketing list automatically.

Creating a marketing list

Perform the following steps to create a marketing list:

1. Navigate to **Marketing** | **Marketing List** and click on the **+ NEW** button. The following form of marketing list will load up:

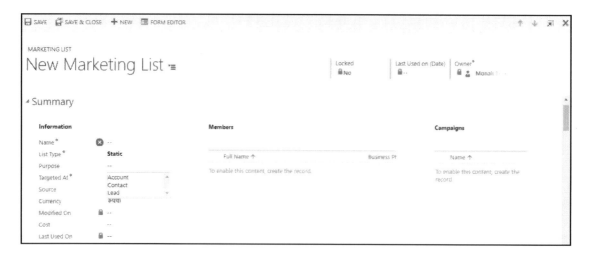

The following are some of the important details of the **Marketing List**:

- **List type**: This defines the type of the marketing list, that is, **Static** or **Dynamic**.
- **Targeted at**: This defines the target audience of the marketing list. It can be **Account**, **Contact**, or **Lead**.
- **Cost**: This is the cost set for the execution of the campaign.
- **Members**: This is a collection of all the records that are to be targeted in the campaign.
- **Campaign**: This is a collection of all the marketing campaigns that target this marketing list.
- **Quick campaign**: This is a collection of all the marketing quick campaigns that target this marketing list.

2. **Adding members in a static marketing list**: After the marketing list is created with **List Type** as **Static**, you must manually add members to the **Members** grid:

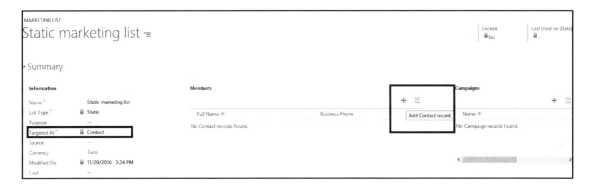

Select members for the **Marketing Lists**:

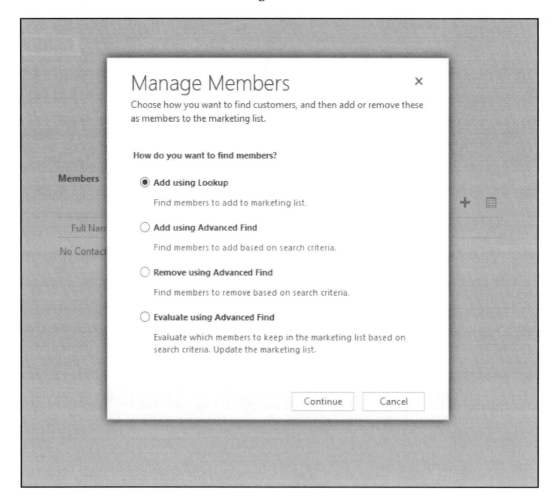

Select members using **Look Up Records**:

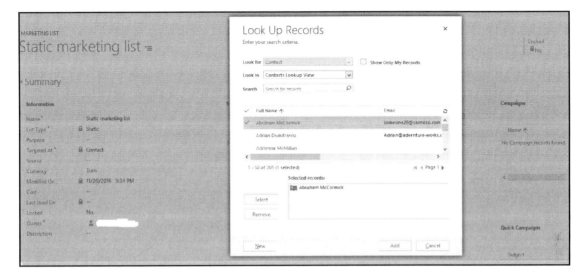

Create a **Static marketing list**, as shown in the following screenshot:

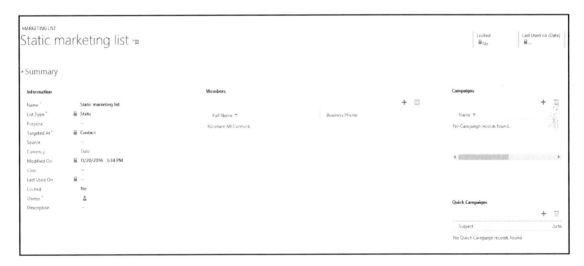

As illustrated in the preceding screenshots, Dynamics CRM also provides the capability to add members using advanced find:

3. **Adding members in a dynamic marketing list**: After the marketing list is created with the list type as **Dynamic**, you need to specify a query. All the records of the target member that fall under the query will be added to the marketing list:

Let's see the second part of the same figure:

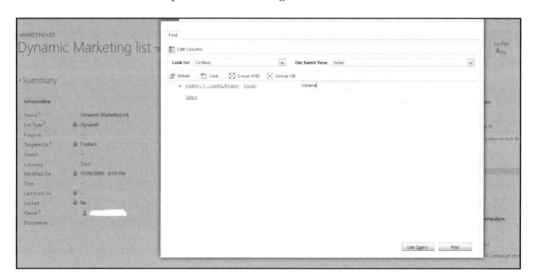

As illustrated in the query, all contacts in `Ireland` will be added to the marketing list.

Campaigns

Dynamics CRM provides a rich set of processes related to the execution of marketing activities. Campaigns are the centerpiece of Dynamics CRM Marketing module. Let's see how a campaign is created and executed:

1. **Creating a new Campaign**: Navigate to **Marketing** | **Campaigns** and click on the **New Campaign** button:

Let's see the second part of the same screenshot:

Let's see the third part of the same screenshot:

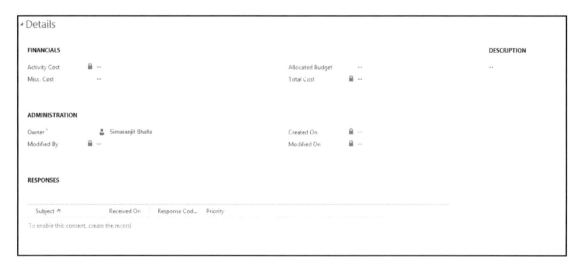

The following are some of the important details on the Campaign form:

- **Basic information**: This consists of the campaign name, campaign code, currency, campaign type, and the expected response percentage. An out-of-the-box campaign box can have values such as **Advertisement**, **Direct Marketing**, **Event**, **Co-branding**, and **Other**.
- **Schedules**: These consist of dates related to the launch of the campaign.
- **Activities**: This grid consists of all the activities related to the campaign, such as out-of-box **Phone Call**, **Appointment**, **Task**, and **Email**.
- **Marketing lists**: This grid consists of all the marketing lists, which are to be targeted by the Campaign.
- **Leads**: This grid consists of the individual leads that are to be targeted in the campaign.
- **Campaign activities**: This grid defines the list of activities that will be executed in the campaign.
- **Financial details**: This section consists of fields related to the execution of the campaign.
- **Response**: The grid consists of all the responses that the customers have given to various campaign activities.

2. **Adding a marketing list to the campaign**: On the campaign form, a user can add the marketing lists, which will be targeted by the Campaign:

The members count indicate the number of records present in the marketing list.

3. **Adding individual leads to the campaign**: On the Campaign form, a user can add the individual lead records that are to be targeted in the campaign:

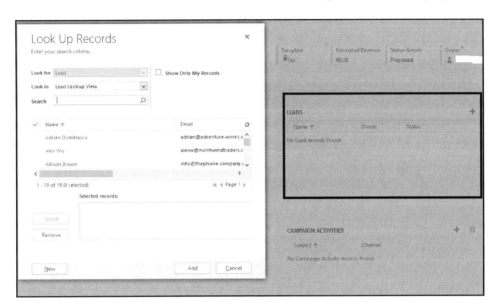

4. **Adding Campaign Activities to the Campaign**: On the Campaign form, you can click on the **Add** button to create **New Campaign Activity**. This will launch a new form for **Campaign Activity**:

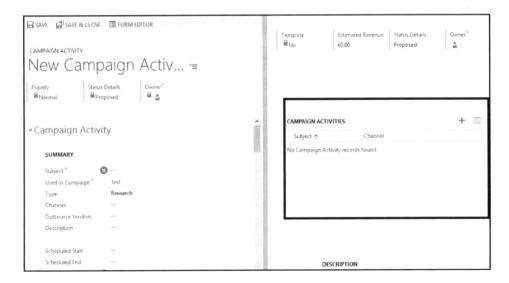

Mentioned below is some of the important information that needs to be filled in the Campaign Activity:

- **Channel**: This defines the mode of Campaign Activity execution. Possible values are **Email**, **Task**, **Phone Call**, **Appointment**, **Fax**, and **Letter**.
- **Scheduled Start**: This is the start time of execution of the Campaign Activity.
- **Scheduled End**: This is the end time of execution of the Campaign Activity.
- **Allocated Budget**: This is the budget that has been allocated for the execution of the Campaign Activity.
- **Actual Cost**: This is the total amount actually spend in execution of Campaign Activity.
- **MARKETING LIST**: The marketing lists will be copied across from the associated Campaign.

Check out the following screenshot:

5. **Approving the campaign**: To start the campaign execution, you must firstly approve the campaign. You need to change the status of the campaign to **Launched**. This will launch the campaign:

6. **Distributing the Campaign Activities**: After the campaign is launched, you need to distribute the predefined campaign activities. This needs to be done on the **Campaign Activity** form:

On clicking the button, appropriate activities will be generated for each member present in the marketing list. As the channel of **Campaign Activity** is **Phone Call**, the click action will open a form for entering the basic details about the phone call activity. Some of the fields, such as **To**, will be read-only, as they are to be generated automatically by the system:

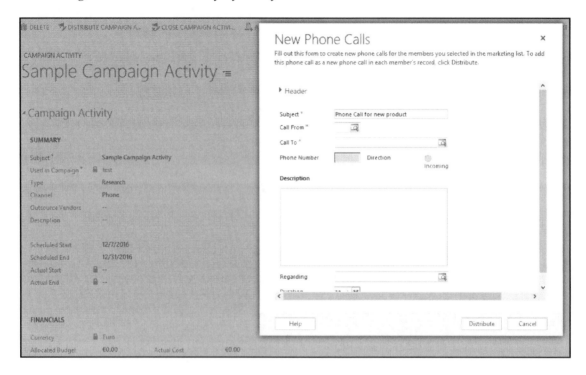

Click on the **Distribute** button after entering all the required information. The system will prompt you the user to enter the owner of the generated activities:

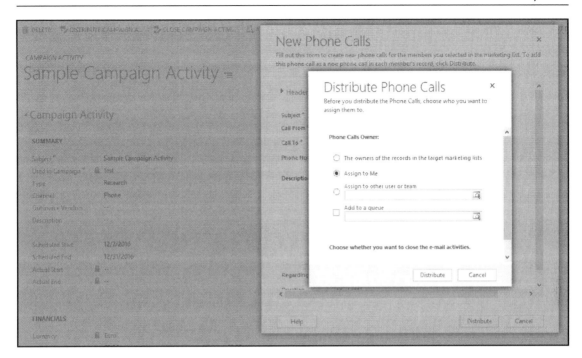

As illustrated in the following screenshot, activities for the members mentioned in the marketing lists will be automatically generated:

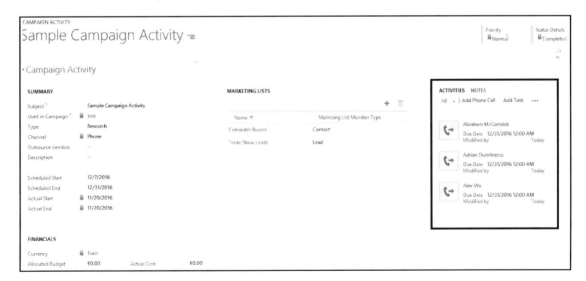

7. **Capturing Campaign Response**: As this is an outgoing phone call activity, you need to manually convert the associated phone call activity to a campaign response:

On clicking the button, a **Campaign Response** form will open:

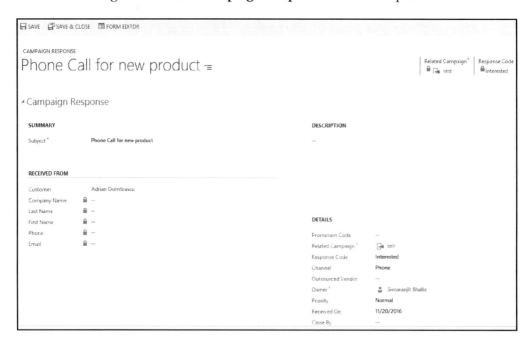

The following are some of the important fields related to **Campaign Response**:

- **Customer**: This is the contact, lead, or account to which the call is made.
- **Response Code**: This is the response that the customer gave. Its possible values are **Interested**, **Not interested**, **Do not Send Marketing Material**, and **Error**.
- **Received On**: This is the date of response receipt.

Once you click and save the form, **Campaign Response** will be updated on the Campaign form:

Quick campaigns

Quick campaigns are very similar to campaigns, except for the following differences:

- Quick campaigns can only be targeted against a single marketing list. On the other hand, a campaign can be executed for multiple marketing lists.
- Quick campaigns can only have a single activity that can be executed against the target members. On the other hand, a campaign can have multiple campaign activities.

Perform the following steps to create a quick campaign:

1. Navigate to a marketing list and create a quick campaign for the marketing list:

2. When you click the **Create Quick Campaign** button, it will launch a **Quick Campaign** wizard. The next step is to complete the wizard:

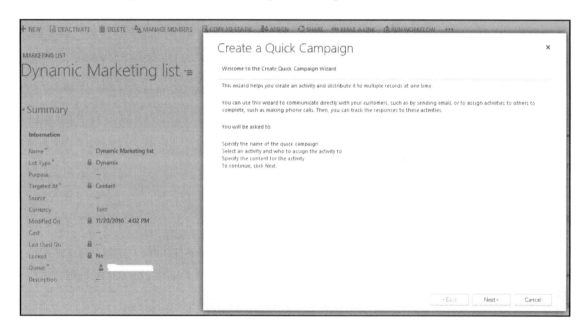

Add a name for the new quick campaign:

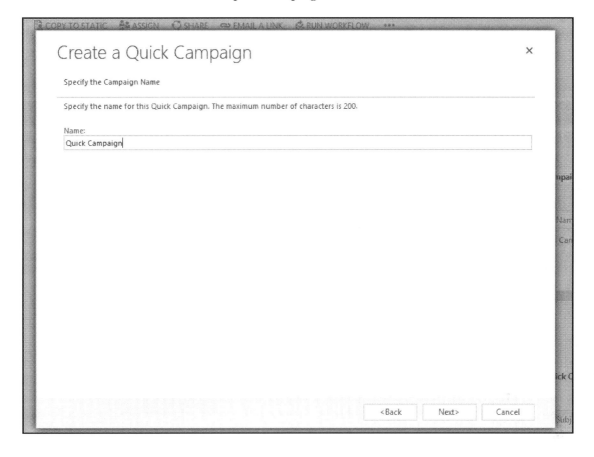

On the next screen, you need to select the activity that will be executed in the quick campaign. Based on the type of activity you select, Dynamics CRM will prompt for the details that the user needs to enter:

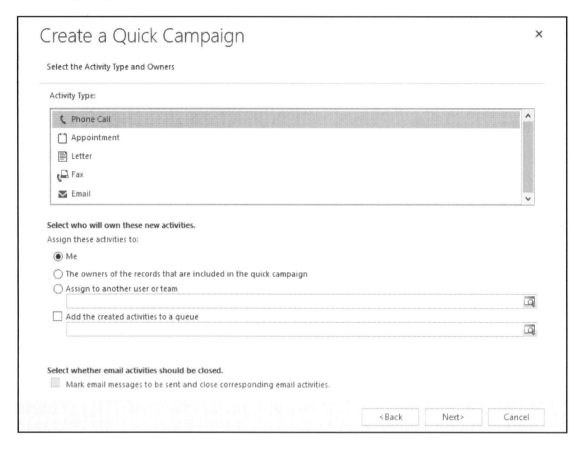

Here's how to add details for the campaign activity:

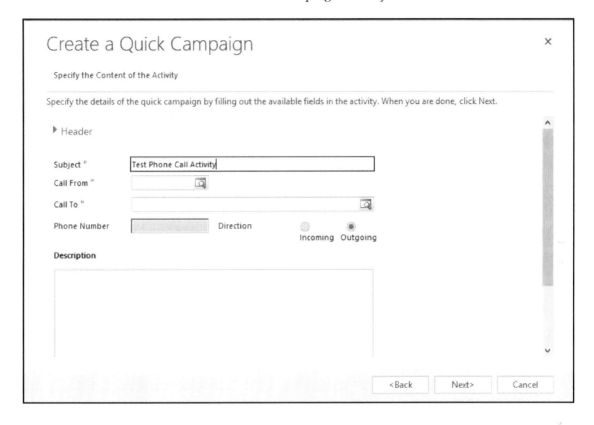

Let's see the second part of the same screenshot:

After the wizard is completed, Dynamics CRM will create the quick campaign and it will get associated with the marketing list:

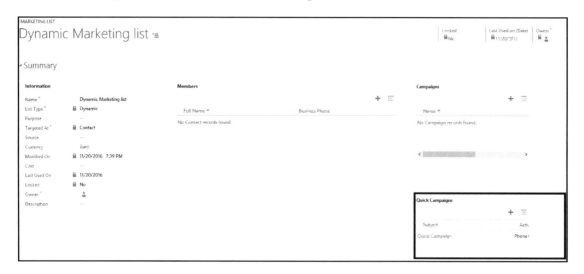

Scenario 1

As a part of the marketing team in Contoso, I need to prepare a list of leads with ages less than 25. I should be able to send a promotional email to these leads and also track their response. Based on their response, I should have the ability to track them.

Perform the following steps:

1. **Create a dynamic marketing list**: The list should be based on leads and advanced queries should include all the leads less than 25 years of age. As the list is a dynamic one, the marketing list will be automatically updated. Create a new **MARKETING LIST**, **Targeted At Lead**, and add members, as shown in the following screenshot:

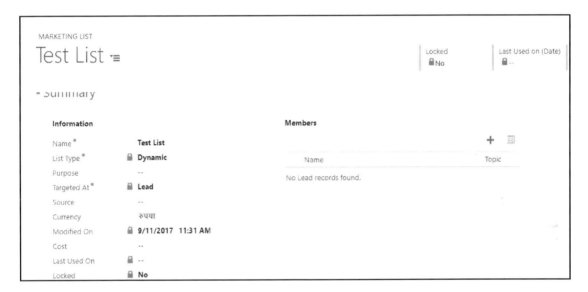

Add a query, as shown in the following screenshot:

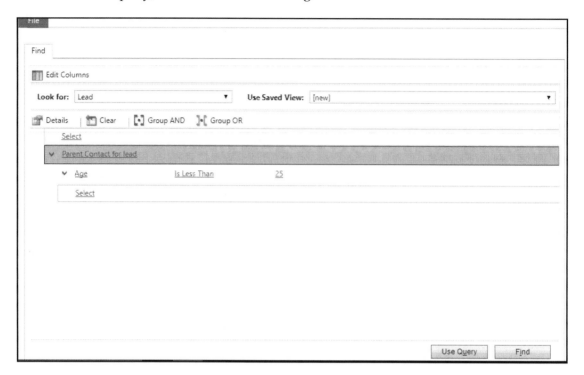

The members will be added to your list, as shown in the following screenshot:

2. **Create an email template**: Based on the content that you wish to share in the promotional email, prepare an email template:

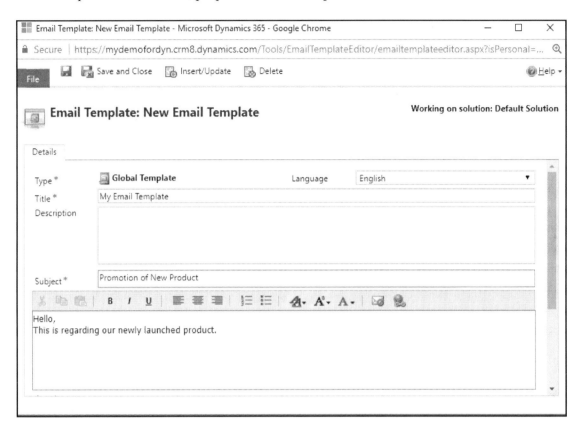

3. **Create a campaign**: Create a campaign and add the marketing list created in the first step.

4. Create a new record and add the marketing list by clicking the + button, as shown in the following screenshot:

Select the marketing list we created in the previous steps:

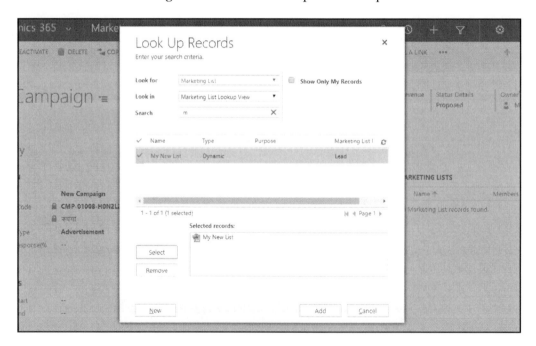

5. Now, for the campaign, create a campaign activity. In the campaign activities grid, add a new email activity. For the email, use the template that we prepared in *step 2*.

6. First, add a new campaign activity, as shown in the following screenshot:

7. Create a new activity and save it:

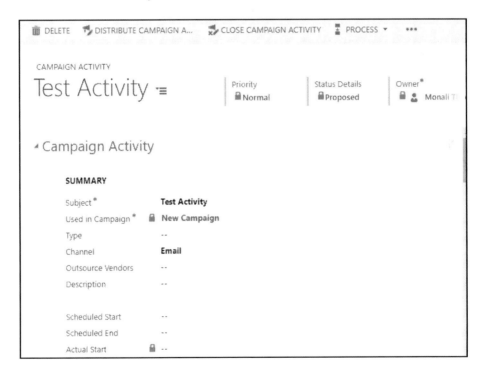

8. Now, on the campaign record, click on the **Distribute Activities** button. This will basically roll out the email records to all the leads present in the marketing list.

9. Navigate to the activity you created and distribute it by clicking the **DISTRIBUTE CAMPAIGN ACTIVITY** button. Select the email template, as shown in the following screenshot:

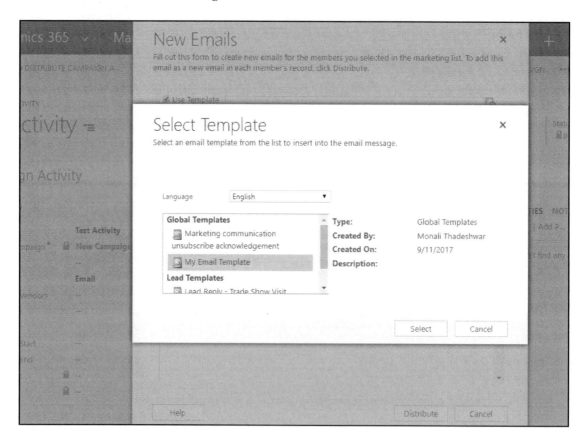

10. Click the **Distribute** button:

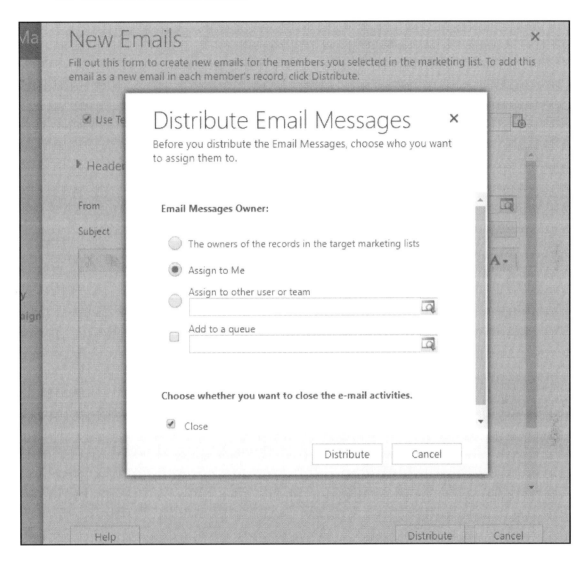

11. When the lead replies to the email campaign, using the tracking option in Dynamics CRM, the response will automatically be synced to Dynamics CRM and will start appearing on the response grid in the campaign.

12. Based on the campaign response, the user can click on the **Qualify Lead** button. This will qualify the lead to an opportunity or contact.

Scenario 2

Contoso is launching a new product. They want to monitor the social channel to gather the runtime feedback on how the public is reacting to their product. They also want their marketing team to reply to the questions/feedback that people are putting regarding their product on a social platform.

Perform the following steps:

1. **Setting Up Microsoft Social Engagement**: **Microsoft Social Engagement** helps users to track and analyze social communications across public networks about specific topics. This is how you can set up social feeds on **Microsoft Social Engagement**:
   1. Log in to **Microsoft Social Engagement** and navigate to **Microsoft Social Engagement | Search Setup**:

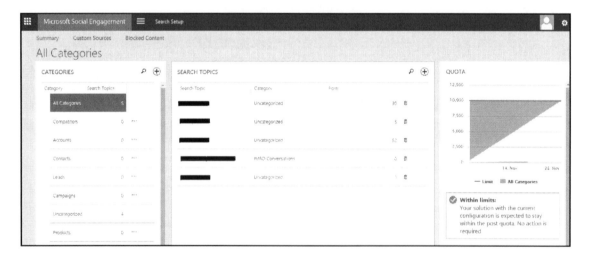

2. You can then create new categories related to competitors, products, or any other required category:

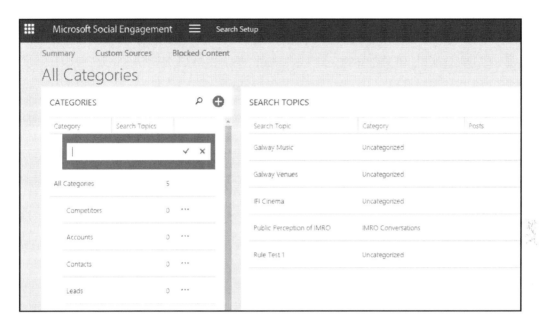

3. For any existing Category, you can add search feeds. Social listening will then monitor the social media for any activity related to these feeds. For doing so, you need to select the category and click the add (+) button on **Search Topics**:

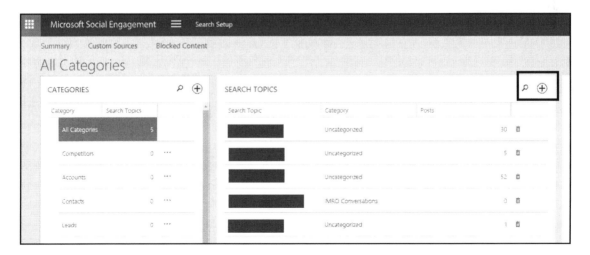

4. You can then add a new search topic or click on any individual search topic to configure the feeds:

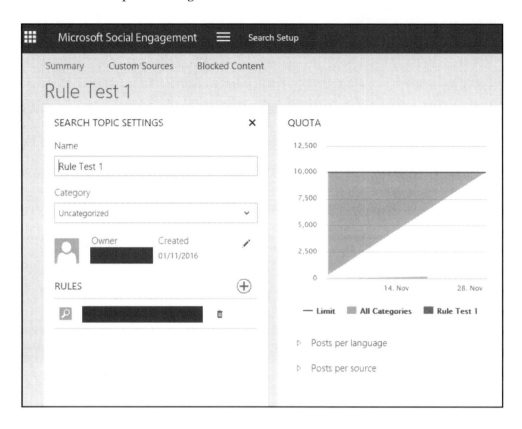

Select the type of search rule:

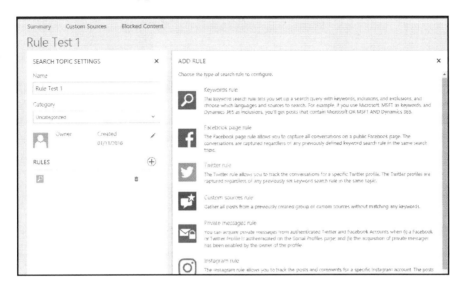

As illustrated in the preceding screenshot, you can configure different rules related to **Keywords rule**, **Facebook page rule**, **Twitter rule**, and so on.

2. After the search criteria has been set up, the user can navigate to the dashboard. The user needs to navigate to **Microsoft Social Engagement** | **Analytics** for monitoring the data:

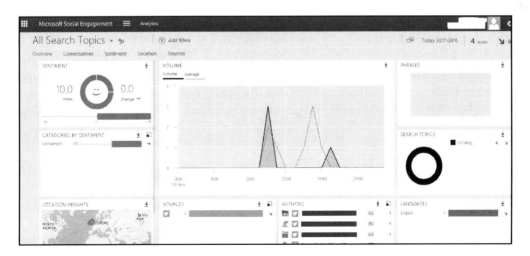

Let's look at some of the entities in **Analytics**:

- **Sentiment analysis**: This shows whether the overall feedback is positive or negative
- **Volume**: This gives the number of feeds happening in social media related to the configured search topics
- **Phrases**: This shows the different search topics that have been configured in the social engagement
- **Categories by sentiment**: This shows the feeds in terms of the different categories
- **Location insights**: This shows the feeds in terms of the locations from which the feeds are coming from
- **Sources**: This differentiates feeds in terms of their source, that is, Twitter, Facebook, and so on
- **Authors**: This shows the different people posting the feed
- **Languages**: This shows the feeds in terms of their native language classification

3. After going through the feeds that come through to the **Social Engagement**, you can reply back to the tweets or the Facebook posts.
4. Based on the conversation or the replies given by the author, you can convert it to an opportunity or a lead.

Scenario 3

John leads the marketing team in Contoso. He wishes to go through different KRAs and see how the campaigns are performing across different parameters.

John logs into the CRM system. As a member of the marketing team, he sets the marketing dashboard as the home page. Let's look at campaign type classification, which involves the differentiation of campaigns in terms of campaign types, such as **Advertisement**, **Direct Marketing**, **Event**, and so on. Check out the following screenshot:

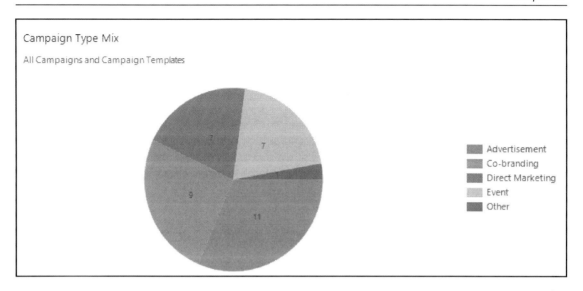

Let's look at the various components:

- **Campaign budget versus actual costs**: This involves comparing the total cost spent across the campaigns in terms of the budgeted cost:

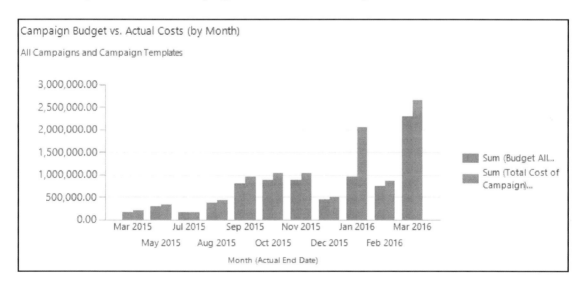

- **Leads by source campaign**: This shows leads generated for each of the campaigns:

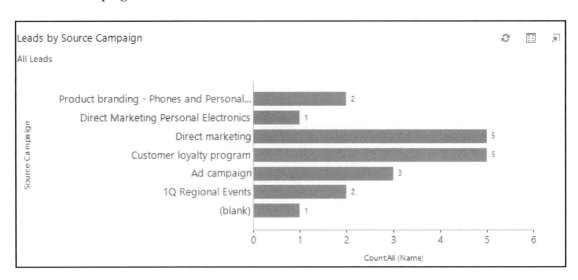

- **Revenue generated by campaigns**: This plots the revenue generated by each campaign:

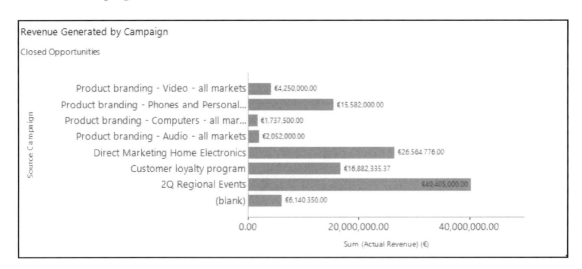

A note on Microsoft Dynamics Marketing

Although **Microsoft Dynamics Marketing** (**MDM**) has been discontinued by Microsoft as a standalone product, it did have several features that were quite useful from a Microsoft perspective. MDM was quite easy to configure and connectors were available to integrate the records with Microsoft Dynamics CRM. The following screenshot shows how information was synced between MDM and Dynamics CRM:

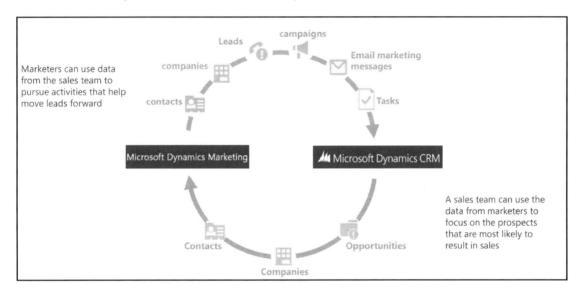

It provided the capability to launch campaigns across different channels, such as social media, SMS, and emails. When the activities were distributed across to people using these channels, it also provided several triggers to monitor the activities done by the contact, such as opening the email, responding to the email, and opening the link provided in the email.

Summary

In this chapter, we discussed the Marketing module of Dynamics CRM 2016. We covered entities involved in the Marketing module and the usage of each entity. You also learned how to prepare a marketing list of leads in the age group below 25 years. In addition, we discussed Microsoft social engagement and the KRAs for the Marketing module.

In the next chapter, we will go through the XRM framework of Dynamics CRM 2016.

5
Working with the XRM Framework

The XRM framework defines a strategic approach of customizing the out-of-the-box features available in Dynamics CRM to make sure that it implements all the business aspects of a system. The central idea of the XRM framework is to extend the standard functionalities provided in Dynamics CRM to suit any business requirement. Businesses could be of varying types, such as public sector, insurance, banking, retail, telecom, and so on.

In this chapter, we will cover the following topics:

- Student management application via the XRM framework of Dynamics CRM 2016
- Understanding custom entities, views, attributes, and so on, in Dynamics CRM 2016
- Understanding calculated fields in Dynamics CRM 2016

Owing to the underlying .NET Framework, Microsoft Dynamics CRM 2016 provides a very powerful tool that can be easily extended to map any business requirement that is not provided out of the box.

In many places in the book, you may have read about the term, out-of-the-box. Out-of-box features mean the components that come packaged with Dynamics CRM 2016, right after an instance is set up. Out-of-box Dynamics CRM 2016 consists of three modules: Sales, Service, and Marketing. These modules consist of standard business processes, which are followed in their respective industries.

Let's explore some scenarios to understand the XRM framework in further detail.

Scenario walkthrough

The following is an illustration that shows how Dynamics CRM can be extended in an education-based institute, for example, a typical school.

Mapping the entities: A typical school management application will consist of the following actors:

- Students
- Teachers
- Parents
- Resources, including classrooms, playground, labs, and so on
- Library books

Apart from the aforementioned actors, there will also be the following processes to enable the daily working of the institute:

- Attendance management
- Test evaluation

The first step is to identify whether there is a possibility of mapping any of the existing out-of-box entities for our usage. Based on our analysis, if that is not possible, we will create a new entity.

Dynamics CRM provides **CONTACT** or **CUSTOMER** as a standard out-of-box entity. By default, it contains attributes such as the first name, last name, and so on. This entity can easily be mapped to either a **Student**, a **Teacher**, or a **Parent**.

As we are using the same entity for all of the students, teachers, and parents, we can use a picklist attribute with the possible values for students, teachers, and parents, in order to differentiate between them. Let's try and understand how we will achieve this. Check out the following screenshot:

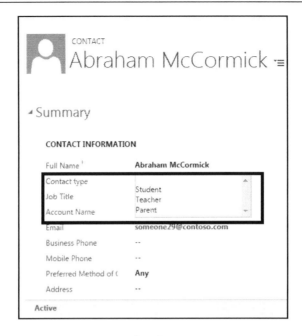

Contact Type

For a data point of view, the **Contact** entity in Dynamics CRM will be a collection of all the students, teachers, and parents associated with the institute. The following diagram highlights the relationship between them:

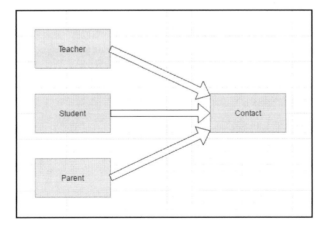

Contact Relationship

Adding resources

Now that we have mapped students, teachers, and parents, the next step is to identify the possible mappings for classrooms, books, and so on. Dynamics CRM provides an out-of-box feature of **Service Management**, which can be easily customized to add the resources required in any typical school:

1. Navigate to **Settings** | **Service Management** | **Service Scheduling** | **Facilities/Equipment**:

Service Management

Article Templates
Create and manage templates for articles in the knowledge base.

Service Scheduling

Business Closure
Create a list of holidays and other times when the business is closed.

Facilities/Equipment
Add facilities and equipment for service scheduling. Change information about resources or delete existing resources.

Sites
Create new sites or office locations where service operations take place. Add and remove resources, change site information, or delete sites.

Service Management

2. Now, click on the **Facilities/Equipment** link. On doing so, you will be redirected to the **Facilities/Equipment** view:

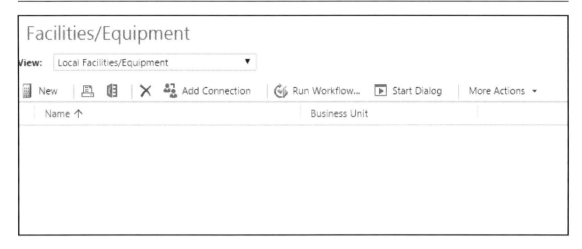

Facilities/Equipment

3. Now, add the appropriate **Facilities/Equipment** requirements for the daily functioning of the institute:

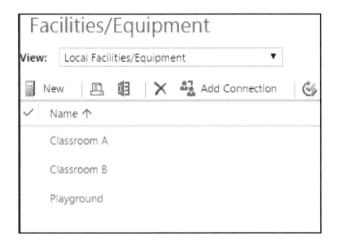

Sample Facilities/Equipment's

This way, we can map all the required equipment, such as classrooms, blackboards, labs, presenters, and so on, to facilities in Dynamics CRM 2016.

For mapping the books available in a library, depending on the attributes required, we can either go for a custom entity, or we can just reuse the same **Facility/Equipment** entity. The following screenshot shows how the records of **Classrooms**, **Labs**, **Playground**, and **Library/Books** will be collectively represented as a **Facility/Equipment**:

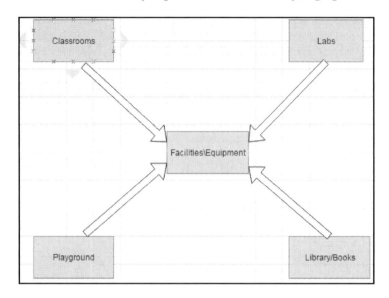

Structure of Facilities/Equipment

Dynamics CRM 2016 provides out-of-box activities such as email, phone, and appointments for associating any interaction with the customer. We can create our own custom entities and define them as activities. Using some custom logic, which we will be learning in the coming chapters, the attendance can be perceived as another form of activity.

Creating custom fields

After we have done the mapping for all the required entities, the next step is to prepare the basic data model for all the actors involved in the solution. Due to business-specific requirements, a user may need to create custom attributes for the entities.

Dynamics CRM allows the user to create attributes of different types. The following section explains the attributes in detail.

Attributing data types

In Dynamics CRM 2016, an attribute could be of the following data types:

- **Single line of text**: This is a string representation, for example, a name.
- **Option set**: This is an attribute that can have values in a picklist, for example, a title can have possible values of **Mr.**, **Mrs.**, and **Miss**.
- **Two options**: This is an attribute that can have only two possible values.
- **Image**: This is an attribute to which we can upload some image.
- **Whole number**: This is an attribute that can acquire an integer value.
- **Floating point number**: This attribute can assume a float value. It is similar to a decimal and is generally used when we are not much concerned with accuracy after the decimal point.
- **Decimal number**: This attribute can assume a decimal value.
- **Currency**: This attribute can assume money-related value. For example, we can create an attribute for representing a salary of 100 dollars per day. The dollar component, that is, the currency component will be saved in a base attribute. The base attribute is created automatically when a currency attribute is created. The value component, that is, 100, will be saved separately from the base component.
- **Multiple line of text**: This is a multi-line string representation, for example, the description of a book.
- **Date and Time**: This attribute can assume a date-time value, such as the date of a class.
- **Lookup**: This attribute links two different entities.
- **Customer**: This attribute links the entity to an account or a customer.

 For a detailed explanation, you can refer to this MSDN link:
https://msdn.microsoft.com/en-in/library/dn817862.aspx

The Calculated and Rollup fields

In Dynamics CRM 2016, we can define attributes as Calculated and Rollup. Calculated fields allow a user to automate mathematical calculations used in the solution. Based on the type of the attribute, Dynamics CRM allows the user to configure an attribute with the type as Calculated or Rollup.

An attribute can be declared as a Calculated attribute if its value can be derived from a mathematical formula, such as the addition or multiplication of two fields.

An attribute can be declared as a Rollup field if its value can be derived using an aggregate function over a set of other records related to that specified record. For example, we can aggregate data from the activities related to the record, such as emails and appointments.

The following screenshot shows how an attribute can be declared with its type as **Calculated** or **Rollup**:

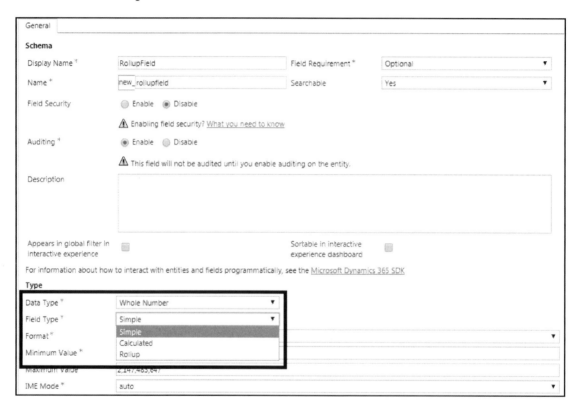

Rollup/Calculated Field Declaration

 This option cannot be rolled back and is only defined when the entity is being created.

Now, while we have gone through how the Rollup and Calculated fields are created, we need to understand some aspects, which we will do in the next section.

What operations can the Rollup fields do?

Rollup fields can be created for the following operations:

- **SUM**: This calculates the sum of a set of related record fields and rolls up to a parent entity field
- **COUNT**: This counts the related records and rolls up to a parent entity field
- **MIN**: This gets the minimum value in a set of related record fields and rolls up to a parent entity field
- **MAX**: This gets the maximum value in a set of related record fields and rolls up to a parent entity field
- **AVG**: This gets the average value in a set of related record fields and rolls up to a parent entity field

The following are some examples where we can use Rollup fields:

- The last modified activity date on an account
- The number of open cases under an account
- The total revenue under all opportunities for an account

The following are some of the limitations of Rollup fields:

- Rollups are only supported for 1:N relationships and not for N:N relationships
- The maximum number of Rollup fields allowed in any CRM organization is 100
- The maximum number or Rollup fields allowed in one CRM entity is 10
- Creating Rollup fields over a Rollup field is not allowed
- A workflow cannot be triggered on Rollup field updates

What types of formula are allowed on Calculated fields?

The Calculated fields can be created for the following formulas. As the names of the formulas are self-explanatory, we will not go through their explanation:

- **ADDHOURS**
- **ADDDAYS**

- **ADDWEEKS**
- **ADDMONTHS**
- **ADDYEARS**
- **SUBTRACTHOURS**
- **SUBTRACTDAYS**
- **SUBTRACTWEEKS**
- **SUBTRACTMONTHS**
- **SUBTRACTYEARS**
- **DIFFINDAYS**
- **DIFFINHOURS**
- **DIFFINMINUTES**
- **DIFFINMONTHS**
- **DIFFINWEEKS**
- **DIFFINYEARS**
- **CONCAT**
- **TRIMLEFT**
- **TRIMRIGHT**

The following are some examples where we can use the Calculated fields:

- As a requirement, we need to capture a follow-up date, which should be a week after the opportunity has been created. Note that there may be more than one way of achieving the requirements, such as in this case, by creating an out-of-box workflow. However, the main idea is just to show how Calculated fields work.
- Applying some sort of predecided criteria and combining the values present in different string objects is another example.

The following are some limitations of the Calculated fields:

- A Calculated field cannot refer to itself in the formula.
- We can configure a Calculated field such that its value is determined by another Calculated field. However, the maximum level of this dependency is five.
- Duplicate detection rules are not triggered on Calculated fields.

Duplicate detection rules in Dynamics CRM allow a user to identify whether there are other records in the system with the exact same attribute values. Unfortunately, we cannot set a duplicate detection job on a Calculated field.

Refer to the following MSDN link, which explains the duplicate detection rules:
`https://msdn.microsoft.com/en-us/library/gg309427.aspx`

- A workflow or plugin cannot be triggered on Calculated field updates.

While discussing the concept of Rollup/Calculated fields, it would be beneficial to go through relationships once.

Relationships

Entity relationships define how two different entities can be related to one another. As illustrated in the following screenshot, three types of relations are possible between entities:

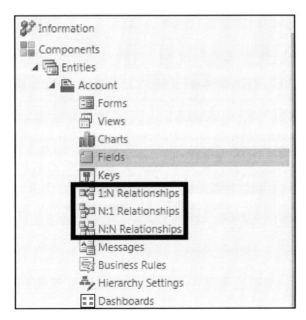

Relationship

The following is a critical aspect of relationships, which allows us to control the main operations in Dynamics CRM:

- **Relationship behavior**: This defines how the child entities will be impacted if any of the following events are executed on the parent record:
    - **Assign**: When the parent record is assigned to another user or a team
    - **Reparent**: When the associated child record is assigned to another parent record
    - **Share**: When the parent record is shared
    - **Delete**: When the parent record is deleted
    - **Unshare**: When the parent record is removed from sharing with the child record
    - **Merge**: When the parent record is merged with another record
    - **Rollup view**: This option is available only when the parent is **Account**, **Contact**, or **Opportunity**, and it is related to the Rollup of the activities field on the related record

    By Default, **Merge** is **Cascade All** for all relation types.

The following are the possible values of relationship behaviors:

- **Parental**: Whenever any of the aforementioned actions is executed on the parent record, the same change also occurs on the child.
- **Referential**: Apart from **Merge**, none of the other actions are executed on the child record.
- **Referential, restrict delete**: The **Delete** operation on the parent will not be allowed if there are any associated child records. **Merge** will be executed on the child records, while the other functions will not be executed on the child record.
- **Configuration cascading**: Apart from **Merge**, the user will be able to control the respective actions on all the child records.

For the sake of explanation, we will define the relations between two entities: **A** and **B**.

1:N relationships

When a 1:N relationship is created between A and B, it signifies that a record of A can have multiple associated records of B. When a 1:N relationship is created between A and B, Dynamics CRM internally creates a lookup attribute in B and an associated navigation link in the record of A. Check out the following screenshot:

1:N Relation example

N:1 relationships

When an N:1 relationship is created between A and B, it signifies that multiple records of A can be associated with a single record of B. Like 1:N, creating an N:1 relationship will create a lookup attribute in A and a navigation link in B.

N:N Relationships

When an N:N relationship is created between A and B, it signifies that a single record of A can be associated with multiple records of B and vice versa. When this relation is created between two entities, it creates a navigation link in both the entities:

Along with the navigation links, it also creates a middle entity with the schema name of the relationship, which can then be used in various requests.

Let's look at some scenarios to better understand the Rollup and Calculated fields.

Scenario 1

The teacher of a class wishes to maintain the attendance records of every student in any given year.

The standard behind designing any solution in Microsoft Dynamics CRM 2016 is to avoid as much custom code as possible. It makes the customizations easy to maintain and upgrade if we end up moving to newer versions of CRM. Here, again, we will try to achieve the same.

As stated in the mapping section, we identified that `Attendance` of any student can be captured as a custom activity record. The following steps explain how the scenario can be achieved:

1. **Creating the attendance entity**: In the following screenshot, review the **Define as an activity entity** check box:

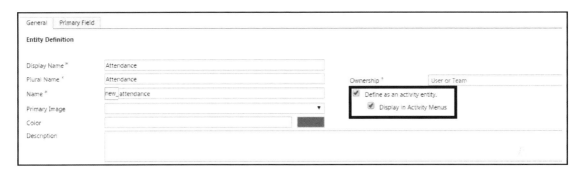

Scenario 1 : Attendance entity

On creating the entity, a 1:N relationship between **Contact** and **Attendance** should get automatically created:

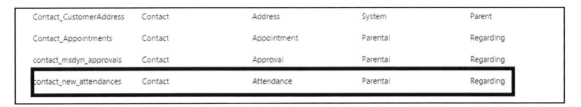

Contact relationship

 When we say that a 1:N relationship exists between entity A and entity B, we mean that one record of A can be connected to multiple records of B; however, one record of B must be associated with only one record of A. On the other hand, when an N:N relationship exists between two entities, it means that one record of B can be connected to multiple instances of A, and vice versa.

2. Now, navigate to **Contact** and create a new whole number field for the previous year's attendance. Note that its field type should be **Rollup**. Refer to the following screenshot:

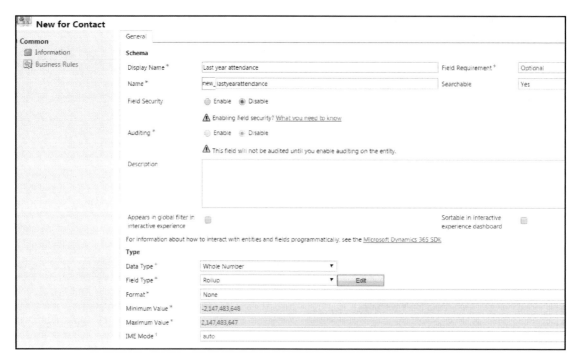

Scenario 1: Attendance Attribute

3. Save the attribute and click on the **Edit** button. A popup for entering the criteria of the Rollup field opens:

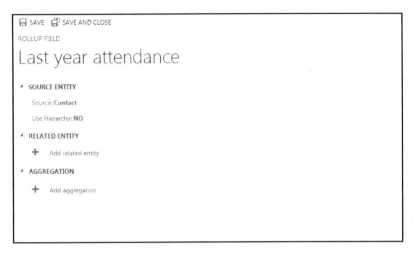

Scenario 1 : Rollup field

4. As shown in the following screenshot, click on the **Related** drop-down menu to select the related entity on which the user wishes to configure the Rollup field:

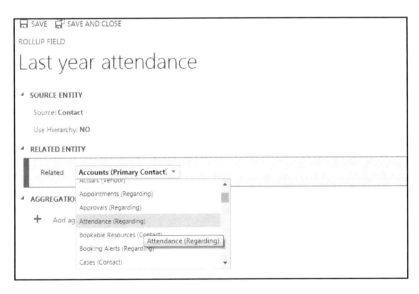

Scenario 1: Rollup field

5. After selecting the **Attendance** entity, we need to define the filter criteria. As the user is only interested in the attendance records of the previous year, we will define the filter criteria accordingly. Refer to the following screenshot, where the start date of the attendance is being set to be greater than a particular date. Therefore, it will only pick the count of attendance records of the current year:

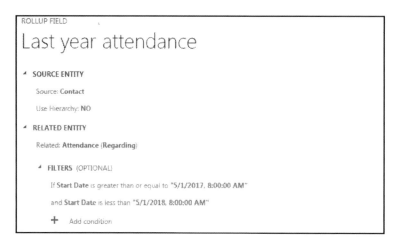

Scenario 1: Attendance filter

6. After the filter criteria are defined, the next step is to define the **AGGREGATION** function. We are only concerned with the actual number of attendance records:

Scenario 1: AGGREGATION

7. Once the criteria are defined, we save and close the screen. The next step is to just add the field to the student form:

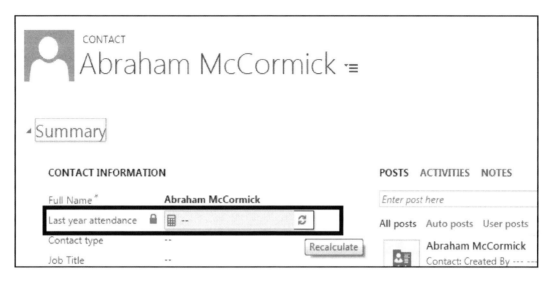

Scenario 1 : Contact form

By default, the field will be refreshed every 12 hours. The user can also click on the refresh icon to refresh the fields manually. The user can also modify the settings to update the Rollup fields to be refreshed in shorter intervals of time. You can also visit the MSDN article for the same at `https://technet.microsoft.com/en-us/library/dn832162.aspx#Rollupcalculations`.

Scenario 2

A user in the same system wishes to maintain the weighted average score of a student for the entire year. The user has devised a formula and wishes the system to maintain the score without any extra input from her side.

The scenario can be achieved using Calculated fields in Microsoft Dynamics CRM 2016. In the earlier versions of Dynamics CRM, the user had to write a custom code in JavaScript, or a plugin, to carry out this logic. However, in this edition of Microsoft Dynamics CRM 2016, we can achieve this functionality without having to write any custom code. The following are the steps for doing the same:

1. The first step is to create individual custom fields for assignments, midyear score, final year score, and weighted average score:

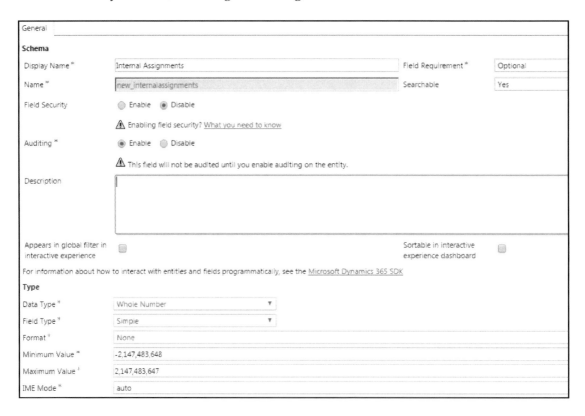

Scenario 2 Assignment field

2. Next, the user needs to create a weighted average field for the total score. The field type should be **Calculated**:

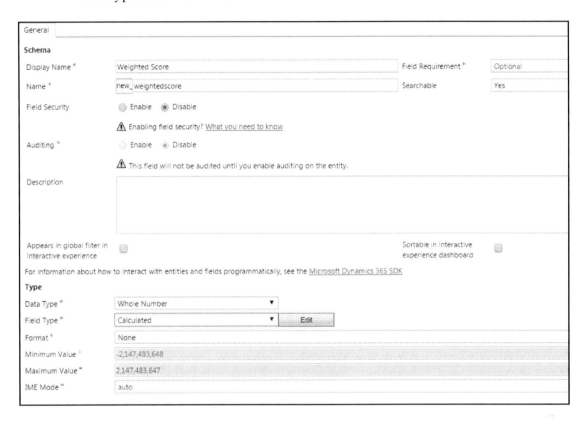

Scenario 2: Calculated field

3. Now save the field. A popup should come up. As we do not need any prevalidated conditions for the scenario, we can leave the condition area blank and just start filling the values in the **ACTION** tab:

Scenario 2: Calculated Field Function

4. Enter the following formula:

   *Weighted Score = new_internalassignments * .2 + new_midyearscore * .3 + new_finalyearscore * .5*

5. Save and close the field:

Scenario 2 Score Formula

6. After the **Weighted Score** field has been created, it can then be used in the student form, or wherever the user wants this field to appear.

Before going further, it is a good idea to discuss the various entity forms available in Dynamics CRM.

Entity forms

Microsoft Dynamics CRM 2016 provides several types of forms, which can be utilized for different purposes. The following form types are available in Microsoft Dynamics CRM 2016:

- **Main form**: This is the main web form that is opened when the user navigates to the record. These forms provide the main user interface for interacting with entity data.
- **Quick-create form**: This form can be configured for data entry by the user.
- **Quick-view form**: This form can be configured on the main forms of entities with a 1:N relationship with parent entity.
- **Mobile form**: This is filled by users browsing the Microsoft Dynamics CRM site via mobile devices. We will explore enhancements for mobile in later chapters.

For the sake of understanding, we will just consider out-of-box contact entities and their respective forms:

1. **Main form**: The main form is the entity form that is opened when the user navigates to the record. Navigate to **Sales** | **CONTACT** and click on any of the records. On doing so, the main form of the contact will load:

Contact Main Form

If the user wishes to update the form, they can click on the form editor button shown in the following screenshot:

Contact Form Editor

On doing so, a popup window will open. In the form, the user can select the fields they wish to have on the form:

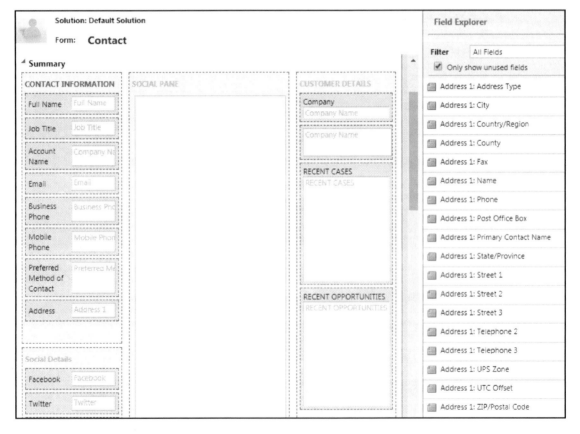

Contact Form Editor

In any form, there are three sections: **Header**, **Body**, and **Footer**. The users have an option of adding fields to these sections. The following screenshot shows how a user can select the sections in which they wish to add/remove fields:

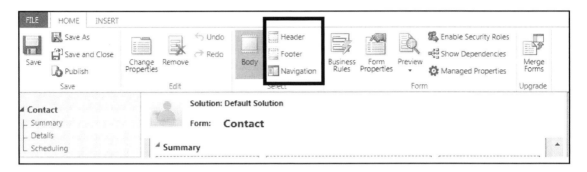

Contact Form Section

Apart from adding fields in these sections, the user can also use the navigation links appearing in the record. The user can just click on the **Navigation** link and then edit the tabs on the left-hand side of the main form:

Contact Navigation links

The user can also add different sections, tabs, sub grids, web resources, and iframes on the main form. The option is available in the **INSERT** tab on the form:

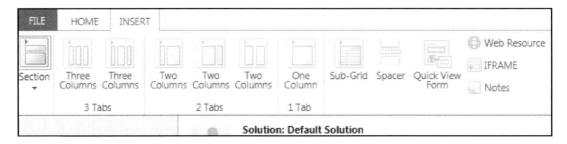

Contact Form Insert tab

Once the user is done with the changes, they can click on the **Publish** button, which will apply the changes made by the user in the environment:

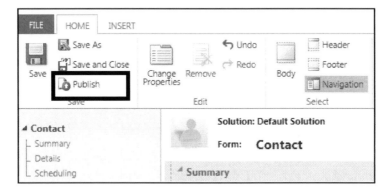

Contact Form Publish Button

The following screenshot describes how users can edit an already existing main form. To create a new main form, the user can navigate to **Settings** | **Solutions** and open a solution containing the entity:

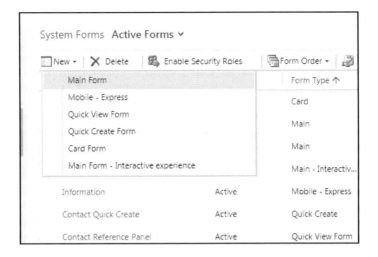

Contact New Main Form

2. **Quick create form**: Quick create forms have been provided by Dynamics CRM to enable users to quickly add data in the system with just the main fields. The following screenshot illustrates how users can access quick create forms of the **Contact** entity:

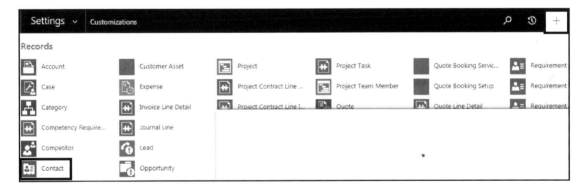

Contact Quick Create Form

This will open the out-of-box quick-create form of **Contact**:

Contact Quick Create Form

If the user wishes to create a new quick-create form, they can just navigate to the appropriate solution and create a new quick-create form.

3. **Quick-view form**: The quick-view form is available for data viewing purposes only. This form can be embedded in any related entity that has a lookup attribute to parent entity. The following screenshot shows how the quick-view form of an account can be embedded in the contact main form. Open the main form of **Contact** and click on the **INSERT** tab:

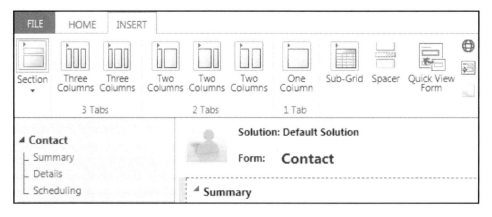

Contact Main Form

Click on **Quick View Form**. Note that a popup for selecting the related parent entity and the corresponding **Quick Create** form opens:

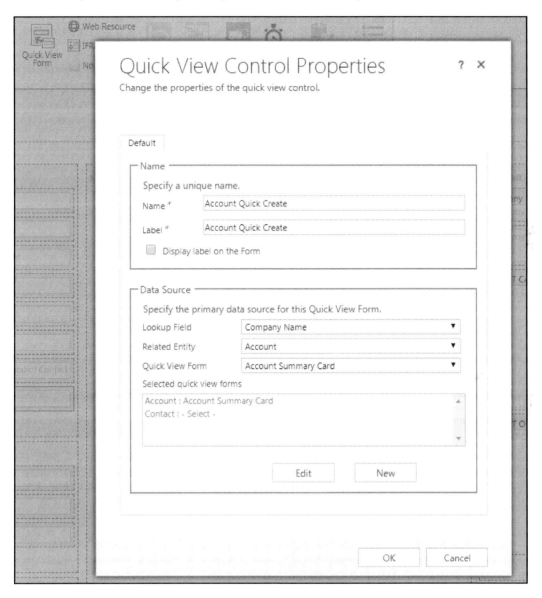

Account Quick Create

Click **OK** and publish the customizations. Now, navigate to the main form of the contact. Note that the quick-view form of the account should appear on the main form:

Quick View Form

Continuing the use case scenario that we have so far discussed in this chapter, let's take an example where the user can utilize the form-level customization feature provided by Dynamics CRM.

Entity views

The following are the main views present for any entity:

- **Active records**: This view shows the active records of the entity.
- **Inactive records**: This view shows the inactive records of the entity.
- **Associated records view**: This view shows the associated records (N:1 and N:N) of the entity with other entities.

- **Lookup view**: This view appears on the 1:N control.
- **Advanced find view**: This view allows users to create queries, and save and export the results. This can also be converted into a personal view so that the query is saved. Bulk operations, such as updation of records, are also possible using the advanced find view.

To modify any existing view or to create a new one, the user can navigate to **Settings** | **Solution** and open a solution containing the entity. The following screenshot explains the steps. For the sake of this example, we will use the out-of-box **Contact** entity:

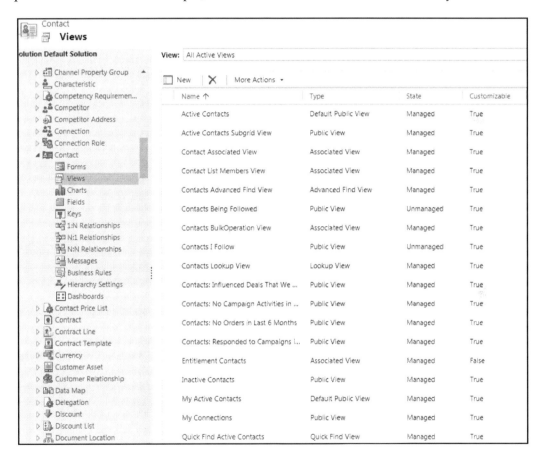

Contact View

To modify an existing view, just double click on **View**:

Active Contact View

To add columns in the view, you can click on the **Add Columns** button appearing on the right-hand side of the popup window. This will open a list of columns that the user can select. Dynamics CRM also provides the capability of adding the attributes of related entities:

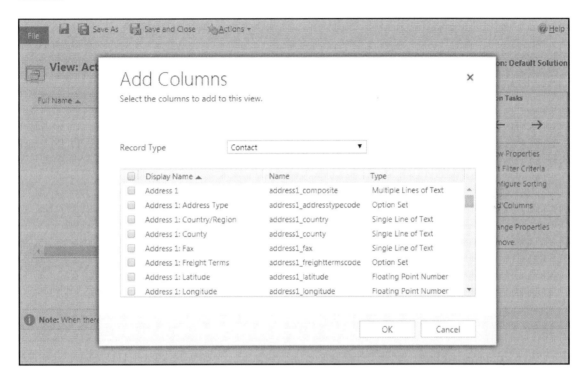

Contact View Add Columns

To edit the filter criteria, that is, conditions that will be applied on the records present in the entity, you can click on the **Edit Filter Criteria** link, and then select the column attribute and the appropriate filter value:

Active Contact View Filter Criteria

You can sort the records coming in the view by clicking on the **Configure Sorting** link. This will open a popup window, where you can select the attributes on which you want the sorting to be applied:

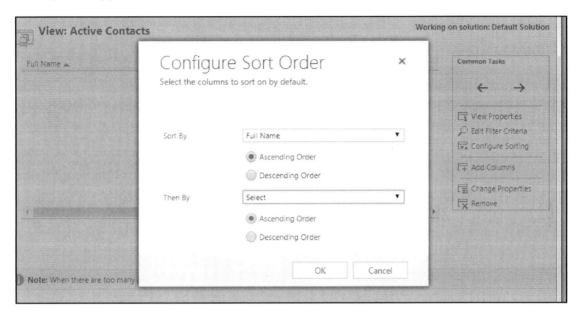

Active Contact View Configure Sorting

You can also alter the length of the columns by double-clicking on the respective column. This will open a popup window where you can then select the width you want for that column:

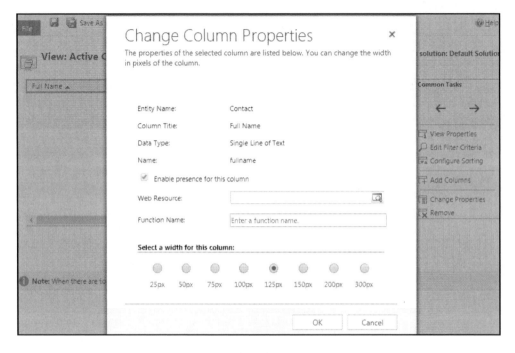

View Column Properties

To create a new column, you can just navigate to the list of views and create a new view:

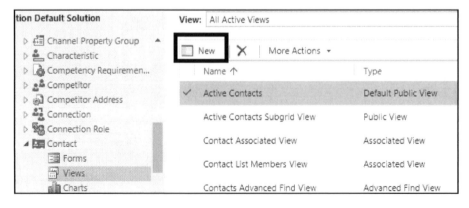

Contact New View

Sample scenarios

Let's consider a few examples related to the student management system.

A user wishes to configure a view, wherein they can refer to all the students with a total marks of less than 40 percent:

1. To create a new view, the user can navigate to the **ADVANCED FIND** dialog:

Entity View Scenario

2. In the **ADVANCED FIND** window, the user can then select the appropriate entity, that is, **Contact**:

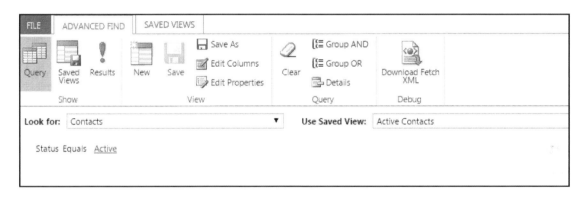

Entity View Scenario

3. As we are creating a new **Saved View**, the user can select **[new]** in the drop-down menu. In our case, we are concerned with the marks obtained by the student. We can select this in the attributes criteria:

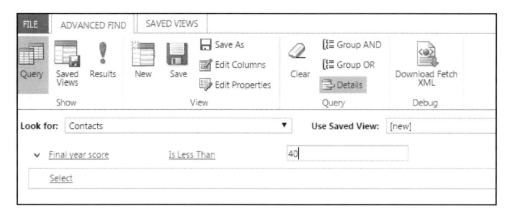

Entity View Scenario

4. After selecting the criteria, the user can click on the **Save As** button. This will open a popup where the user can enter the view name:

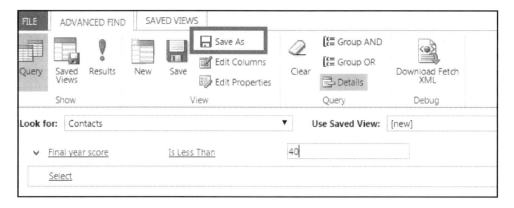

Entity View Scenario

5. In the popup screen, the user can enter the name of the view and save it:

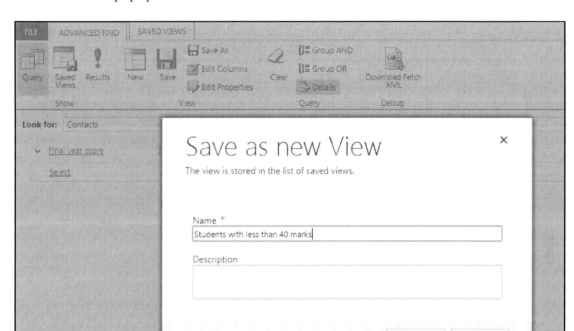

Entity Scenario View

Summary

In this chapter, we discussed the XRM framework of Microsoft Dynamics CRM 2016. You learned how to effectively leverage out-of-box functionalities and entities to create the XRM functionalities of Microsoft Dynamics CRM 2016. In addition, we explored the Calculated field, Rollup field, and quick-create forms in Microsoft Dynamics CRM 2016.

6
Analytics with CRM

This chapter is focused on introducing and using advanced analytical features available with Dynamics CRM 2016. We will cover some features available within the Microsoft Dynamics CRM 2016 product offering, provide ways to enhance the Analytics experience using other Microsoft product offerings, and then, see how this can be interconnected with Microsoft Dynamics CRM 2016.

In this chapter, we will cover the following features of Dynamics CRM 2016:

- Word templates in Microsoft Dynamics CRM 2016
- Excel templates in Microsoft Dynamics CRM 2016

Word templates

Word templates provide a means to create reusable templates in Microsoft Word and to save them to Microsoft Dynamics CRM 2016. These Word templates can then be used to generate standardized Word documents based on the CRM data. The following table describes the supported versions of Word that can be used to generate or open a document generated via the Word template feature of Microsoft Dynamics CRM 2016:

Creating a Word template	Using documents generated via the Word template
Microsoft Office 2013, Microsoft Office 2016	Microsoft Office 2010, Microsoft Office 2013, Microsoft Office 2016

Scenario

John works in an organization where he has to deal with a lot of documentation on a daily basis and format the documents as per the company's standard format. Therefore, he needs to create Word templates so that he can reuse the same templates repeatedly.

In the following section, we will look at the steps for creating a Word template and using it in Dynamics CRM.

Creating a Word template

A Word template can be generated in three different places in Dynamics 365:

1. Navigate to **Settings** | **Templates** | **Document Templates**:

2. The following is the **Templates** panel; select **Document Templates**:

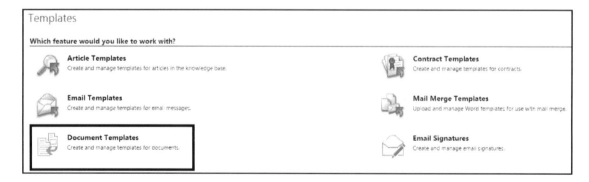

3. Click on **+NEW** to proceed:

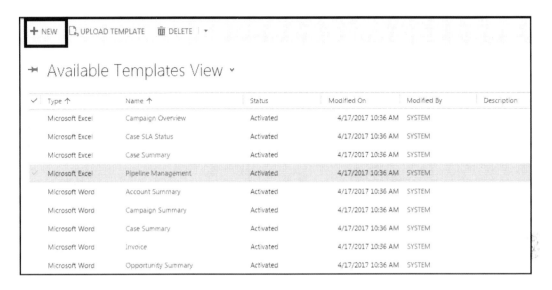

4. We can create both Excel and Word templates. As we are discussing Word templates, so we will select **Word Template** for this example:

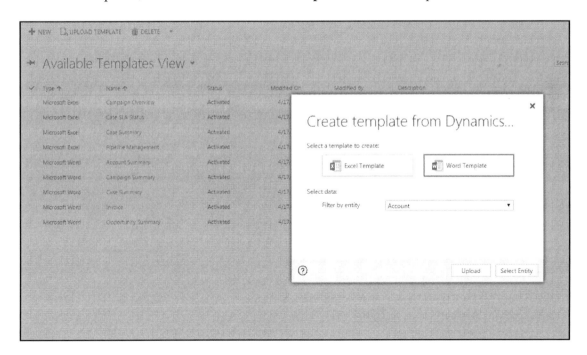

5. We can upload an already existing template, as well as create a new one. Let's look at how to create a new Word template. Examine the following image and read the context following it:

The relationships defined in the preceding screenshot define the entities available when the template is defined later. Now, we can select the relationships that we want to be available in the template. After selecting the required options, we can click on the **Download Template** button. Please note that for this option, you must have enough permissions in the corresponding security roles to view the **Settings** page, which means that you must either be a system administrator or a system customizer.

An alternative way of creating the template

Another way of generating a Word template is to generate it while being on any of the entity records. Let's look at how it can be generated for an account:

1. While on the account record form, click on More (...), | **Word Templates** | **Create Word Template**:

Check out the following screenshot to see how can selected the **Word Template** option:

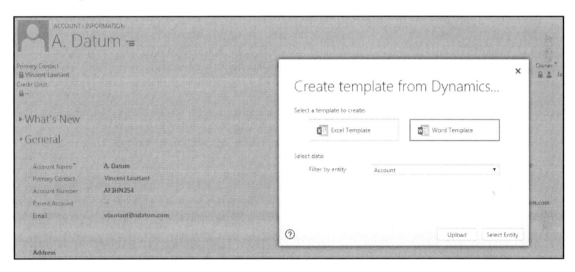

Doing this will open a screen where you can select the relationships that are to be included in the template.

Another way for generating the word template would be from a list of records. Navigate to the view for the entity for which the user wants to generate the document template. Select one record and click on More (**...**) | **Word Templates** | **Create Word Template**:

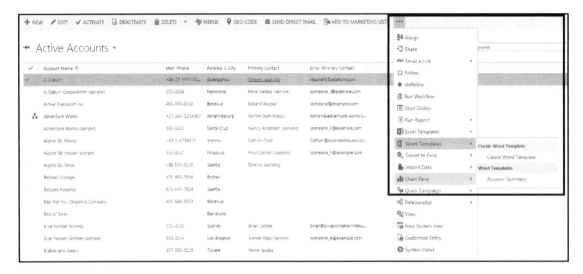

Hence, we have now created a Word template. Now, let's see how to work on the generated document template.

2. The next step is to edit the document template. Open the document in Microsoft Office. Note that the document is completely blank:

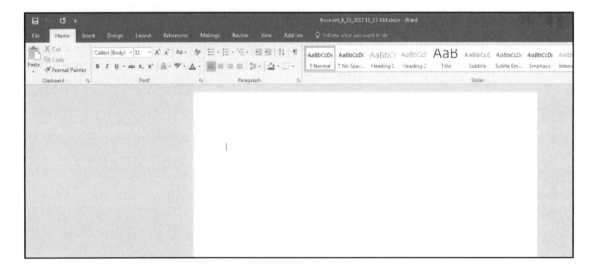

3. To see and add Dynamics 365 XML data, you will need to enable the **Developer** tab. The steps are as follows:

    1. Navigate to **File | Options | Customize Ribbon** and enable **Developer**:

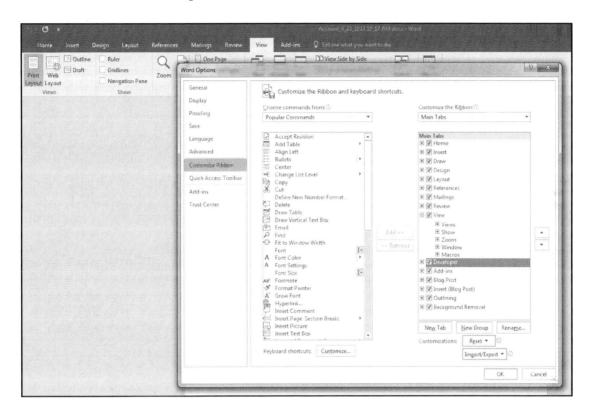

2. Click on **OK**, review that a new tab **Developer** is added on word, as follows:

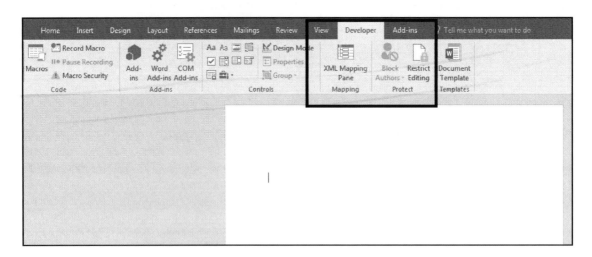

3. Click on the XML Mapping Pane. On the right-hand pane, review that a drop-down menu for selecting **Custom XML Part** appears. Select the XML part related to Dynamics CRM. Note that, on doing so, all of the attributes related to the entity for which the template was generated along with the relations selected start appearing, as shown in the following screenshot:

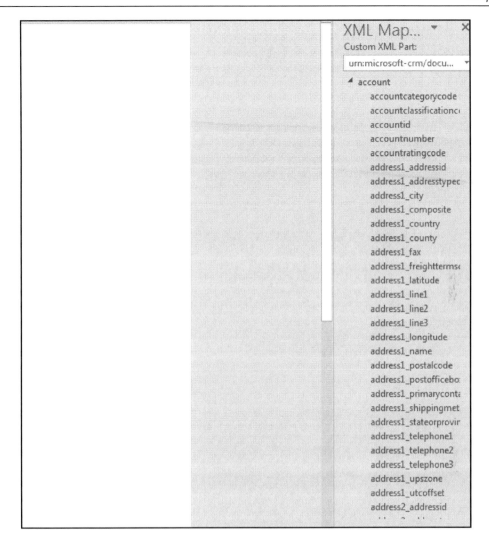

Now, you can insert custom controls in the attribute by right-clicking on **Attribute** | **Insert Custom Control**, and then selecting the custom control type. The control will govern the layout of the attribute in the template.

Types of controls

The following are the different types of controls that can be added:

1. Rich text
2. Plain text
3. Picture
4. Checkbox
5. Combo box
6. Dropdown list
7. Date picker

In the following example, we have inserted seven attributes of all of the possible types in the document template:

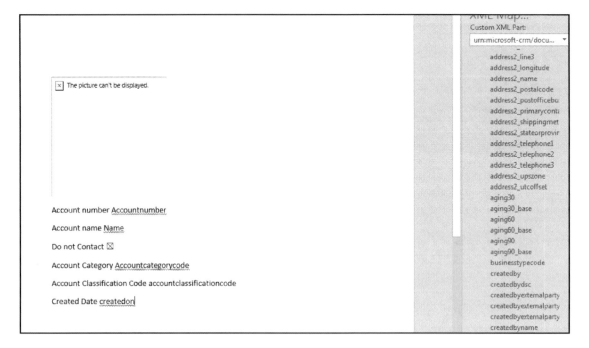

You can also click on the **Design Mode** property (highlighted in the following screenshot) to edit the document:

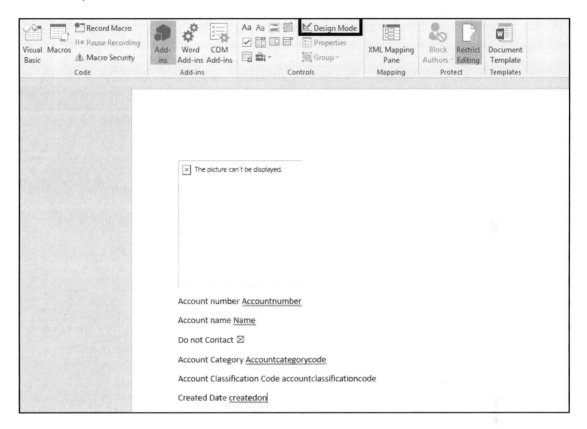

You can also insert the data relevant to the related entities or relations, which were added while creating the template. For doing so, you can just scroll to the relevant relations that need to be added and right-click on **Insert Content Control** | **Repeating**. Check out the following screenshot to see how the final template will appear:

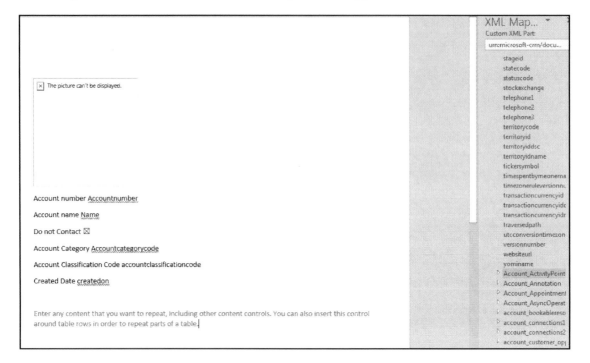

Uploading the template to Dynamics CRM

After the document template has been prepared, the next step is to upload the template back into Dynamics CRM. The following steps show how it is done:

1. Navigate to **Settings** | **Templates**:

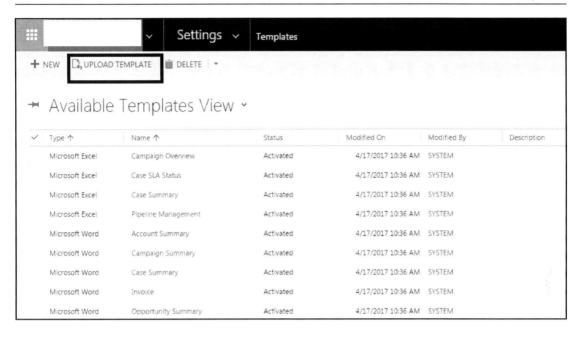

2. Click on **Upload Template**:

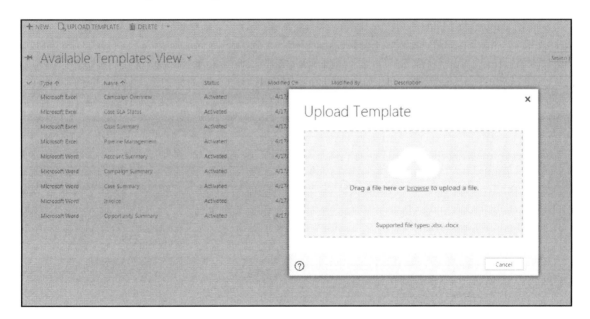

3. Click on the browse button and select the document modified in *Step 3*:

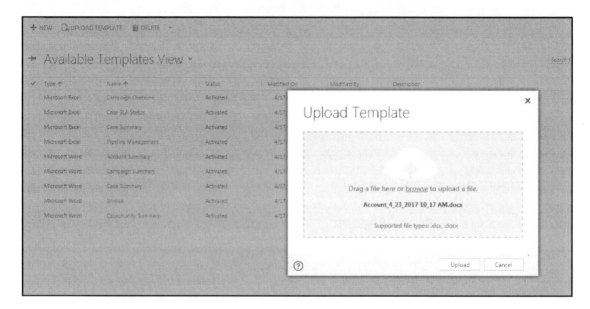

4. Click on the **Upload** button; the following screen appears:

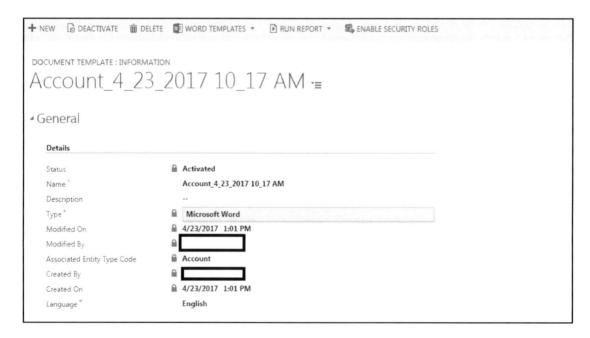

5. Just like in *Step 1*, you can also upload templates on any of the record forms or while being on any of the entity views:

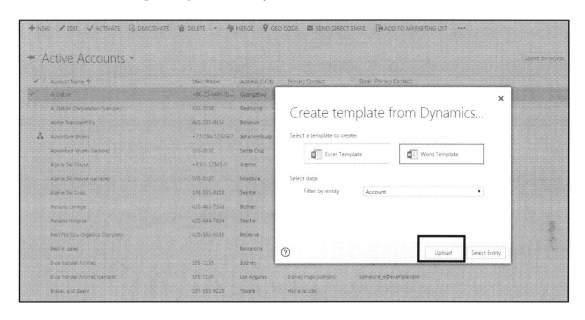

Using the uploaded document templates in Dynamics

After the word templates have been imported into Dynamics CRM, the next thing we'd like to do is generate information using the templates:

1. Navigate to the record form for which you want to generate the document using the uploaded template. Navigate to More (...) | **Word Templates**:

2. Check whether the uploaded template appears in the list of **Word Templates**.
3. Click on the template name to download the document.
4. Open the document to view its contents:

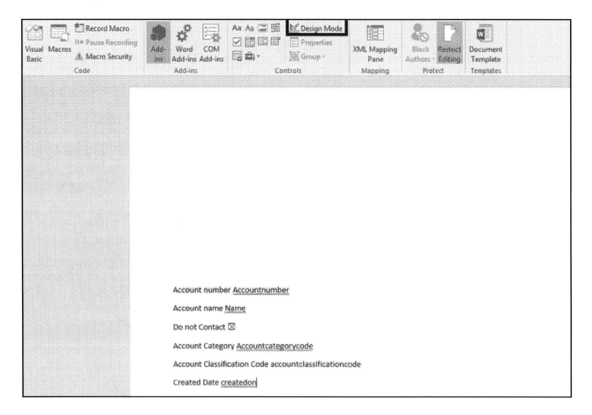

Excel templates

Just like Word templates, we can also generate Excel templates in Dynamics CRM. The only difference between Word and Excel templates is that, while the Word template is for information relevant to one entity record, Excel templates are for information relevant to a set of entity records. Let's look at how an Excel template is generated:

1. Navigate to the entity view for which you want to generate the Excel template:

2. Click on the **Excel Templates** button:

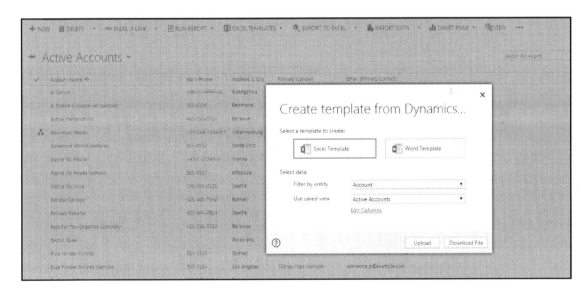

3. Select the template type as **Excel Template**, select the entity, and view names from the respective drop-down menus. Now, click on the **Download File** button:

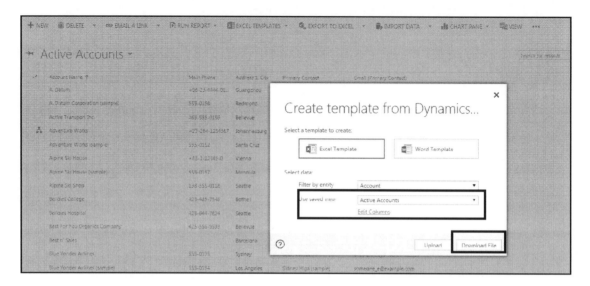

As illustrated in the preceding screenshot, you can also click on the **Edit Columns** link for editing the columns that you want to be present in the Excel template.

Customizing data present in the document

Perform the following steps to customize the document that is created:

1. Open the created Excel template:

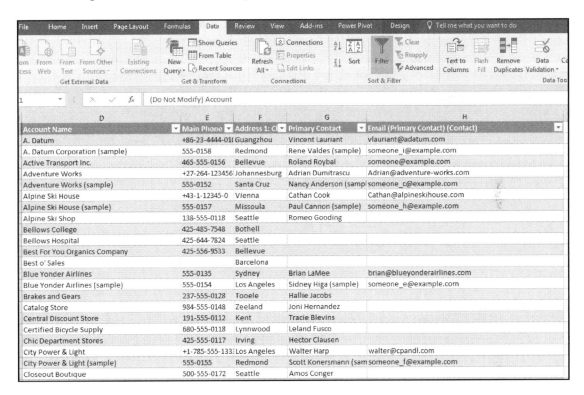

2. Now, you can enable editing in the document and add some new user-defined columns in the template. For example, in the preceding Excel document, we can add a new column, whose value should be a combination of **Main Phone** and **City**. Check out the following screenshot:

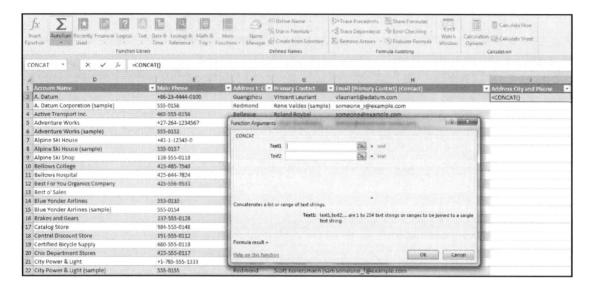

3. In the same manner, we can add more text values:

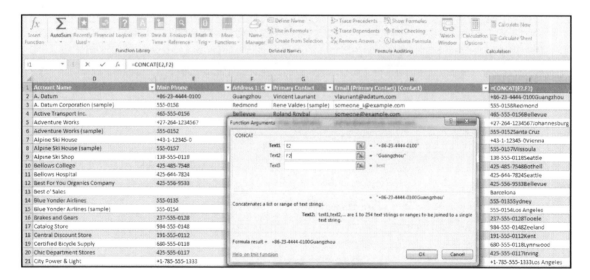

Click **OK** and see that the value in the newly added column is generated automatically. Please note that Microsoft Excel provides a rich set of features such as pivot table, chart, calculated columns, and many more. All of these features can also be utilized in the Excel template. For doing so, you can just navigate to **Insert** | **Charts**, as shown in the following screenshot:

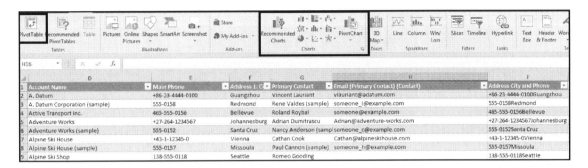

Uploading the template

After you save the template, the next step is to upload the document template in Dynamics CRM. As in the Word template, you can either upload the template from **Settings** | **Templates** or on the view of the main entity:

The following screenshot is pretty self-explanatory:

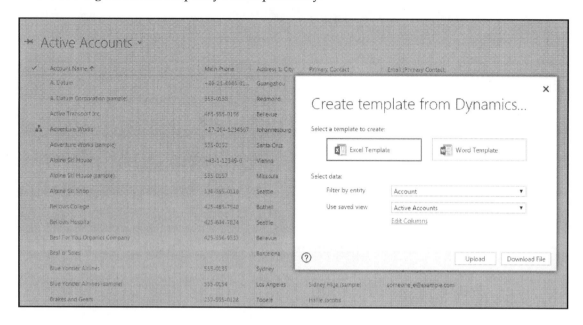

See the **Upload Template** window, where you can drag and drop your file:

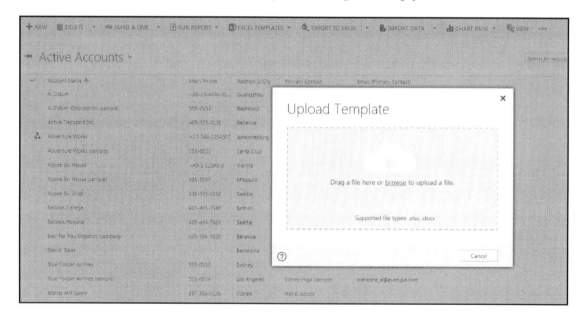

Check out the following screenshot to see how the window appears after the template has been uploaded:

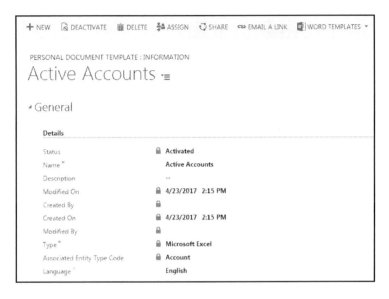

Generating documents using the template

After the document has been generated, the next task is to utilize the Excel templates for generating the documents:

1. Navigate to the entity view for which the document template has been uploaded. Click on **EXCEL TEMPLATES** and review that the newly uploaded template is available in the list of **Personal Excel Templates**:

2. You can select either of the two options, that is, whether to download the Excel document or open it in Excel. The online Excel is opened, as shown in the following image:

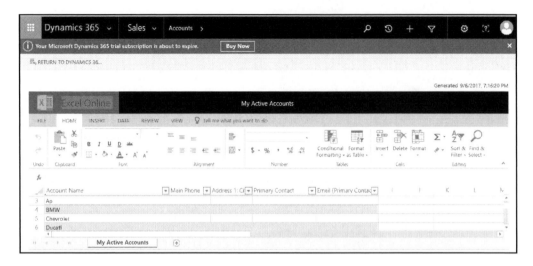

Configuring the security roles in templates

You can also configure the security roles for the templates; perform the following steps:

1. Navigate to **Settings | Templates** and select the template for which you want to configure the security role:

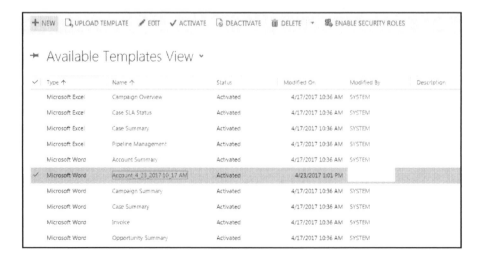

2. Click on the **Enable Security Roles** button:

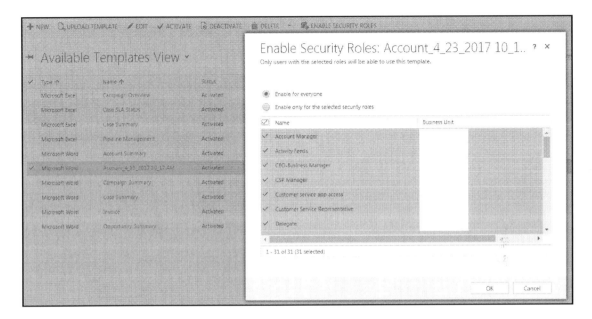

3. Now, select the roles for which you want the template to appear.

Summary

In this chapter, we discussed the new features in Microsoft Dynamics 2016 and explored two major templates: Word and Excel. We also looked into their configurations.

In the next chapter, we will cover Workflow development with Microsoft Dynamics CRM 2016 and understand the types of Workflows with several examples.

7
Workflow Development with Dynamics CRM

Workflows are the handlers for the events fired by Dynamics CRM. The events that a workflow can support are limited compared to plugins. Using workflows, we can either utilize workflows using a native drag and drop interface, or extend the standard behavior of Dynamics CRM using customizations or with custom code written in the .NET framework.

In this chapter, we are going to cover the following topics:

- Workflow and types of workflow
- Examples on workflows

Types of workflow

Logically speaking, workflows can be classified as follows:

- **Out-of-box workflows**: Out-of-box components are provided by default in Dynamics CRM. Out-of-box workflows provide a wide range of options for CRM events such as Create, Update, and Delete, or they can be run on demand. This workflow can be configured by using the customization option without the need for writing code.
- **Custom workflows**: Custom workflows allow other workflows to be extended using .NET and write more complex automation to be done because of triggering the workflow. The component is termed as Custom Workflow activity.

Another classification of workflow has been existing since the launch of Microsoft Dynamics CRM's 2013 version. This is based on whether a workflow will be executed immediately or will be processed a bit later in the background:

- **Background workflows**: Background workflows are not triggered immediately because of some action in Dynamics CRM. They have rather triggered asynchronously and are processed by an asynchronous processing service in CRM.
- **Real-time workflows:** Synchronous workflows were introduced first in the Microsoft Dynamics CRM 2013 version. Synchronous workflows trigger immediately as soon as the particular event is triggered in Dynamics CRM.

Please note that real-time workflows can be converted to background workflows and vice versa. It is recommended that you carefully select this choice, as it has impacts on the system performance and usability. By default, workflows are created as background workflows unless specified during creation.

Workflows and plugins can both be utilized to accomplish the same functionality, as both essentially run on the server side to do automation or processing. Recommended usage of workflows or plugins for a scenario is mostly decided by the following factors:

Criteria	Plugins	Workflows
Administration	The plugin is a technical component and needs the involvement of a technical professional when changes are required.	Workflows are customizable components, and an advanced user of CRM can easily make changes to out-of-box workflows
On-demand usage	Plugins cannot be triggered on demand.	Workflows can be triggered on demand
Triggers	Plugins can be triggered on a lot of CRM events, including complex messages. For example, plugins can even be triggered on the retrieval of any entity type.	Workflows can only be triggered for Create, Field Change, Status Change, Assign to Owner, and On Demand
Nested child process	No	Yes

Scenario walkthrough

In this section, we will go through some scenarios to highlight how workflows are used in Dynamics CRM. Through these scenarios, you'll get a clear idea of how and where to use workflows, according to various requirements.

Scenario 1

Michael is a sales manager for Contoso Corporation and is worried about the state of sales management in Contoso. He has noticed that the sales representatives make frequent changes to the leads created in the system during the Qualify stage of a lead. This gives him issues about the data of leads that he reports daily, and the company forecasts are struggling. Michael wishes to lock the editing of the leads by the sales representatives once a lead is created in the Develop stage. So, the only time a sales representatives can enter information about a lead is during the first-time entry. If they wish to make changes to the leads later, they need to contact Michael.

The following steps illustrate how Michael can utilize out-of-box workflows to achieve this requirement:

1. The first step will be to navigate to **Settings** | **Processes**:

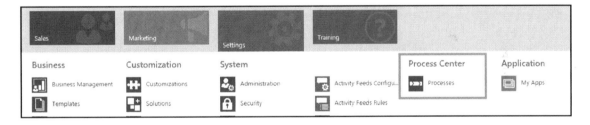

2. Click on the **New** button on the **Processes** entity grid ribbon that you see:

3. The **Create Process** window will pop up. Select **Category** as **Workflow**, untick the checkbox for **Run this workflow in the background (recommended)**, which is selected by default, and select **Entity** as **Lead**:

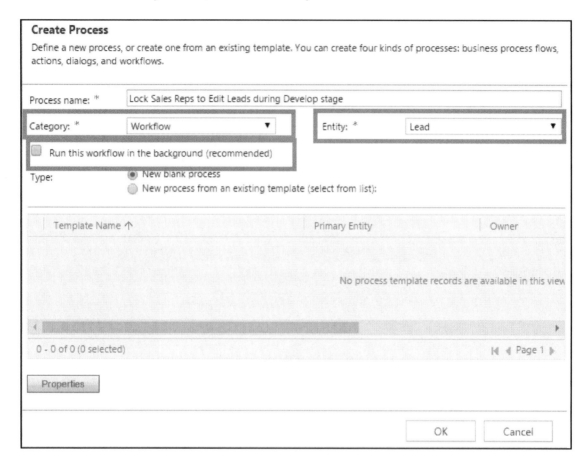

4. The **Create Process** window will pop up. Select **Scope to Organization** so that it is applicable to all of the users of the CRM system. Other options available for scope are those that are applied as per the security model configured in the CRM system:

- **Users**
- **Business Unit**
- **Parent Child Business Unit**

Also, select the checkbox for **On fields Change** and click **Select**:

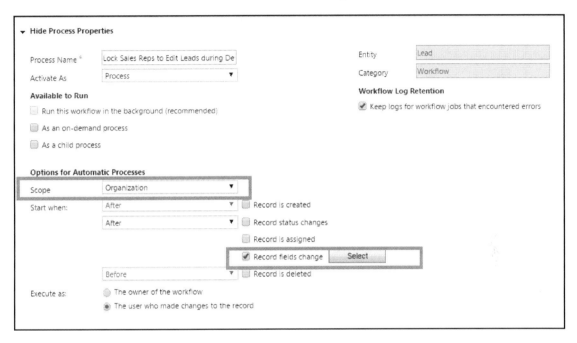

5. The **Select Fields** option will pop up, as shown in following image. Select all of the fields available. This selection is used to configure the trigger for the workflow. In this configuration, a workflow will be triggered for all of the field changes. Other triggers available for the workflow are as follows:
   - **Record is Created**
   - **Record Status change** (from **Active** to **Inactive**, or vice versa)
   - **Record is Assigned**
   - **Record is Deleted**

Once the required fields are selected, click **OK**:

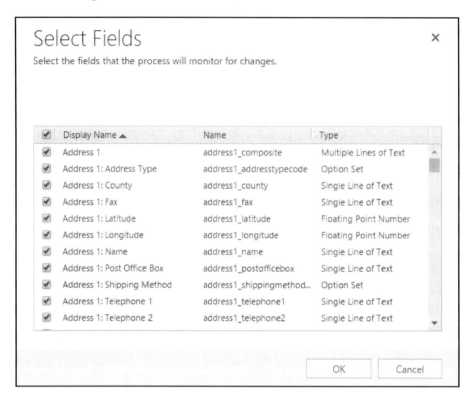

6. The next step is to configure what needs to happen every time fields change on the lead record.

   Scroll down a bit on the workflow editor window and you will be able to see the **Add Step** button. On the available menu, select **Check Condition**.

   This part allows us to select what actions or automation need to be applied once the event is selected in the workflow is triggered. The main steps that can be used are as follows:

   - **Create Record**: Create a new entity record, related entity record, and so on
   - **Update Record**: Update the current entity record or any related entity record
   - **Assign Record**: Assign the current entity record, related entity record, and so on

- **Send Email**: Send email notification
- **Stop Workflow**: Stop the current workflow
- **Change Status**: Change the status of the current entity record

Check out the following screenshot:

Now, click on **Add Step**. After clicking **Add Step**, you will be presented with an area to comment about the step. It is recommended that you use this area to describe the current step. Then, click the condition area below that:

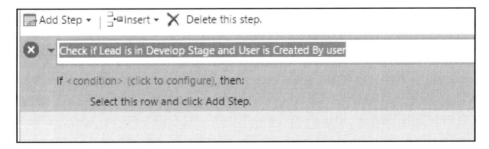

Select the conditions for this workflow action to be triggered. In our case, the conditions for the current process stage category are **Qualify** and **Modified by (User)** (user modifying the record), which are created by the user or the sales representative for the configuration applied in Contoso corporation's CRM system. Once done, click **Save and Close**:

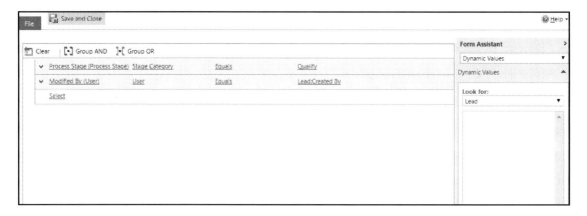

Navigating back to the steps flow, select the next available step row below the condition, click **Add Step** again, and select the **Stop Workflow** step:

On the next step, select the dropdown for the status of the stopping workflow. The default value will be **Succeeded**; change that to **Canceled**. Also, do not forget to mention some meaningful comments about this step. Click **Set Properties**:

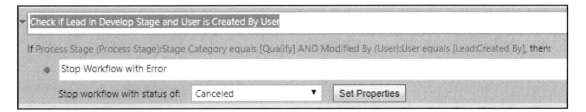

7. Mention a meaningful message for the status and click **Save and Close**:

8. On the top of the workflow, note that there is a button to **Activate** the workflow. Once activated, this workflow will start working:

9. On confirmation, a pop-up window will appear; click **Activate**:

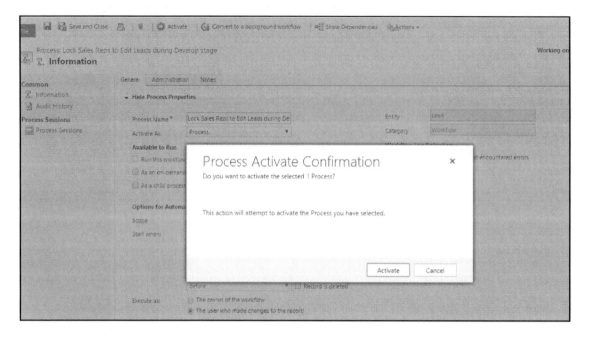

The following error will pop up to the user because of this workflow:

Let's now see this workflow in action. Navigate to any leads created by the sales representative in the system and try to edit an existing lead during the Develop stage. You will receive the preceding error.

Using the synchronous workflow along with the validation available to identify the stage category has enabled Michael to lock multiple edits to the lead record, thereby improving lead management more effectively.

Scenario 2

Michael, who is a sales manager in Contoso Corporation, had locked multiple edits to leads during the Develop stage, as described in *Scenario 1*. This worked very well initially for his reporting needs. However, over time, he has noticed that this has been more of an overhead for him, as more and more sales representatives now contact him even if they wish to update fields such as address, phone number, and so on. Michael analyzes his reporting requirements again and wishes to re-engineer the current process in a way that the only field that can be locked to change will be the **Budget** amount, as that is the field he uses for his sales pipeline reporting.

The following steps illustrate how Michael can easily change the out-of-box workflow he created in *Scenario 1* to achieve this requirement:

1. Navigate to **Settings** | **Processes**:

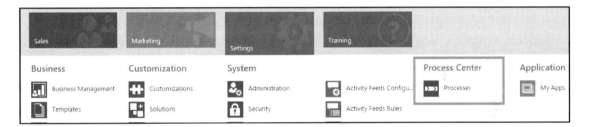

2. Locate the existing process and double-click on it:

3. Note that there is a **Deactivate** button to deactivate the workflow. Activated workflows cannot be changed. So, click the **Deactivate** button to change this workflow to the **Draft** status, so it can be edited:

4. Next, untick the checkboxes for **Record is assigned** and **Record status changes**, and keep the checkbox for **Record field changed**. Click **View**:

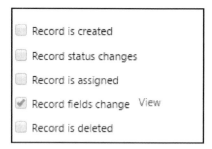

5. On the **Select Fields** window, uncheck all of the other fields and only select the **Budget Amount** field; click **OK**:

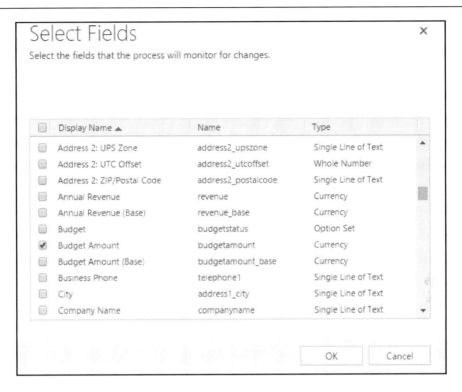

6. Next, go to the Stop workflow status message and change the message to suit the current scenario:

7. Save and **Activate** the workflow.

Now, the workflow will not trigger on all of the field updates. However, if a sales representative tries to edit the **Budget Amount**, he/she is presented with the following error:

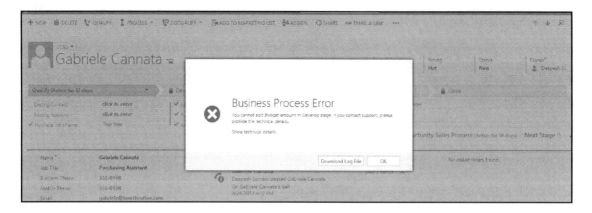

Scenario 3

Michael continues to utilize all of the great features of Microsoft Dynamics CRM 2016. Another feature that Michael has utilized is **Business Process Flow**. He has created two kinds of business processes for lead qualification depending on the budget of the lead, as shown in the following screenshot:

However, every time a lead is created based on the estimated budget, Michael has to manually verify the budget and assign it to the right business process in case the sales representative has made any mistake in assigning the right business process during record creation. Michael wishes to automate the selection of business process flows when a lead is saved the first time, depending on the following factors:

- If the estimated budget of the lead is above 1 million, then the lead has to be assigned to high budget
- If the estimated budget of the lead is below 1 million, then lead has to be assigned to low budget

The following steps illustrate how Michael can easily change the out-of-box workflows he created in *Scenario 1* to achieve this requirement:

1. Navigate to **Settings** | **Process** and click **New Process**. Fill the details as shown in the following screenshot and click **OK**:

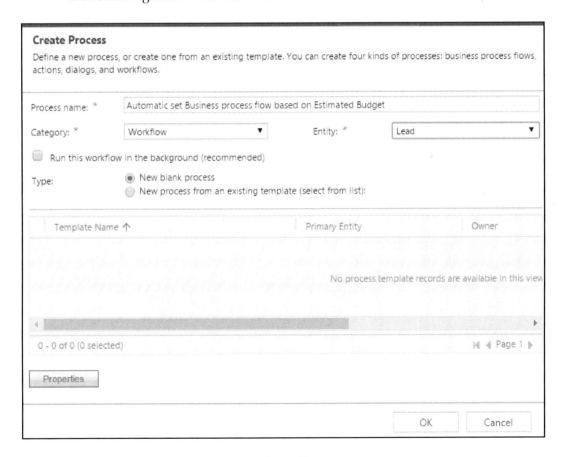

2. On the **Create Workflow** window, set **Scope** to **Organization** and select the checkbox for **Record is created**:

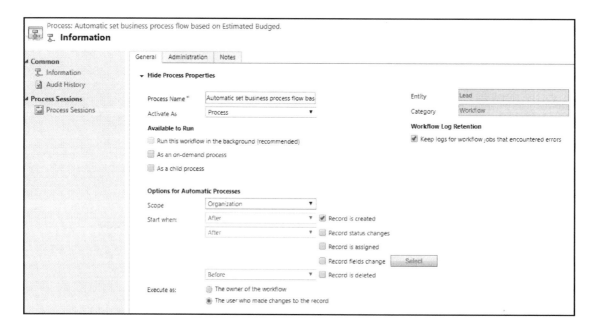

3. Next, scroll down to the **Create Workflow** window, click **Add Step**, and select the **Check** condition. Put the comments and click **Condition link**:

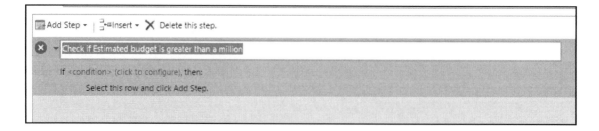

4. Put the condition for lead budget amount greater than 1 million and click **Save and Close**:

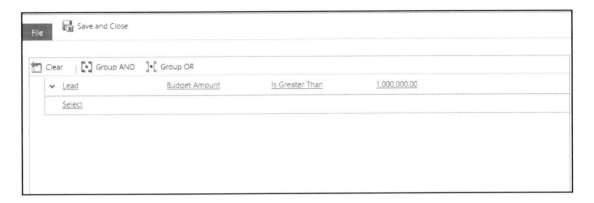

5. Select the step under the condition, click **Add Step**, and pick **Perform Action**:

6. Choose the **SetProcess** option as **Action** and click on **Set Properties**:

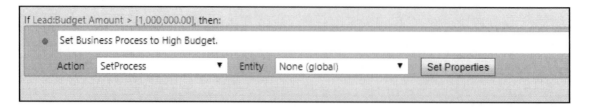

7. On the **Properties** window, set **NewProcess** to **High Budget Business Process** and **Target** to **Lead Record**. Press **Save and Close**:

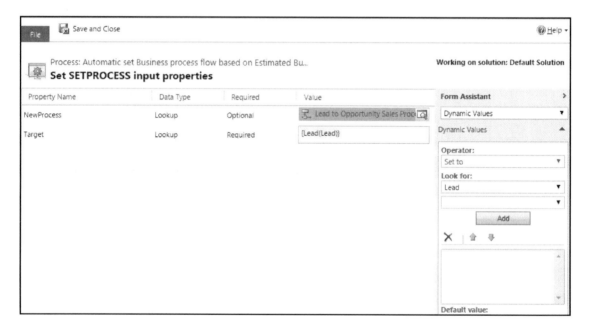

8. Keep the entire condition selected on the workflow editor window and select the **Conditional Branch** option on **Add Step**:

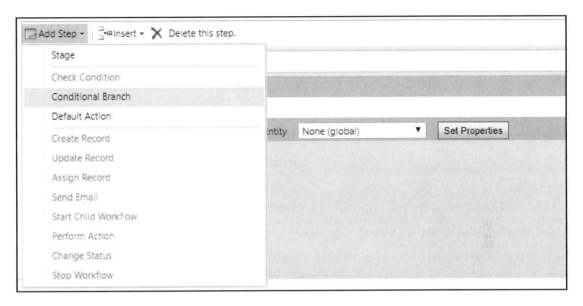

9. Click the **Otherwise Condition**, and fill the condition as follows. Click **Save and Close**:

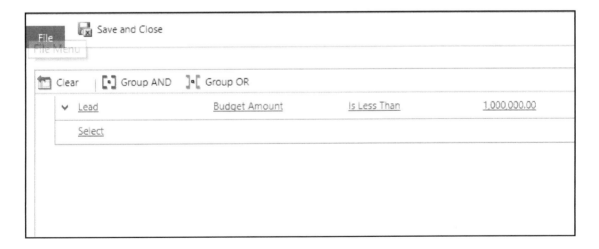

10. On the next step for the otherwise condition, select **Add Step** as **Perform Action** and then select **SetProcess**:

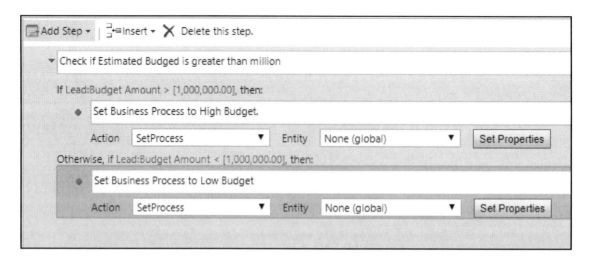

11. Next, select **Set Properties**. On the **Properties** window, set **NewProcess** to **Low Budget Business Process** and **Target** to **Lead Record**. Press **Save and Close**:

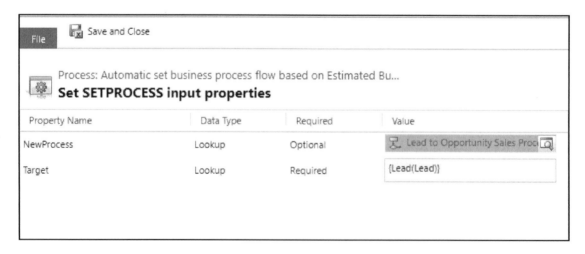

12. Click **Save** on the workflow and **Activate** the workflow:

Go and explore the workflow in action for yourself. It will set the business process flow automatically. Michael is pleased to see this and, now, he doesn't need to worry about whether the correct business process flow is being set, since the system will automatically take care of it.

Scenario 4

Sarah is a customer service manager at Acme Ltd. Acme Ltd utilizes parent and child cases to categorize bigger customer issues and solve them faster. Sarah wishes to change the priority of the parent case so that if even one of the **Child** cases is set to **Critical** priority, then the **Parent** case should also be set to **Critical** priority.

The following steps illustrate how Sarah can easily configure an out-of-box workflow to achieve this requirement:

1. Navigate to **Settings** | **Process** and click **New Process**. Fill the details as shown in the following screenshot and click **OK**:

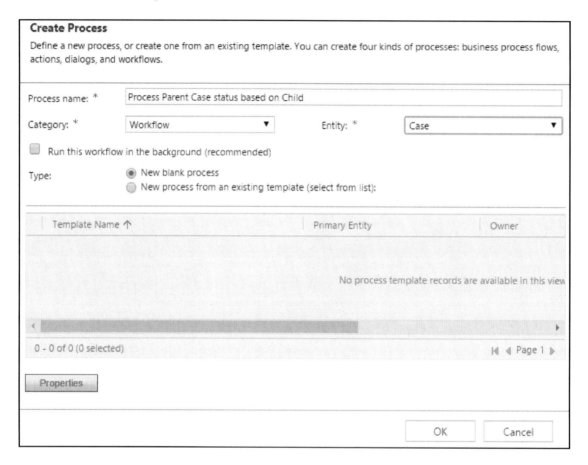

2. On the **Create Workflow** window, set **Scope** to **Organization** and select the checkboxes for **Record is created** and **Record fields change**:

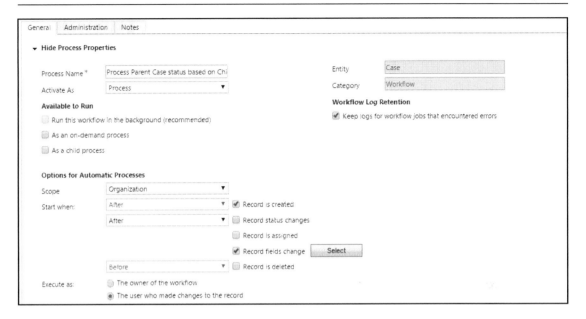

3. Next, select **Records fields change**. On the **Select Field** window, select the **Priority** field:

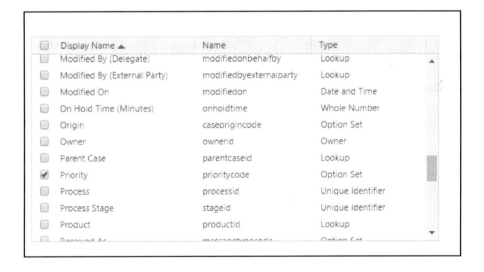

4. Next, go to **Add Steps** and select **Add New Step**. Select **Check Condition**, add comments for reference, and click the condition as follows:

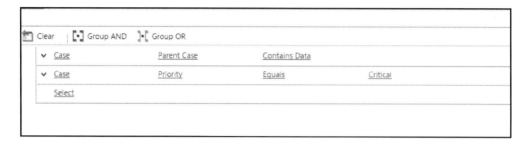

5. Finally, the steps will appear as follows. Select the row below the condition and click **Add New Step**:

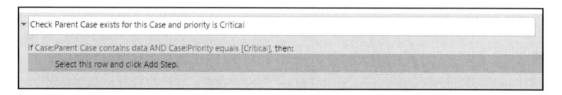

6. On **Add New Step**, select **Update Record**:

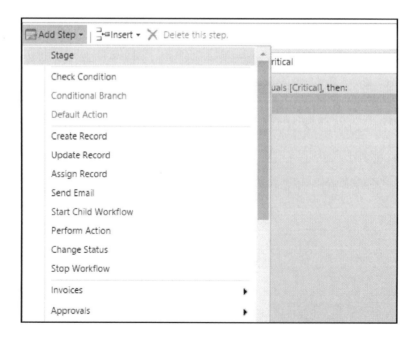

7. On the **Update Record** step, select the entity as **Parent** case. Click **Set Properties** and map the **Priority** field on the **Parent** case to **Child** case priority. Click **Save and Close**:

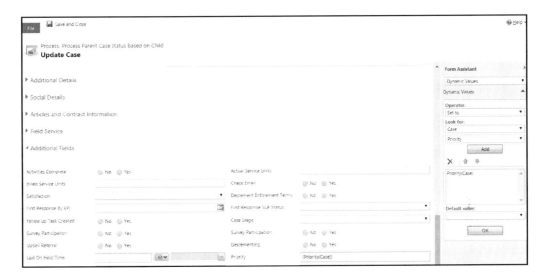

8. Finally, the workflow will appear as follows:

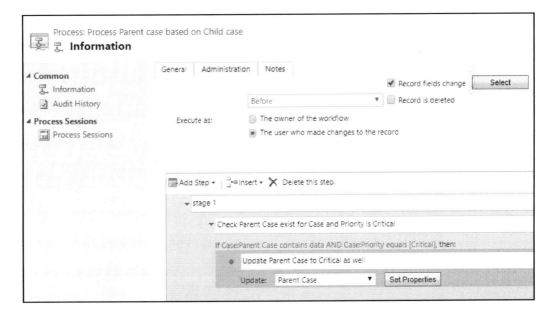

9. Save and activate the workflow by clicking **Activate**:

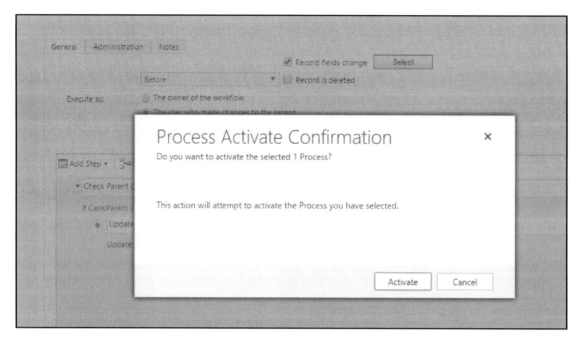

Now, let's see this workflow in action. Here, a **child** case is created with **Critical** priority:

As soon as the **child** case is created, the **Parent** case priority is automatically updated to **Critical** as well:

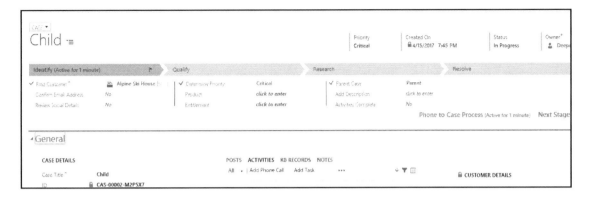

Sarah is very pleased with the results and wishes to utilize this workflow for managing critical cases better.

Further exercises

Try and send an email notification to Sarah when a **Parent** case is updated to **Critical**.

Summary

In this chapter, you learned about workflows in Microsoft Dynamics CRM 2016, when to use workflows and when to opt for plugins, and the new features in workflows in CRM 2016. We also had an overview of the classifications of workflow types and looked at the possible actions that can be implemented with workflows. I urge you to try and explore custom workflow activities for further reading.

In the next chapter, we will go through client-side scripting in Microsoft Dynamics CRM 2016, wherein we will cover client script enhancements, WEB API, and key press events in Microsoft Dynamics CRM 2016.

8
Client-Side Scripting

This chapter is focused on introducing and using client-side enhancements available with Microsoft Dynamics CRM 2016. We will cover some client-side script functions with examples and then also discuss the WEB API in the later part, which is a new way of querying CRM data directly from JavaScript.

Generally, in Microsoft Dynamics 365, JavaScript is used to perform actions in the form of scripts and ribbon commands, and in web resources.

In this chapter, we will go through the following:

- Client-side script functions with examples
- Form scripts and validating data using JavasSript
- Creating JavaScript web resources
- The Web API - a new way of querying CRM data directly from JavaScript

Now, let's look at the some scenarios for an in-depth coverage of the enhancements that can be done using JavaScript.

Scenario 1

Mark is the manager for Contoso Corporation. Contoso Corporation is a package delivery organization, delivering parcels in parts of San Francisco, CA. He notices a lot of small issues with respect to the data quality being put up by different employees who enter data into the system. One of the issues he notices is with respect to ZIP codes. He wishes to aid the employees as they type in the various ZIP codes into the contact's address field so that there are lesser chances of error while the entry is being done by the staff. The following is a list of ZIP codes handled by Contoso Corporation:

- 94102,94104.94103
- 94105,94108,94107

Let's look at the solution that Mark can utilize to provide assistance to his employees so that there are fewer chances of errors creeping in.

Resolving the scenario

Mark can implement the requirements by using the following script enhancements, introduced in Microsoft Dynamics CRM 2016:

- **Keypress handler**: Microsoft Dynamics CRM 2016 has introduced methods to add some JavaScript for `keypress` events on any input fields in Microsoft Dynamics CRM 2016. Three methods can be used to assist in this regard:
    - `addOnKeyPress`: This method can be used to add a function as an event handler for the `keypress` event. The syntax is as follows:

        ```
        Xrm.Page.getControl(field name).addOnKeyPress(
        name of function);
        ```

    - `removeOnKeyPress`: This method can be used to remove a function as an event handler from the `keypress` event. The syntax is as follows:

        ```
        Xrm.Page.getControl(arg).removeOnKeyPress(
        function name);
        ```

    - `fireOnKeyPress`: This method can be used to call a `keypress` handler. The syntax is as follows:

        ```
        Xrm.Page.getControl(field name).fireOnKeyPress();
        ```

- **AutoComplete handler**: Microsoft Dynamics CRM 2016 has introduced methods to add JavaScript to assist in autocomplete on any input fields, such as text or number fields, in Microsoft Dynamics CRM 2016. Two methods can be used to assist in this regard:

  - `showAutoComplete`: This method allows us to add autocomplete options on any field. The syntax is as follows:

    ```
    Xrm.Page.getControl(field name)
    .showAutoComplete(object);
    ```

    The object parameter in the preceding syntax is an array of possible handlers, as follows:

    ```
    var resultset = {
      results: [{
        id: <value1>,
        icon: <url>,
        fields: [<fieldValue1>]}],
      commands:{
        id: <value>,
        icon: <url>,
        label: <value>,
        action: <function reference>
      }
    }
    ```

  - `hideAutoComplete`: This method allows us to remove autocomplete from any field. The syntax is as follows:

    ```
    Xrm.Page.getControl(field name).
    hideAutoComplete ();
    ```

Source code

Now, let's understand the complete code first. The comments explain each relevant step within the code:

```
function suggestZipCodes() {
  //defined possible ZipCode
  ZipCodes = [
    { name: '94102' },
    { name: '94103' },
    { name: '94104' },
    { name: '94105' },
    { name: '94107' },
```

```
        { name: '94108' }
      ];
    var OnZipCodekeyPress = function (fld) {
      var ZipCodetxt = Xrm.Page.getControl
      ("address1_postalcode").getValue();
      resultSet = {
        results: new Array(),
        commands: {
          id: "ZipCodecmd",
          label: "Search in Bing",
          action: function () {
            window.open("http://bing.com"); //Open Bing URL
          }
        }
      };
      var ZipCodetxtLowerCase = ZipCodetxt.toLowerCase();
      for (i = 0; i < ZipCodes.length; i++) {
        if (ZipCodetxtLowerCase ===
        ZipCodes[i].name.substring(0,
        ZipCodetxtLowerCase.length).toLowerCase()) {
          resultSet.results.push({
          id: i,
          fields: [ZipCodes[i].name]
          });
        }
        if (resultSet.results.length >= 10) {
          break;
        }
      }
      if (resultSet.results.length > 0) {
        //Show Auto Complete
        fld.getEventSource().showAutoComplete(resultSet);
      }
      else {
        //Hide Auto Complete
        fld.getEventSource().hideAutoComplete();
      }
    };
    Xrm.Page.getControl("address1_postalcode").addOnKeyPress
    (OnZipCodekeyPress);
}
```

Now, let's look at the steps to be performed after completing the code:

1. Navigate to **Settings** | **Customization** | **Customize the System** and select **Web Resources**. Click **New**:

2. Name the web resource as `zipCodeAutoComplete`. Select **Type** as **Script(JScript)** and paste the preceding code in the **Text Editor** link:

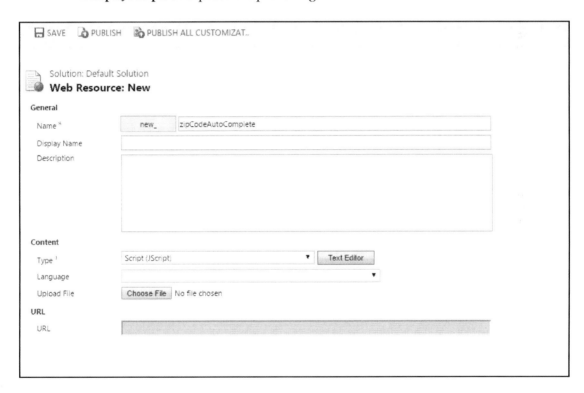

3. On clicking the **Text Editor** button, you will be able to paste the code into it:

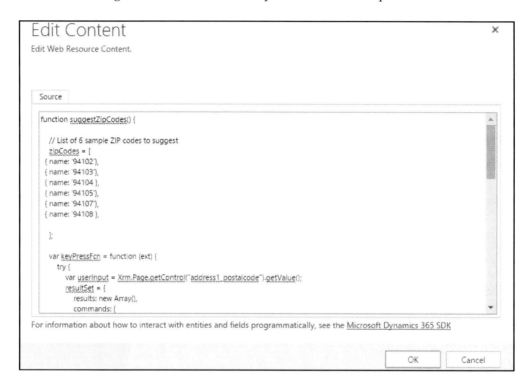

4. Click **OK**. On the main screen, click **Save and Publish**. Next, navigate to **Contact** entity | **Forms**. Open the **Contact** main form by double-clicking on it:

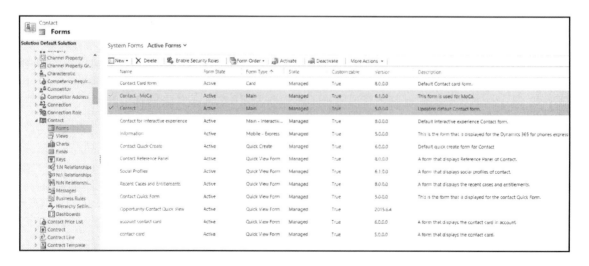

5. Click on the **Form Properties** ribbon button on the form editor:

6. Attach the WebResource script (created earlier to form libraries) by clicking **Form Properties** and attach the method name to the **On Load** event handler:

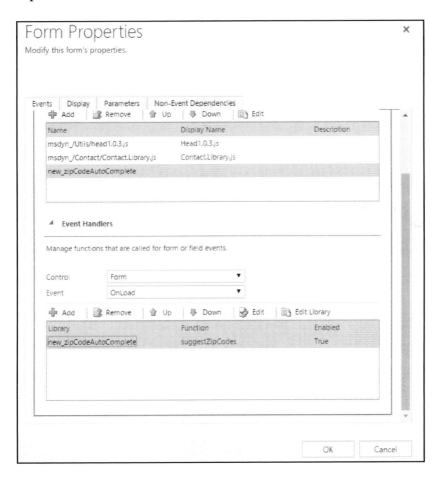

7. Click **OK**. Then click on **Save and Publish** to publish the form.

8. Now, as soon as any employee types in to the ZIP code field, he or she is presented with options for assistance, diminishing the chances of error:

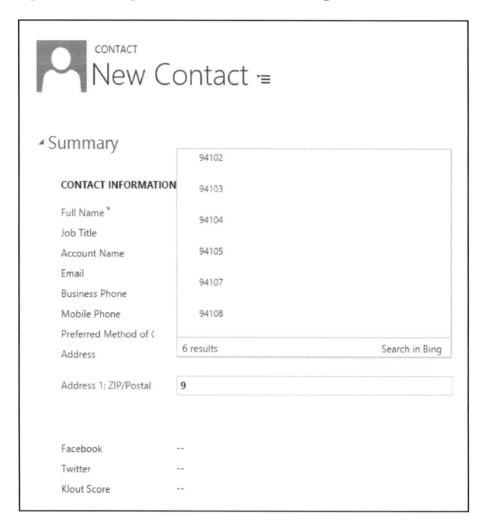

This is how we can get autocomplete selection for ZIP codes in our forms.

Microsoft Dynamics 365 Web API

This section introduces the new Web API introduced in Microsoft Dynamics 365. Prior to Microsoft Dynamics 365, the following were the different services provided by Dynamics CRM for executing different operations:

- **Organization service**: This service has been available since Microsoft Dynamics CRM 2011 and is mainly used for server-side operations. Due to this, the service is tightly coupled with the tools and assemblies provided in the .NET framework. It uses WCF to SOAP endpoints. The request and response have a SOAP format and can return a maximum of 5,000 records in one request.
- **Organization data service**: This service has been available since Microsoft Dynamics CRM 2011 and is mainly used for client-side operations. It supports the JSON format for request and response and, thus, can easily be handled in client-side scripting. It uses REST endpoints and can return a maximum of 50 records in an operation. It has been deprecated with Microsoft Dynamics CRM 2016.

In Microsoft Dynamics 365, the organization data service has been deprecated and replaced with the Web API. The main purpose of the API is to provide parity with the organization service and try to reduce as many constraints as possible. The following are the main characteristics of the Web API:

- It implements OData version 4.0, which is the open standard for building and consuming RESTful APIs over rich data sources, such as DOC, HTML, and PDF.
- It supports a wide variety of devices, platforms, and programming languages, such as .NET and C++.
- The request and response have the JSON format. Therefore, we can easily work with it in JavaScript.

In upcoming sections, we will explore various Web APIs in further detail.

Authentication with the Web API

Any request executed via the Web API will need to be authenticated with the Dynamics CRM instance. The only exceptions are the requests that are executed inside the web resources and plugins deployed in the organization itself.

The possible scenarios are as follows:

- **With JavaScript/ plugins**: When the Web API is used in web resources embedded in entity forms or ribbon commands, the user does not need to provide explicit authentication parameters while executing the API.
- **When executing code outside Dynamics CRM on an on-premise server**: In these cases, the code needs to pass the network credentials while calling the API. The following is a code snippet showing how to pass the credentials in `HTTPWebRequest`:

```
HttpWebRequest request =
(HttpWebRequest)WebRequest.Create(url);
request.Method = "GET";
request.Credentials =
new NetworkCredential(UserName, PassWord);
```

- **When executing code for Dynamics 365 online or an on-premise internet-facing deployment**: The authentication needs to be handled via OAuth. The following is a code snippet showing how the credentials are passed:

```
UserCredential userCredential = new UserCredential("
<office 365 user name>", "<Office 365 Password>");
```

Scenario 2

John is working with a requirement according to which he needs to populate the category and subcategory of a selected product on the form. He is using JavaScript for this. There are three different lookups on the form: **Product**, **Category**, and **Sub Category**. Now, as per John's requirement, when a user selects a product in the lookup field, the category and subcategory of the product need to be populated on the `onchange` event of the product lookup on the form. Therefore, we can make a Web API call from JavaScript to retrieve both the category and the subcategory of a selected product and can further set those values for lookups using JavaScript functions.

Why use Web API?

Using JavaScript is one of the most convenient ways to perform operations on data in Dynamics 365; you can do this with the help of the Web API.

The Web API sends and receives data in JSON format, which is easy to convert into objects in JavaScript. So, most developers use the Web API for performing CRUD operations with data in Dynamics 365.

We will use an `XMLHttpRequest` object to perform operations with the Web API. Now, what is `XMLHttpRequest`? `XMLHttpRequest (XHR)` is a native object supported by all the browsers that enable AJAX techniques to make web pages dynamic.

Now, as stated earlier, we have three lookups on the form for this scenario: **Product**, **Sub Category**, and **Category**:

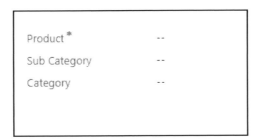

Our requirement states that, whenever a user fills the first lookup, that is, **Product**, the remaining two should be populated as shown in the following output:

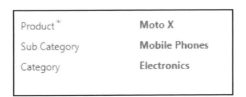

To achieve this, we will fetch the details of the selected product using the Web API. The **Product** form contains the lookups for both **Category** and **Sub Category**; our Web API query will be as follows:

```
Xrm.Page.context.getClientUrl() + "/api/data/v8.2/dyn_customproducts(" +
productId +
")?$select=_dyn_category_value,dyn_name,_dyn_subcategory_value";
```

`Xrm.Page.context.getClientUrl()` is a function to get the client URL of the current organization. The `productId` object is the ID of the selected product for which the details are to be fetched. The `dyn_customproducts` object is the logical name for the custom entity, **Product**, and the fields to be selected are `_dyn_category_value`, `dyn_name`, and `_dyn_subcategory_value`.

Now, we need to initialize `XMLHttpRequest` as follows:

```
var req = new XMLHttpRequest();
```

After initializing the `XMLHttpRequest` object, you need to open it before sending or setting any properties for it. The parameters of an open method are HTTP request methods (`GET`, `PUT`, `POST`, `DELETE` and so on), URL, and a Boolean parameter that indicates whether the operation is to be performed asynchronously.

When you use a web resource, you do not need to specify the username and passwords for authentication, as the user is already authenticated.

As we need to retrieve the entity details, we will use the `GET` HTTP request method:

```
req.open("GET",encodeURI(Xrm.Page.context.getClientUrl() +
"/api/data/v8.2/dyn_customproducts(" + productId +
")?$select=_dyn_category_value,dyn_name,_dyn_subcategory_value"), true);
```

The next step is to set the headers and event handlers for the opened request. After `XMLHttpRequest` is opened, you can set multiple request headers. We will set the following request headers for our operation:

```
req.setRequestHeader("OData-Version", "4.0");
```

To avoid ambiguity with OData versions, using this request header is necessary:

```
req.setRequestHeader("Accept", "application/json");
```

It is mandatory to use the `"Accept"` header value of the `"application/json"` request header for every operation you perform because the response given by the Web API will be in the JSON format:

```
req.setRequestHeader("Content-Type", "application/json; charset=utf-8");
```

If your request includes JSON data, you need to use the `"Content-Type"` request header:

```
req.setRequestHeader("Prefer", "odata.include-annotations=\"*\"");
```

If your query returns any formatted values, you need to include `"odata.include-annotations"`.

Event handlers

We must include event handlers before sending a request to detect when the operation is complete. Your request passes through several states before the response is returned. The `onreadystatechange` property detects when the request is complete. When the `readystate` property equals 4, the request is complete. You can check the status property at this time.

The response of our request in JSON format is as follows:

```
{
  "@odata.context":"https://dynamistydemo.crm.dynamics.com/api/data/v8.2/$metadata#dyn_customproducts(_dyn_category_value,dyn_name,_dyn_subcategory_value)/$entity","@odata.etag":"W/\"1159697\"","_dyn_category_value":"a37f34ea-0272-e711-8115-fc15b4286724","dyn_name":"Moto X","_dyn_subcategory_value":"f99c268d-0372-e711-8115-fc15b4286724","dyn_customproductid":"9a38421c-0472-e711-8115-fc15b4286724"
}
```

Therefore, here is the complete code of the GET request that we need to send:

```
function retrieveProductInfo()
{
  //Gets attribute for product.
  var product = Xrm.Page.getAttribute("dyn_product");
  //Attribute name of Category field
  var categoryField = "dyn_category";
  //Attribute name of Sub Category Field.
  var subCategoryField = "dyn_subcategory";
  //Variable to store product ID
  var productId;
  //Check if Product attribute is null
  if (product != null)
  {
    //Assign the selected product Id
    productId = product.getValue()[0].id.replace(/[{}]/g, "");
  }
  //Initializes request object
  var req = new XMLHttpRequest();
  //Opens the request
  req.open("GET", Xrm.Page.context.getClientUrl() +
  "/api/data/v8.2/dyn_customproducts(" + productId + ")?
$select=_dyn_category_value,dyn_name,_dyn_subcategory_value", true);
    //Set the request headers
    req.setRequestHeader("OData-MaxVersion", "4.0");
    req.setRequestHeader("OData-Version", "4.0");
```

```
req.setRequestHeader("Accept", "application/json");
req.setRequestHeader("Content-Type", "application/json;
charset=utf-8");
req.setRequestHeader("Prefer", "odata.include-annotations=\"*\"");
//Function to detect changes of readystate
req.onreadystatechange = function ()
{
  if (this.readyState === 4)
  {
    req.onreadystatechange = null;
    //Checks if request was completed succesfully
    if (this.status === 200)
    {
      //Parses the JSON response
      var result = JSON.parse(this.response);
      //Get the CategoryId
      var categoryId = result["_dyn_category_value"];
      //Gets Category Name
      var categoryName = result["_dyn_category_value@OData.
      Community.Display.V1.FormattedValue"];
      //Gets logical name of Category entity.
      var categoryLogicalName =
      result["_dyn_category_value@Microsoft.
      Dynamics.CRM.lookuplogicalname"];
      //Get the SubCategoryId
      var subcategoryId = result["_dyn_subcategory_value"];
      //Get the SubCategory Name
      var subcategoryName = result["_dyn_subcategory_value@OData.
      Community.Display.V1.FormattedValue"];
      //Get the logical name of SubCategory Entity
      var subcategoryLogicalName =
      result["_dyn_subcategory_value@Microsoft.
      Dynamics.CRM.lookuplogicalname"];
      //Calls the funtion to set lookups
      SetLookupValue(categoryField, categoryId,
      categoryName, categoryLogicalName);
      SetLookupValue(subCategoryField, subcategoryId,
      subcategoryName, subcategoryLogicalName);
      }
      else
      {
        Xrm.Utility.alertDialog(this.statusText);
      }
    }
  };
  req.send();
}
//Function that sets lookups
```

```
function SetLookupValue(fieldName, id, name, entityType)
{
  if (fieldName != null)
  {
    var lookupValue = new Array();
    lookupValue[0] = new Object();
    lookupValue[0].id = id;
    lookupValue[0].name = name;
    lookupValue[0].entityType = entityType;
    if (lookupValue[0].id != null)
    {
      Xrm.Page.getAttribute(fieldName).setValue(lookupValue);
    }
  }
}
```

So, by performing the preceding steps, the linked entities that were used to set the other two Lookup fields on the form can be retrieved through the Web API.

Scenario 3

Andy is working on a solution in which he needs to populate the fields of an entity into an option set. He wants to load the option set dynamically. To retrieve the fields of a particular entity, you can query the metadata using the Web API. All the attributes of an entity can be retrieved using the metadata query. In this scenario, it is demonstrated how the attributes of a **Contact** entity can be retrieved using a Web API call.

Retrieving metadata using the Web API

Microsoft Dynamics 365 is a metadata-driven application. Sometimes, you need to query the metadata while working with requirements such as those mentioned in this scenario. For this purpose, you can easily query the metadata using the Web API. We will use the `EntityDefinitions` entity to retrieve the metadata of the **Contact** entity. The URL will be as follows:

```
clientURL +
"api/data/v8.2/EntityDefinitions(LogicalName='contact')/Attributes"
```

We will create an HTML web resource and the following is the code to retrieve the metadata using the Web API. You will need to create a HTML control for selection in the web resource, as you cannot append items into the option set. So, we'll use the `$(document).ready`, function of JQuery, which will be executed on the page load. The Web API call is made inside this function, which will retrieve all the fields of the **Contact** entity. After retrieving the fields, the option set is appended with the retrieved fields:

```
<html>
  <head>
    <meta charset="utf-8" />
    <title></title>
    <script type="text/javascript" src="ClientGlobalContext.js.aspx">
    </script>
    <script type="text/jscript" src="
    https://dynamistydemo.crm.dynamics.com//
    WebResources/mcs_jquerymin"></script>
    <script type="text/jscript">
      //Function called when the web resource is loaded
      $(document).ready(function () {
      //Initializing requet
      var req = new XMLHttpRequest();

      //Opens request
      req.open("GET", window.parent.Xrm.Page.context.getClientUrl() +
      "/api/data/v8.2/EntityDefinitions(LogicalName='contact')
      /Attributes", true);

      //Sets request Headers
      req.setRequestHeader("OData-MaxVersion", "4.0");
      req.setRequestHeader("OData-Version", "4.0");
      req.setRequestHeader("Accept", "application/json");
      req.setRequestHeader("Content-Type", "application/json;
      charset=utf-8");
      req.setRequestHeader("Prefer",
      "odata.include-annotations=\"*\"");

      //Function to detect ready state change
      req.onreadystatechange = function () {
        if (this.readyState === 4) {
          req.onreadystatechange = null;

          //Check if request completed successfully
          if (this.status === 200) {
            var result = JSON.parse(this.response);
            var index = 1;
            for (var i = 0; i < result.value.length; i++) {
```

```
                    //Gets schemaname from response.
                    var schemaName = result.value[i].SchemaName;
                    $("#Entities").append("<option value='" + index +
                    "'>" + schemaName + "</option>");
                    index = index + 1;
                  }

                }
                else {
                  Xrm.Utility.alertDialog(this.statusText);
                }
              }
           };
           req.send();

        });
    </script>

    <style type="text/css">
      .select {
        font-size: 12px;
        font-family: Segoe\000020UI;
        color: #444444;
        margin: -8px;
      }

      .control {
        margin-left: 108px;
        font-size: 12px;
        height: 23px;
      }
    </style>
</head>
<body>
    <div class="select">
      <label for="Entities">Fields</label>
      <select name="Entities" id="Entities" class="control">
        <option value="0">--<options>
      </select>
    </div>
</body>
</html>
```

Here is the output of the preceding code:

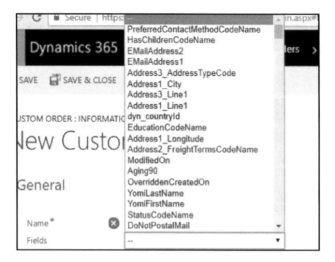

As you can see in the preceding screenshot, the option set is loaded with the field names of the entity.

Scenario 4

Rob is a CRM developer in an organization; he comes across a requirement that needs him to deactivate the **Contact** form if the parent account status is inactive. He figures he can use JavaScript to solve this problem. We will make a Web API call for the account to check its status and then deactivate the form using a JavaScript function.

First, we will retrieve the `statuscode` field of the parent account. Then, we need to check if the status of the parent is inactive; if yes, then we need to deactivate the form. We will write a JavaScript function for this. The whole process is shown in the following code:

```
function checkAccountStatus()
{
  //Fetch parent account
  var accountAttribute = Xrm.Page.getAttribute("parentcustomerid");
  var accountId;

  //Check if account is not null
  if (accountAttribute != null)
  {
    //Get value of account attribute
    accountId = accountAttribute.getValue();
```

```
if (accountId != null)
{
  //Gets the account Id
  accountId = accountId[0].id.replace(/[{}]/g, "");

  //Initializes new request.
  var req = new XMLHttpRequest();
  //Open the request
  req.open("GET", Xrm.Page.context.getClientUrl() +
  "/api/data/v8.2/accounts(" + accountId + ")?
  $select=name,statuscode", true);
  //Sets the Request Headers
  req.setRequestHeader("OData-MaxVersion", "4.0");
  req.setRequestHeader("OData-Version", "4.0");
  req.setRequestHeader("Accept", "application/json");
  req.setRequestHeader("Content-Type", "application/json;
  charset=utf-8");
  req.setRequestHeader("Prefer",
  "odata.include-annotations=\"*\"");
  //Function to detect ready state
  req.onreadystatechange = function ()
  {
    //Check if request is completed
    if (this.readyState === 4)
    {
      req.onreadystatechange = null;

      //Check if status code is 200 for success
      if (this.status === 200)
      {
        var result = JSON.parse(this.response);
        var name = result["name"];
        var statuscode = result["statuscode"];

        //checks if statuscode is inactive i.e 3
        if (statuscode == 2)
        {
          deactivateForm();
        }
      }
      else
      {
        Xrm.Utility.alertDialog(this.statusText);
      }
    }
  };
  req.send();
}
```

```
    }
  }

//Function to deactivate the form
function deactivateForm()
{
  var allAttributes = Xrm.Page.data.entity.attributes.get();
  for (var i in allAttributes)
  {
    if (allAttributes[i].getName() != null)
    {
      var attribute = Xrm.Page.data.entity.attributes.get(
      allAttributes[i].getName());
      if (attribute != null)
      {
        var name = attribute.getName();
        if (name != null)
        {
          var control = Xrm.Page.getControl(name);
          if (control != null)
          {
            Xrm.Page.getControl(name).setDisabled(true);
          }
        }
      }
    }
  }
  Xrm.Page.ui.setFormNotification('Information:Form Disabled!',
  'INFORMATION');
}
```

Here is the output of the preceding code:

Summary

This chapter was focused on introducing and using client-side enhancements available with Microsoft Dynamics CRM 2016. We also covered some of the client-side script functions with examples. You learned how to use JavaScript functions to validate data for automations and to create web resources. Also, we discussed the Web API in the later part, which is a new way of querying CRM data directly from JavaScript.

In the next chapter, you will learn about new mobile enhancements in Dynamics CRM. You will get a better understanding of mobile and tablet enhancements, the supported platforms, the browsers for mobile and tablet apps, installing the Microsoft Dynamics CRM 2016 phone App, previewing form customization changes on a phone, and the tablet look-and-feel available with Microsoft Dynamics CRM 2016.

9
Enhancements for Mobile

Microsoft Dynamics CRM 2016 enhances the capabilities of the sales and service teams at any time by providing enhancements in the mobility features of Microsoft Dynamics CRM 2016. Microsoft Dynamics CRM 2016 provides support for mobile applications across a range of devices, such as tablets and phones. Microsoft Dynamics CRM 2016 also supports multiple platforms.
We will have a look at some of the recent developments.

In this chapter, you will learn the following topics:

- Customizing the look and feel of mobile forms
- The Dynamics CRM mobile app for Android
- Supported platforms for the mobile app
- New visual controls in Microsoft Dynamics CRM 2016

Microsoft Dynamics CRM 2016 mobile application requirements

The following table summarizes the support for Microsoft Dynamics CRM 2016 for different types and versions of mobile OS:

Sr. no	Mobile platform	Supported version	Minimum RAM requirements
1.	iOS	8.1 and above	1 GB RAM
2.	Android	4.4 5.0 6.0	1 GB RAM

3.	Windows	8.1 10	1 GB RAM

Microsoft Dynamics CRM 2016 tablet application requirements

The following table summarizes the support for Microsoft Dynamics CRM 2016 for different types and versions of tablet OS:

Sr. no.	Tablet platform	Supported versions	Minimum RAM requirements	Minimum supported resolution	Other requirements
1.	iOS	8.1 and above	-	-	iPad third generation or later 9 inch (diagonal) or larger screen size.
2.	Android	4.0 4.3 4.4 5.0 6.0	1 GB RAM	-	Screens larger than 7 inches Optimized for screen sizes of 9 and 10 inches.
3.	Windows	8 or later	1 GB RAM	1366 x 768 resolution (720p)	-

The following combinations are tested and validated for the Microsoft Dynamics CRM 2016 app for tablets on Android:

- Samsung Galaxy Tab 4 over Android 4.4
- Samsung Galaxy Tab S over Android 4.4
- Google Nexus 10 over Android 4.2, 4.4 and 5.0
- Samsung Galaxy Tab 3 over Android 4.2.2
- Asus Transformer Pad Infinity TF700 over Android 4.2
- Samsung Galaxy Note 10 over Android 4.3

Microsoft Dynamics CRM 2016 tablet web browser support

Microsoft Dynamics CRM 2016 supports the default web browser in the following combinations of mobile OS and platform:

S. no.	Tablet platform	Supported version
1.	Windows	8 or later (on supported Windows tablets)
2.	iOS	7 8 9
3.	Android	4.2.2 4.3 4.4 5.0 * 6.0 (on supported Android tablets)

However, the following features are not available when using Microsoft Dynamics CRM 2016 from a web browser on the supported combinations that are listed in the preceding table:

- Pinch and zoom
- Reports
- System settings
- Advanced find
- Process dialogs
- Skype for business presence
- Entities that use classic forms

It is recommended that you use tablet application to utilize all the features available for Microsoft Dynamics CRM 2016 using tablets.

Scenario 1

Roy is the CRM administrator at Acme Ltd. He wants to explore the mobile capabilities that are available, preview the account entity form, and check the look and feel of the form in Microsoft Dynamics CRM 2016 mobile and tablet applications.

The following steps are required for the CRM administrator:

1. Navigate to **Settings** | **Customizations** | **Customize the System**:

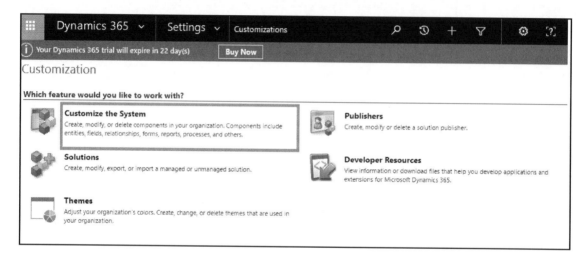

2. A popup window will open with all the customization components of the system (**Solution: Default Solution**). Expand the entities. Select **Account** and pick **Forms**:

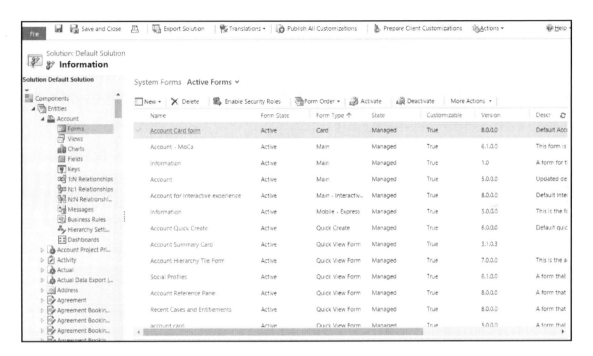

 Note: Default Solution is a container containing all the customization elements and code elements that are configured in the CRM system.

3. Double-click the **Information** form to open it with a form editor:

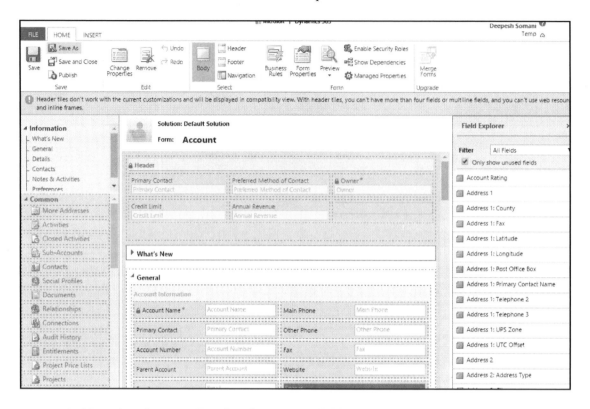

4. Note that there is a **Preview** button available. Click on it to expand it, select **Mobile Client**, and you will be presented with two options—one for **Tablet** and another for **Phone**:

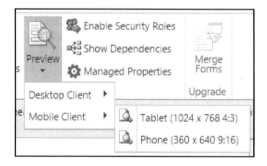

5. Pick **Tablet** experience. The following screen will be presented across to you while the preview is being generated. Please wait for the preview to be generated:

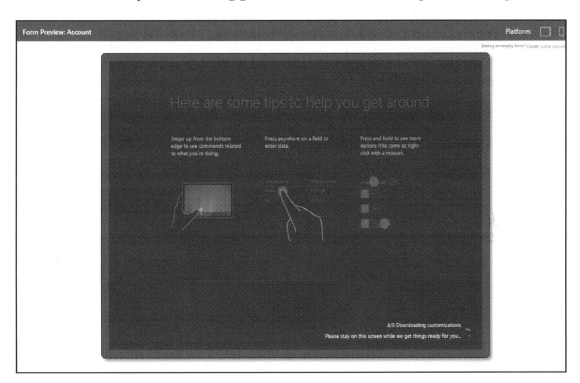

6. Once the customization preview for **Tablet** is ready, Roy can see the look-and-feel of the Microsoft Dynamics CRM 2016 form in a tablet interface:

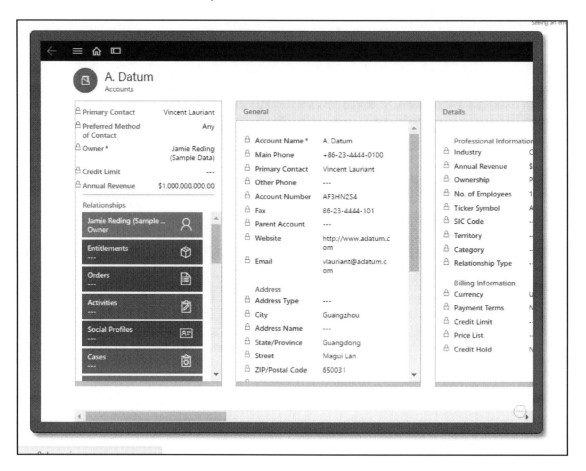

7. Roy can also quickly check for the appearance in the mobile application by changing the platform icon (top-right of the screen) to the mobile icon:

8. On Selecting the mobile icon, Microsoft Dynamics CRM 2016 starts generating the screen layout preview of the **Account** form in the mobile app for Microsoft Dynamics CRM 2016:

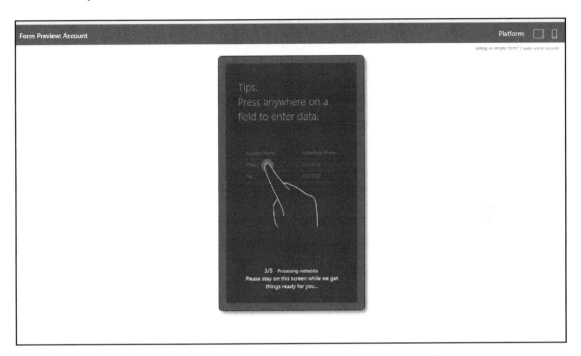

9. Once the customization preview for mobile is ready, Roy is able to quickly view the look-and-feel of the Microsoft Dynamics CRM 2016 form in the mobile app:

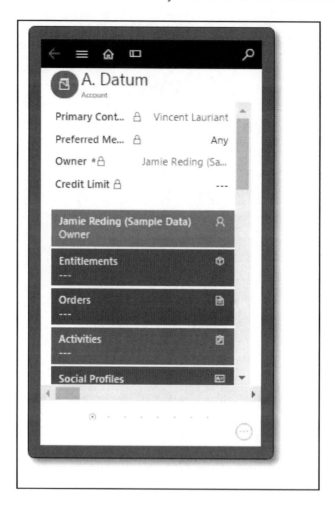

This new enhancement to preview mobile and tablet forms without the need to download, install, and configure the app on a mobile or tablet device makes Roy a lot more productive and efficient in configuring the Microsoft Dynamics CRM 2016 forms for mobile and tablet apps.

Scenario 2

Roy is very happy with the mobile and tablet previews available for the **Account** form and wishes to configure the Microsoft Dynamics CRM 2016 app for phones on his Android device and to connect it against his organization's Microsoft Dynamics CRM 2016 online instance. Here are the steps he needs to follow:

1. Navigate to the Google Play app on your Android phone and search for dynamics crm - you will be presented with multiple apps for Dynamics CRM:

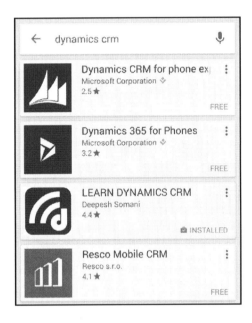

2. Select **Dynamics 365 for Phones** and click **Install**:

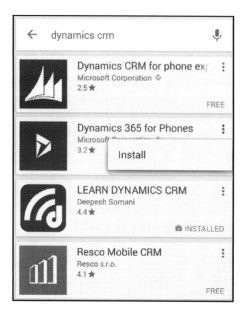

3. Certain permissions need to be given before the **Dynamics 365 for Phones** will start downloading. Please **Accept** for giving the necessary permissions:

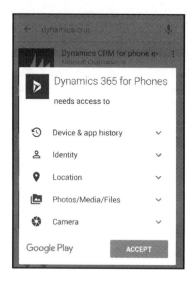

4. The **Dynamics 365 for Phones** app will start downloading now. Once the app is downloaded and installed, select **Open**:

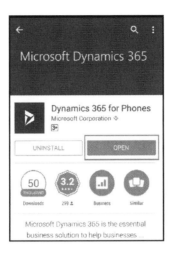

5. The **Dynamics 365 for Phones** app will now ask the user to enter the CRM organization URL to connect to. Please specify your organization URL in the intended format and tap on the arrow:

In order to connect on-premise CRM to mobile apps, the **Internet Facing Deployment (IFD)** is required.

6. In the next step, you need to enter the username and password for the app to get configured and connected. Specify the required credentials and click **Sign in**:

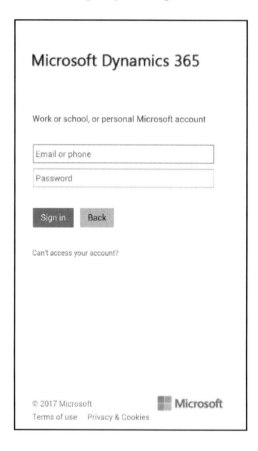

7. The Dynamics CRM phone app will start the configuration process now. You will need to wait on the following screen until the configurations are completed:

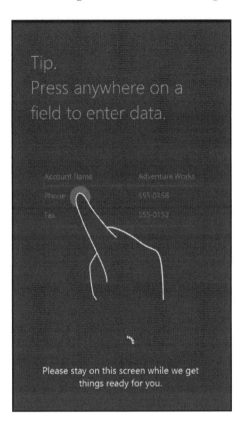

8. Once the configurations are completed, you will land on a CRM dashboard:

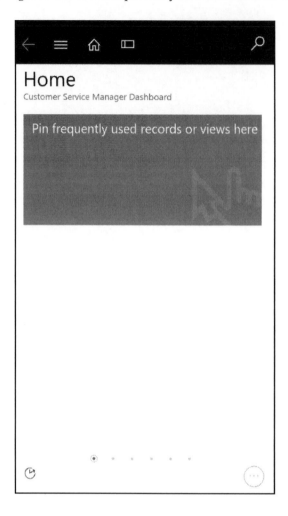

9. Tapping the second button on top will expand a list of entities that can be selected. Pick **Accounts**:

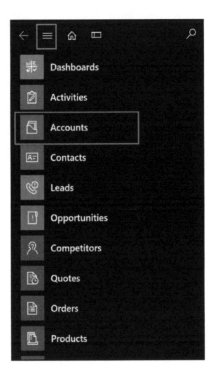

10. You are now presented with a list of accounts:

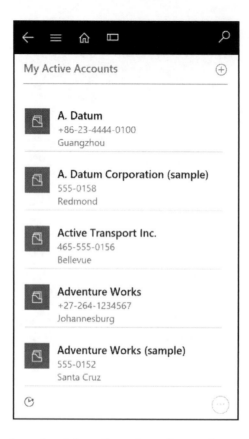

These steps enable Roy to download, install, and configure the app on a mobile or tablet device. Similar steps need to be followed to install the Dynamics CRM app on iOS or Windows platforms. The Dynamics CRM tablet app can also be configured on Android, iOS, and Windows platforms using the preceding steps.

Visual controls in Microsoft Dynamics CRM 2016

Microsoft Dynamics CRM 2016 introduces controls for mobile and tablet applications that help the users to enter and use CRM apps faster. These controls are designed considering the touch-friendly environment provided by modern smart phones and tablets.

The main advantage of these visual controls is that they are very user-friendly and they make operating easier while using the app on phones or tablets. These controls are more interactive, and typing is not the only alternative. They also control the format of data displayed in a consistent way.

The following types of visual controls are introduced with Microsoft Dynamics CRM 2016:

- **Linear slider**: The linear slider control displays any numeric or currency field as a slider. The following image shows this control:

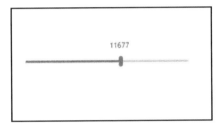

- **Option set:** The option set control displays an option set field in mobile and tablet apps. The following image shows control:

- **Flip switch**: The flip switch control displays a two-option field, such as a switch control, in mobile and tablet apps. The following image shows this control:

- **Radial knob:** The radial knob control displays numeric or currency fields as a radial in mobile and tablet apps. The following image shows this control:

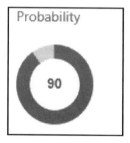

- **Pen control:** The pen control is used to input multiple lines of text in text fields to capture pen input, such as signatures. The maximum length of the field is 15,000. Signature input cannot be changed once it is inputted. The following image shows this control:

- **Calendar control:** Calendar control is used to give a calendar view on entity grids. The following image shows this control on the phone app:

- **Website preview:** The website preview control is used to map to a URL field to show a preview of the website URL provided. The following image shows this control:

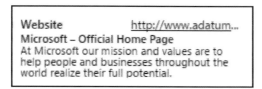

- **Number input:** The number input field is used for numeric or currency fields. The following image shows this control:

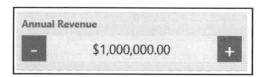

- **Input mask**: The input mask control is used in the case of any single line of text field, where the input must be entered in a specific format, such as in the case of a credit card. The following image shows this control:

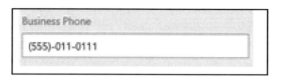

- **Linear gauge:** Linear gauge is used to create a linear gauge input for numeric or currency fields. The following image shows this control:

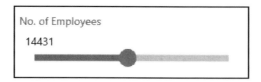

- **Arc knob:** Arc knob is used to create arc-like inputs and visual fields for numeric or currency fields. The following image shows this control:

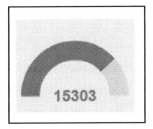

- **Autocomplete:** Autocomplete can be used to create an autocomplete input, which can be mapped to any option set or view. The following image shows this control:

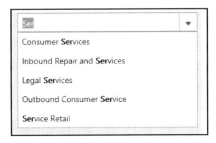

- **Multimedia control:** The multimedia control is used to map to a URL field that contains the audio or video link to be played. The following image shows this control:

- **Star rating:** The star rating control is used for a whole number field. The maximum number of stars is 5. The following image shows this control:

- **Bullet graph:** Bullet graph is a visualization control for any numeric or currency field. This is useful in cases where there is a need to show such field types. The following image shows this control:

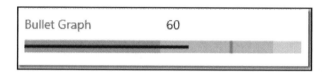

The following table summarizes the control type against the supported mode and the corresponding field type:

S.No.	Control type	Supported modes	Supported CRM field types
1	Linear slider	Edit, Read	Whole number, currency, floating-point number, decimal
2	Option set	Edit, Read	Option set
3	Flip switch	Edit, Read	Two options
4	Radial knob	Edit, Read	Whole number, currency, floating-point number, decimal
5	Pen control	Edit, Read	Multiple lines of text
6	Calendar control	Edit, Read	NA, Supported for entity grids
7	Website preview	Read	Single-line URL
8	Number input	Edit	Whole number, currency, floating-point number, decimal
9	Input mask	Edit	Single-line of text
10	Linear gauge	Edit, Read	Whole number, currency, floating-point number, decimal

11	Arc knob	Edit, Read	Whole number, currency, floating-point number, decimal
12	Autocomplete	Edit	Single line of text
13	Multimedia control	Read	Single-line URL
14	Star rating	Edit, Read	Whole number
15	Bullet graph	Read	Whole number, currency, floating-point number, decimal

A scenario for visual controls

Sarah is the CRM manager for Contoso Corporation. Contoso Corp. utilizes Microsoft Dynamics CRM 2016 for their sales team. They are also using a mobile application for Dynamics CRM 2016. Sarah wants to configure the visual controls of Microsoft Dynamics CRM 2016 for the following, so that the staff is better assisted to complete their tasks:

- Timeline control for opportunities
- Pen control for opportunities

Configuring the timeline control

Here, we will go through the configuration of a timeline control in Dynamics CRM:

1. Navigate to **Settings** | **Customizations** | **Customize the System**:

2. The default solution will pop up in a window. Expand **Entities** | **Opportunity** and select **Controls**:

3. On the **Controls** tab, select **Add Control**:

4. Select **Calendar Control** and click **Add**:

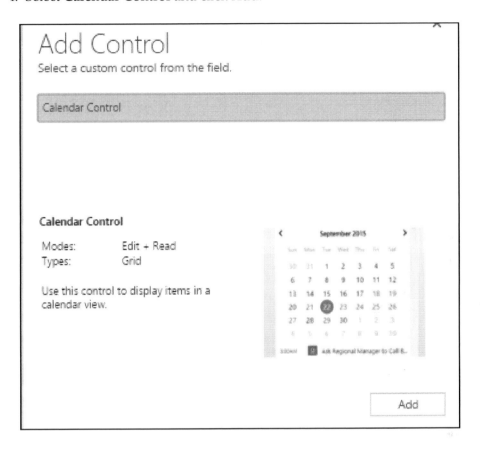

5. On the **Controls** tab. Please select the radio button choices for phone and tablet for the control. Note that **Start Date** and **Description** are required properties for this control. Fill in the properties and bind them to fields. In our case, **Start Date** is bound to the **Modified on** field and **Description** is bound to the **Name** field:

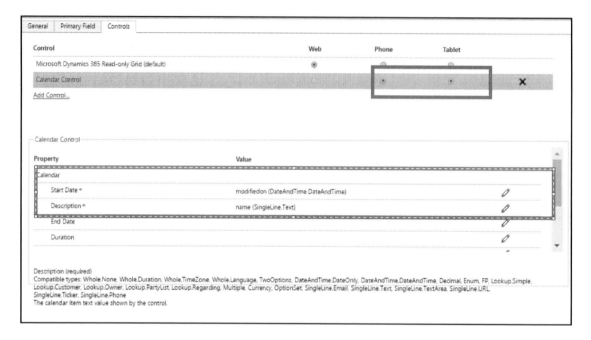

Control		Web	Phone	Tablet	
Microsoft Dynamics 365 Read-only Grid (default)		●	○	○	
Calendar Control			●	●	✕
Add Control...					

Calendar Control

Property	Value	
Calendar		
Start Date ∗	modifiedon (DateAndTime.DateAndTime)	🖉
Description ∗	name (SingleLine.Text)	🖉
End Date		🖉
Duration		🖉

Description (required)
Compatible types: Whole.None, Whole.Duration, Whole.TimeZone, Whole.Language, TwoOptions, DateAndTime.DateOnly, DateAndTime.DateAndTime, Decimal, Enum, FP, Lookup.Simple, Lookup.Customer, Lookup.Owner, Lookup.PartyList, Lookup.Regarding, Multiple, Currency, OptionSet, SingleLine.Email, SingleLine.Text, SingleLine.TextArea, SingleLine.URL, SingleLine.Ticker, SingleLine.Phone
The calendar item text value shown by the control.

Optionally, you can also fill in other properties on the control such as End Date, Duration, and so on.

6. Click **Save** and then **Publish**:

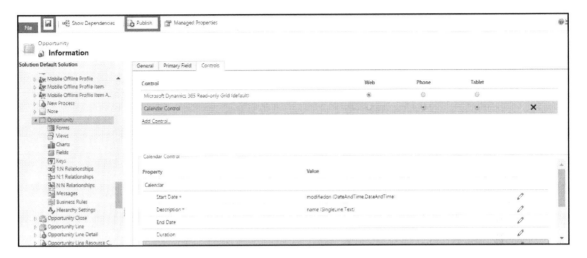

7. Sarah now navigates back to the Dynamics 365 phone app installed on her phone to check the user experience for her sales team. The **Dynamics 365 for Phones** instantly suggests her to download the new customizations. Tap **Download**:

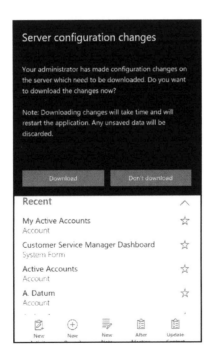

8. The Dynamics CRM phone app will now download the customizations. Once completed, navigate to **Opportunities**:

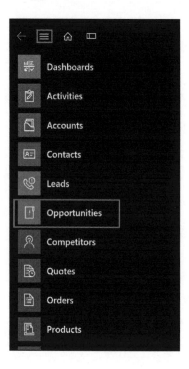

9. Instead of a list, **Opportunities** will now be presented in a calendar format:

Configuring the Pen Control

Sarah now wants to add pen control so that opportunities can be signed by the customers when the Contoso sales representative visits them equipped with the Dynamics 365 phone app.

Perform the following steps to configure the pen control:

1. Navigate to **Settings** | **Customization** | **Customize the System**:

2. Expand entities. Select **Opportunity**, expand **Opportunity** | **Select Fields** and click **New**:

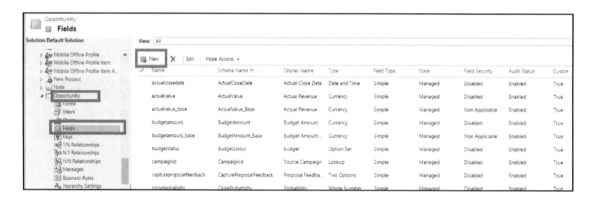

3. Create a new multiline text field called `Signature`. Fill in the name as `Signature` and **Type** as **Multiple Line of Text**. Click **Save and Close**:

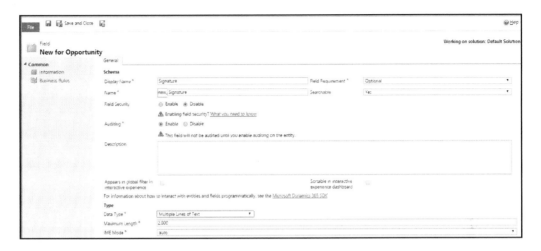

4. Click **Publish All Customizations**:

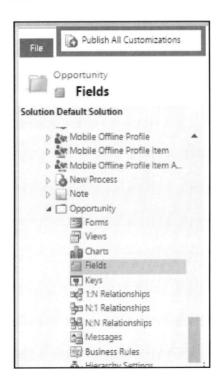

5. Go to **Opportunity** | **Forms** and select the **Opportunity** form by double-clicking it:

6. Drag the newly created **Signature** field on the form from the right-hand side list of the available unused fields:

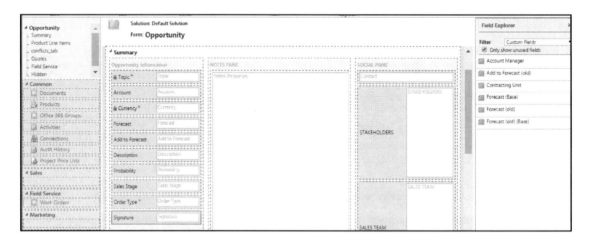

7. Double-click on the **Signature** field to open **Field Properties**, select the **Control** tab, and press the **Add Control** button:

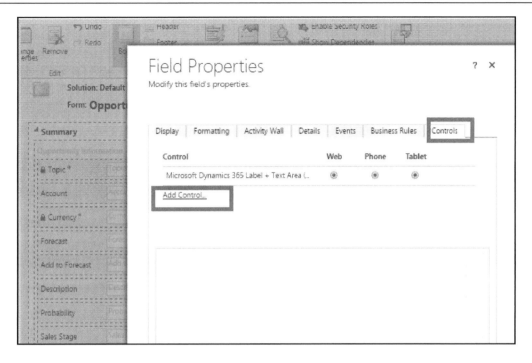

8. Select **Pen Control** and click **Add**:

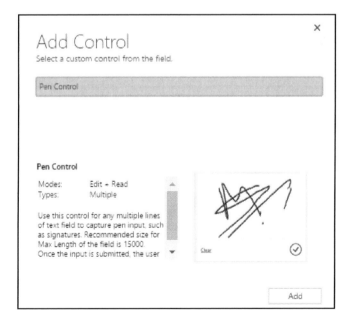

9. On the **Controls** tab, select the radio button for **Phone** and **Tablet** against **Pen Control** and click **OK**:

10. Click **Save** and then click **Publish** on the form:

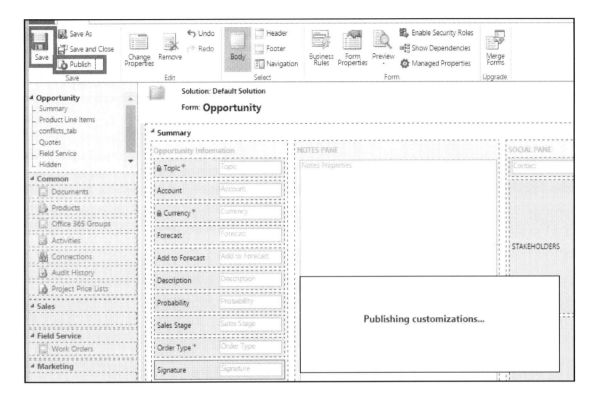

11. Sarah now navigates back to the Dynamics 365 phone app installed on her phone to check the user experience for her sales team. She taps the test opportunity from the calendar to open the **Opportunity** form. On tapping the **Signature** field, the control is available:

Summary

In this chapter, you learned mobile and tablet enhancements, supported platforms and browsers for mobile and tablet apps in Microsoft Dynamics CRM 2016, how to install the Microsoft Dynamics CRM 2016 phone app, how to preview form customization changes in phone and tablet, new visual controls, and how to configure calendar and pen control.

In the next chapter, you will learn about developing plugins in Dynamics CRM. We will be covering topics such as event-execution pipeline, isolation modes, and plugin development.

10
Plugin Development with Dynamics CRM

Plugins are the handlers for the events fired by Dynamics CRM. Each action executed in Dynamics CRM, such as create, update, delete, publish customizations, and so on. is an event. Using plugins, we can extend the standard behavior of Dynamics CRM with a custom code written in the .NET framework.

Dynamics CRM provides a list of all the supported messages and entities for plugins. They are available in the following MSDN site:
`https://msdn.microsoft.com/en-us/library/gg328576.aspx`

In this chapter, we will go through the following topics:

- **Event execution pipeline**: Through the event execution pipeline, one can get an idea about the different stages where plugins can be registered and the types of operations that can be performed using a plugin
- **Isolation modes**: Isolation modes are the modes in which you can register a plugin
- **Plugin Development**: We will cover some scenarios to develop a plugin for a better understanding of how plugins can be developed

A plugin can be written in both online and on-premise environments. Mentioned here are some of the functionalities that could be accomplished via a plugin:

1. Executing some server side data validation
2. Accessing some external third party system and relaying information between the two

3. Executing some server side complex business logic
4. Using the Microsoft Azure bus service, we can also write an Azure-aware plugin that can then be used for setting up integration to third-party applications

Event execution pipeline

Every action in Microsoft Dynamics CRM 2016 results in a call made to the organization's web service. The message contains business entity information and core operation information. These messages are passed through a standard execution pipeline or stages where it can be modified by any custom logic written by users. This custom logic is a plugin.

Pipeline stages

The event pipeline is divided into multiple stages out of which four are available to register custom-developed or third-party plugins.

Mentioned here are the four stages in the plugin execution pipeline in which we can register custom code:

Event	Stage Name	Stage Number	Description
Pre-Event	Pre-Validation	10	The plugins registered in this stage are executed before the main operation. The events are executed outside of the main database transaction.
Pre-Event	Pre-Operation	20	The plugins registered in this stage are executed before the mail operation. The events are executed within the database transaction.
Platform Core Operation	Main Operation	30	This stage is only meant for internal use and no plugins can be registered in this stage. Main operations such as create and update are executed in this stage.

Post-Event	Post-Operation	40	The plugins registered in this stage are executed after the main operation. The events are executed within the database transaction.

Database transaction

Depending upon the stage in which we register the plugin, the plugin will either be executed inside or outside the database transaction. Any plugin registered in stage 20 and 40 will be inside the database transaction. However, any plugin registered in the pre-validation stage, that is, *10*, will be executed outside the main database transaction.

Due to this, pre-validation and pre-operation plugins differ in terms of how they perform exception handling. Mentioned here are two scenarios where instead of pre-operation, the user should use the pre-validation plugin:

- As a requirement, while deleting an account, we need to make sure that the account should be deleted only if there are no subcontacts present in it.
- If we write a plugin and register it on the PreOperation of the delete message on account, we will always get zero associated contacts. Due to this PreOperation will not suffice the requirement. However, if we register the same code as a PreValidation plugin, it will work correctly.

The following diagram explains the relationship between Contact and Account:

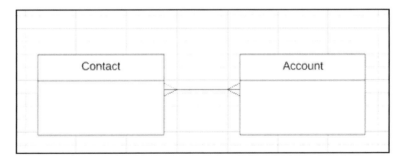

And here's a diagram that helps you understand the logic to verify the subcontacts before deleting the account:

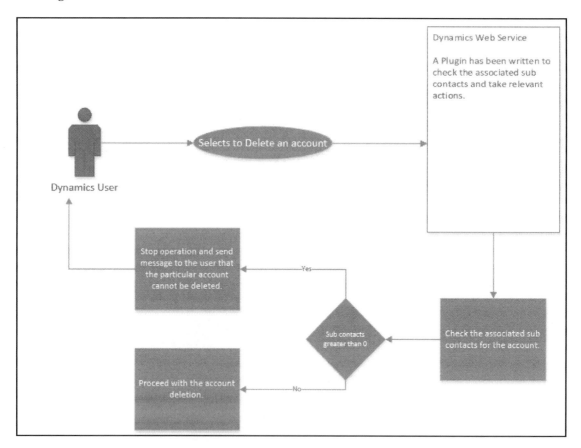

Plugin isolation mode

Plugin isolation mode signifies the level of security restrictions imposed on the plugin execution pipeline. The isolation mode is specified on the assembly level and not on the individual plugin step.

When a plugin assembly is registered, it can either be registered in an **isolated** or **sandbox** mode or in a **none** mode. The sandbox is more secure and some actions are restricted.

When a plugin is registered in a sandbox mode, although a plugin can still access the Dynamics CRM organization service and execute requests in accordance with Dynamics SDK, some of the functionalities such as accessing database or file directory are restricted. However, the plugin will still be able to access Azure Cloud Services endpoint. When a plugin is registered in the **none** mode, the aforementioned restrictions on a plugin won't apply. Mentioned here are some of the key differences in the two modes of plugin isolation

Difference	Sandbox	None
Restricted features	A plugin registered in the sandbox mode will not be able to access the following features: • Access to the file system • System event log • Certain network protocols • Registry • Access to external database	A plugin registered in the *none* mode can access the features that are restricted for the sandbox mode
Dynamics CRM online support	Dynamics CRM online supports the execution of plugins only registered in the sandbox mode.	Dynamics CRM online does not support the execution of plugins registered in the none mode
Dynamics CRM on premise support	Dynamics CRM on-premise supports the registration of plugins in both the modes.	Dynamics CRM on-premise supports the registration of plugins in both the modes
Run time statistics and monitors	Dynamics CRM collects runtime statistics and monitors plugins that execute in sandbox. If the process that hosts the plugin exceeds the CPU threshold, memory, or becomes unresponsive, the process will be killed by the platform.	No statistics and monitors are collected by Dynamics CRM for plugins registered in none

Writing a plugin

Plugins are custom classes that implement the IPlugin interface. The class can be written in any .NET framework-compliant language such as Microsoft Visual C# or Microsoft Visual Basic .NET. The following screenshots illustrate how users can create a plugin project.

1. Firstly, the user can create a new class library project:

Creating a Plugin Class Project

2. After the project is created, the user can add a new **Class...** item to the project. The new class would act as the `plugin` class:

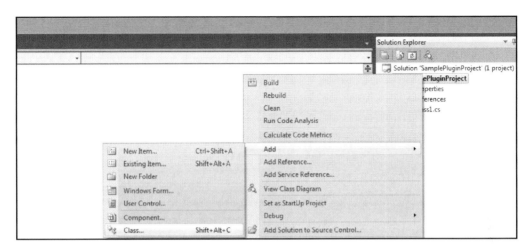

3. Here's how we can add a new class file to the solution:

Selecting the appropriate item type

4. All the plugin projects must have a reference for the `Microsoft.Xrm.Sdk` and `Microsoft.Crm.Sdk.Proxy` assemblies.

   If a person is writing a plugin for the first time, they must download the appropriate Dynamics SDK matching the target environment. You can refer to this MSDN link for downloading the SDK:
   `https://www.microsoft.com/en-us/download/details.aspx?id=50032`

5. Here's how we can add assembly references:

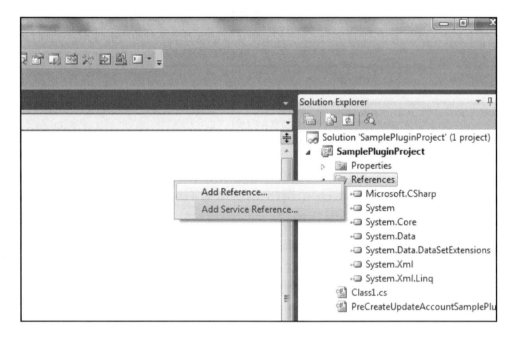

6. Here's how we can add the required assembly references:

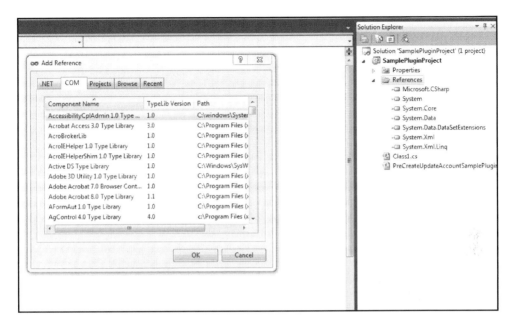

7. Browse or select the required references, in this case, **Microsoft.Xrm.Sdk.dll**:

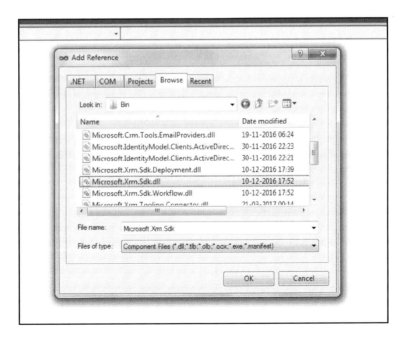

8. Add the **Microsoft.Xrm.Sdk.dll** reference:

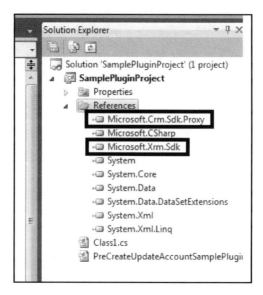

9. The next step would be to add the respective using statements in the plugin class. Also, any plugin must implement the IPlugin interface:

```
using System;
using System.Collections.Generic;
using System.Linq;
using System.Text;
using Microsoft.Xrm.Sdk;
using Microsoft.Crm.Sdk.Messages;
using Microsoft.Xrm.Sdk.Query;

namespace SamplePluginProject
{
  public class PreCreateUpdateAccountSamplePlugin : IPlugin
  {
    public void Execute(IServiceProvider serviceProvider)
    {
    }
  }
}
```

10. When we implement the `IPlugin` interface, we must also define the `Execute` method. This method would be the starting point when control would be transferred to the `plugin` class.

11. After adding the method, build the project to ensure that everything is correct.

12. After the project builds successfully, to deploy the assembly in Dynamics CRM, we must sign the assembly. We can do this by navigating to the properties of the project:

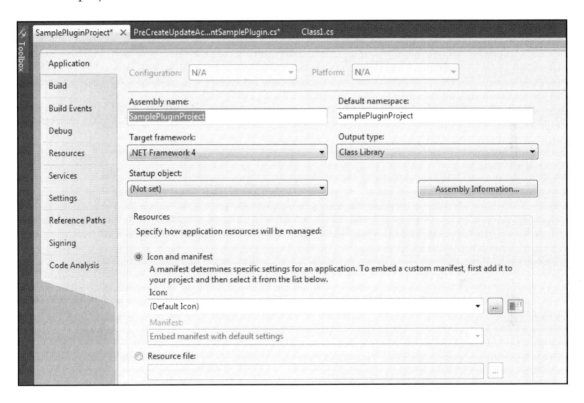

13. Set the assembly name for the project:

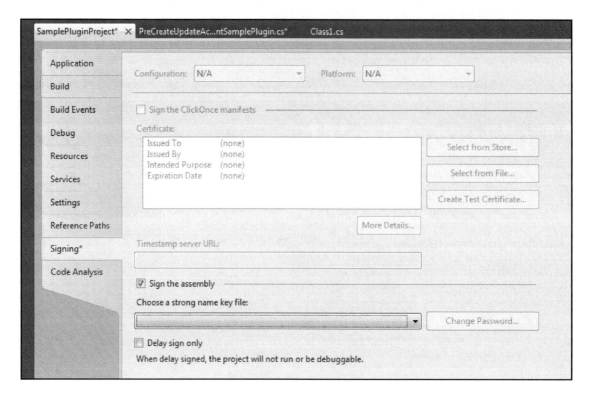

14. Sign the assembly:

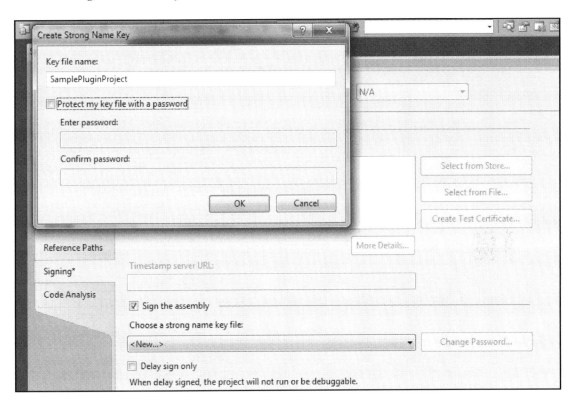

15. After the plugin assembly has been generated successfully, the next step is to deploy the plugin assembly in Dynamics CRM. All plugin deployments take place using a standard tool, *Plugin Registration Tool*, provided by Microsoft in the SDK. It just requires the .NET framework to be installed on the system from which the user is planning to deploy the plugins. As a first step, the user will need to navigate to the file explorer directory where the plugin registration tool has been downloaded:

Name	Date modified	Type	Size
▸ Local Disk (C:) ▸ crm 2016 sdk ▸ SDK ▸ Tools ▸ PluginRegistration ▸			
AssemblyRegistration.dll	23-05-2016 21:41	Application extens...	53 KB
CrmLibraries.dll	23-05-2016 21:42	Application extens...	824 KB
DebugPlugin.dll	23-05-2016 21:41	Application extens...	50 KB
ImageRegistration.dll	23-05-2016 21:41	Application extens...	41 KB
Microsoft.Crm.Sdk.Proxy.dll	23-05-2016 21:33	Application extens...	259 KB
Microsoft.Expression.Interactions.dll	23-05-2016 21:41	Application extens...	106 KB
Microsoft.IdentityModel.Clients.ActiveDi...	23-05-2016 21:33	Application extens...	205 KB
Microsoft.IdentityModel.Clients.ActiveDi...	23-05-2016 21:33	Application extens...	61 KB
Microsoft.ServiceBus.dll	23-05-2016 21:34	Application extens...	3,573 KB
Microsoft.Xrm.Sdk.Deployment.dll	23-05-2016 21:33	Application extens...	96 KB
Microsoft.Xrm.Sdk.dll	23-05-2016 21:33	Application extens...	520 KB
Microsoft.Xrm.Sdk.Workflow.dll	23-05-2016 21:33	Application extens...	58 KB
Microsoft.Xrm.Tooling.Connector.dll	23-05-2016 21:33	Application extens...	198 KB
Microsoft.Xrm.Tooling.CrmConnectCont...	23-05-2016 21:33	Application extens...	1,939 KB
Microsoft.Xrm.Tooling.Ui.Styles.dll	23-05-2016 21:33	Application extens...	95 KB
PluginCommonControls.dll	23-05-2016 21:41	Application extens...	109 KB
PluginProfiler.Debugger	23-05-2016 21:41	Application	67 KB

16. The user then needs to click on `PluginRegistration.exe`:

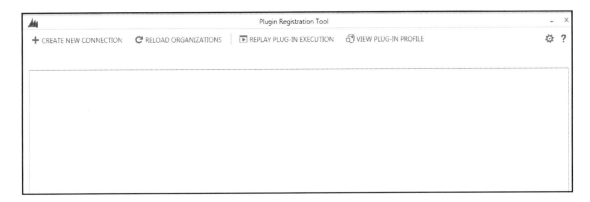

17. The user should then click on the **Create New Connection** button. On doing so, a popup window for entering the user credentials should open up:

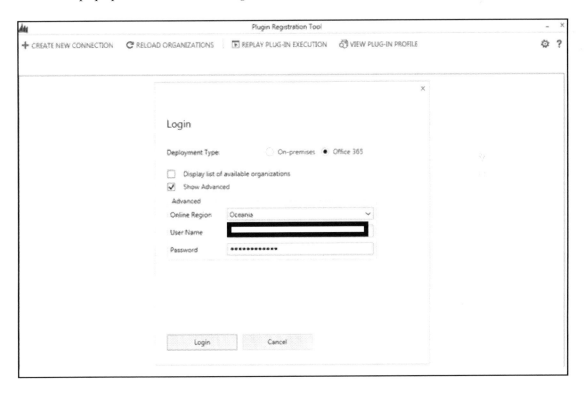

Please note that the user must enter the credentials for a user with the **System Customizer** role. Otherwise, the user will not be allowed to register the assembly.

The user should next click on the **Login** button. If the credentials are correct, the user should be redirected to the next screen, wherein he/she will be able to see all the plugins and custom workflow assemblies that have been registered in the Dynamics CRM organization:

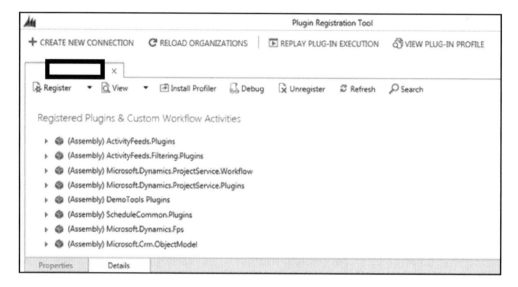

18. After this, the user can now register the plugin assembly created in the previous step. As illustrated in the following screenshot, the user can firstly click on the **Register** button, which should open a dropdown wherein the user can click on **Register New Assembly**:

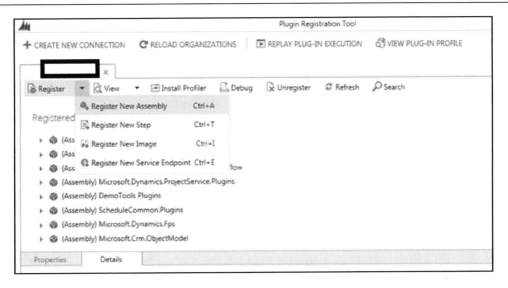

On doing so, a window popup screen should load. The user can now navigate to the plugin assembly created in the preceding steps:

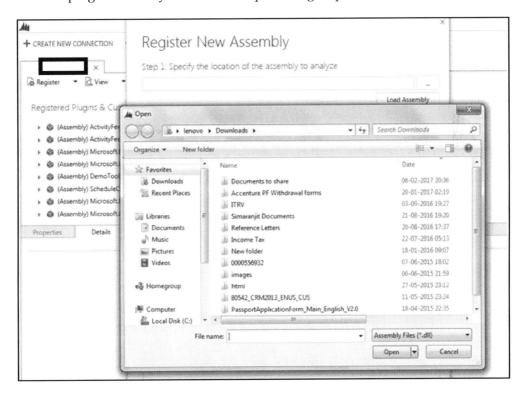

Register the plugin assembly into the CRM:

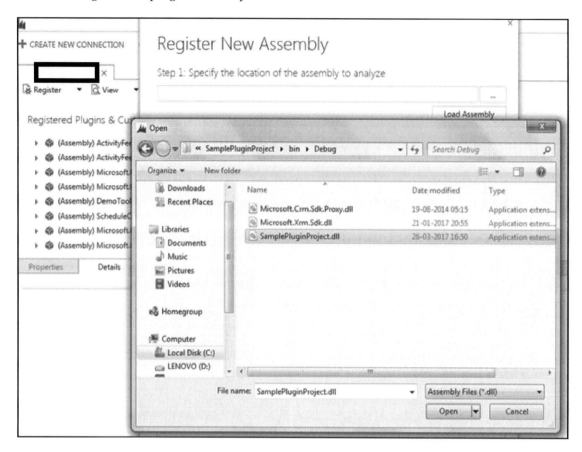

Once the user clicks on the **Open** button, review that the assembly should get loaded. Also, all the classes that implement the IPlugin interface should also appear on the screen:

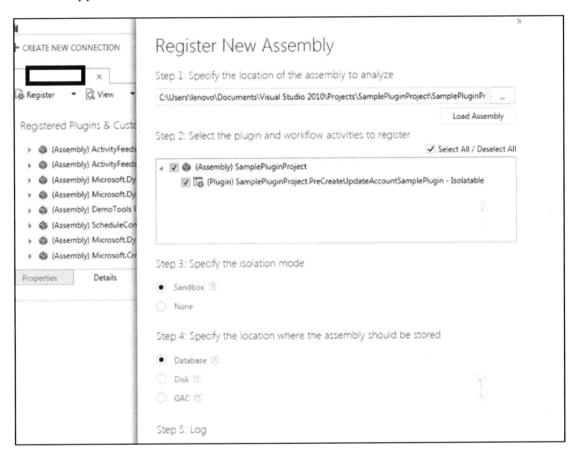

Note that, as explained earlier, the isolation mode for online deployment can only be sandbox. For on-premise, depending upon the required functionality in the plugin, we can either choose sandbox or none.

When we register a plugin assembly, Dynamics CRM needs to store it somewhere so that it can be loaded whenever the associated event gets triggered. There are three options for the same:

- **Database**: The assembly is stored in the Dynamics CRM DB. All assemblies wherein the isolation mode is sandbox will always be stored in the database. One major advantage of using the database approach is that the assembly is automatically distributed across multiple CRM servers in a data center cluster. However, in case we are referencing some external assemblies, then we will need to firstly merge the assemblies using some external tool such as ILMerge.
- **Disk**: If the user selects this option, the assembly will be copied in the CRM bin folder. This option is only available for Dynamics CRM on-premise, where we do have access to the CRM bin folder.
- **GAC**: As in the case of disk deployment, the option is only available for Dynamics CRM on-premise. When we use this deployment, the assemblies are copied to the GAC.

With this, we have defined the outer structure of the plugin project. The next step would be to write the plugin class, which would govern all the event handlers.

1. After all the steps are done, the user can click on the **Register Assembly** button. If everything is fine, the user should receive a success message:

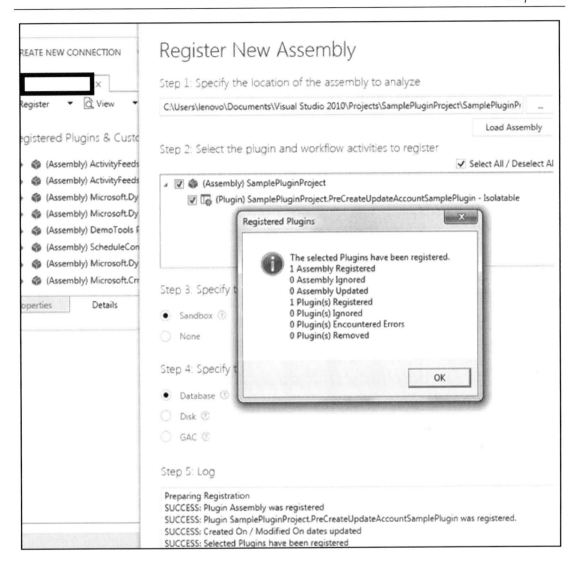

2. Once the user clicks on the **OK** button, he/she should again be navigated to the main page, where he/she will see the list of registered assemblies. Review that the newly registered assembly should also be there:

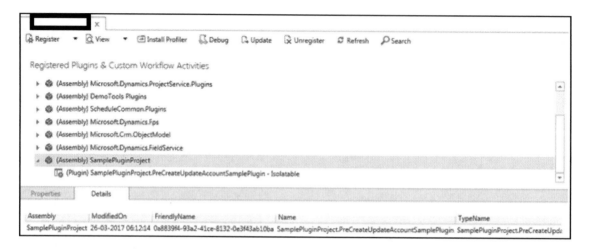

Registering a plugin step

To register a new step in the plugin class, the user can just right-click on the plugin class appearing under the plugin assembly. One the user does that, the following screen should load up:

Mentioned here are some of the key terms along with their definitions:

- **Message**: This describes the event on which we are registering the plugin. Possible values can be `Create`, `Update`, `Delete`, `Retrieve`, `RetrieveMultiple`, `AddListMembers`, and so on. Basically, most of the actions that are happening in Dynamics CRM will have an associated message on which we can write a plugin.

- **Primary entity**: This is the Dynamics CRM object on which we want to register the plugin. The user can register plugins on all the custom entities that they create in Dynamics CRM. Apart from those custom entities, users can also register plugins on out-of-box entities such as account, contact, campaign, marketing list, and so on.

- **Secondary entity**: This is only applied to a very limited number of messages, such as `SetRelated` and `RemoveRelated`. When we register a plugin on the `SetRelated` message, the entity defined in the primary entity becomes the parent and the entity defined in the secondary entity becomes the child entity.

- **Filtering attributes**: These are only used in update messages. The idea of the filtering attribute is to only trigger the plugin when the attributes defined in the filtered attributes list is updated.
- **Event handler**: This is the name of the plugin class.
- **Step name**: This field is auto populated based on the entity and the message that we select.
- **Run in the user's context**: By default when we register the plugin, the plugin always executes as per the calling user security profile. This means that any call that the plugin may make to the Dynamics CRM organization service will be as per the security permissions of the calling user.
  However, in certain cases, we may want the plugin to always execute as per the security context of a user. In such a case, the user may select this option and deliberately select the required user in the drop-down list.

- **Execution order**: In some cases, for an entity, we may have to register more than one plugin in the same event pipeline stage. Due to this, if we want the plugins to follow a certain order of execution, we must define the execution order of the plugins accordingly.
- **Event pipeline stage of execution**: As discussed previously, we can register a plugin in three events, `PreValidation`, `PreOperation`, and `PostOperation`, depending upon whether we want the plugin to execute before the main operation, after the main operation, or in a different transaction altogether.
- **Execution mode**: A plugin can be executed either synchronously or asynchronously. If there is any operation for which we must wait for the execution to complete, we must register the plugin in a synchronous mode. Otherwise, if there is some complex logic that may take some time, we can set it asynchronously. note that in Dynamics CRM, the timeout setting for a plugin or the time that a plugin should finish execution in is 2 minutes. If it takes more than 2 minutes, the execution will automatically be stopped by the event pipeline.

- **Deployment**: This specifies where the user would like the plugin to be deployed. There are two possible options:
    1. On the server
    2. On Dynamics CRM for Outlook with offline access
    3. Both the possible options
- **Secure and unsecure configuration**: Secure and unsecure configurations are used to pass arguments to the plugin. Secure configurations can be read only by CRM administrators. On the other hand, insecure configurations can be read by any user in the CRM.

- **Delete AyscOperation if StatusCode = Successful**: When a plugin executing asynchronously completes an operation, a record of the system job is created in Dynamics CRM. It can be accessed from **Settings** | **System Jobs**:

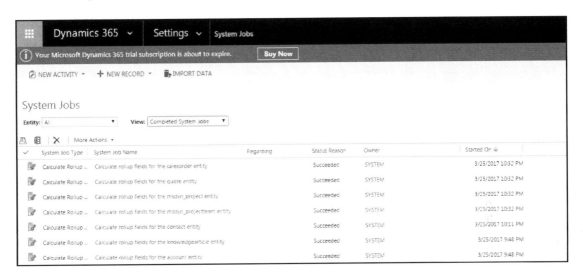

If the user checks this option, it's an indication to the user about deleting the system jobs if the status of the asynchronous plugin is successful.

Scenario walkthrough

This section highlights how plugins are used in Dynamics CRM. For ease of understanding, we will continue with the same school management scenario that we explored in Chapter 5, *Working with the XRM Framework..*

Scenario 1

The teacher of a class wishes to capture some key information for any student registering in the management system. The school management has several school buses in its roaster. Each roaster pertains to a region. Based on the post code and city of the student's home, they are classified into various regions. The school maintains that list of master data in Dynamics CRM. They wish that the system automatically updates the region of the student when the post code and city details are entered in the student's record.

The first step would be maintaining a master data for region, post code, and city. Given the concepts of data normalization and ease of data entry, we will consider the following entities in the Dynamics CRM system. The list of attributes against the entity are also described in the table:

1. Region:

Attribute	Data Type
Region Name	Single line of text

2. Bus region roaster:

Attribute	Data Type
Region	Lookup to Region
Post Code	Single line of text
City	Single line of text

Here is a screenshot of region:

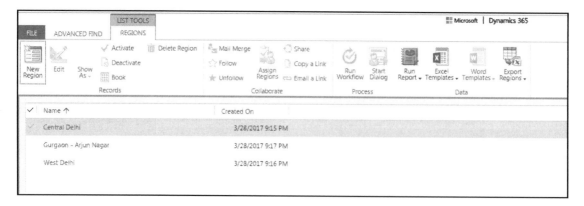

Here is a screenshot of the list of regions:

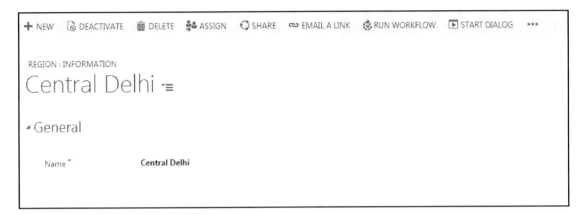

Here is a screenshot of the bus region roaster:

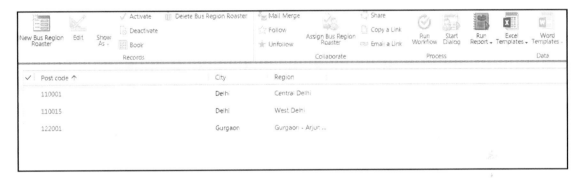

Here is a screenshot of the bus regions:

On the student main form, as mentioned in the following screenshot, there are fields of home city and post code. Along with that, we also have a read-only field of **Region**:

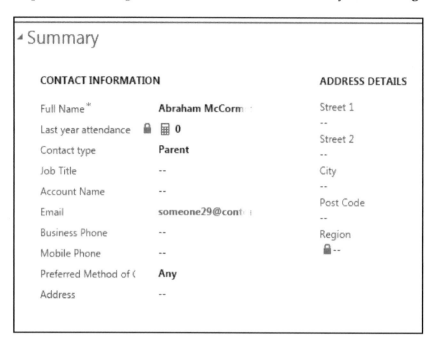

The next step would be to design the logic of the custom plugin that should fill the region field in the student form:

1. The first step for the same is firstly identifying the entity and messages on which the plugin would trigger:
   - As the entity for which we are going to enter information is **Contact**, we can safely assume that the primary entity for the plugin would be `contact`.
   - There could be two possible scenarios in which we will need to populate the **Region** field. The first would be on the **Create** field of student. When the student record is being created in Dynamics CRM, the plugin logic should read the values of city and post code and populate the **Region** lookup. Another scenario for the same would be when users are updating the student record. However, we will only need to recalculate the region lookup when the user is updating the **Post Code** or **City** field. In all other cases, there won't be any need to trigger the repopulation logic.

2. Now, since we have identified the message and the primary entity on which we need to write the plugin, the next step would be to write the plugin.

As a starting step, we can create the plugin project in the same way as we described earlier. After the plugin project is created, we will add a new class to the project, and as described previously, we will implement the IPlugin interface. The following are the steps that we will need to follow for creating the `plugin` class:

1. Firstly, we will just add a new class item, `PreCreateUpdateStudent`, in the same visual studio project that we created earlier. As a reference, we will use the late binding code terminology as C# as the base development language. The following is the complete code of the plugin class:

```csharp
using System;
using System.Collections.Generic;
using System.Linq;
using System.Text;
using Microsoft.Xrm.Sdk;
using Microsoft.Crm.Sdk.Messages;
using Microsoft.Xrm.Sdk.Query;

namespace SamplePluginProject
{
  public class PreCreateUpdateStudent : IPlugin
  {
    public void Execute(IServiceProvider serviceProvider)
    {
      // Plugin Context object
      Microsoft.Xrm.Sdk.IPluginExecutionContext context =
      (Microsoft.Xrm.Sdk.IPluginExecutionContext)
      serviceProvider.GetService(typeof(
      Microsoft.Xrm.Sdk.IPluginExecutionContext));
      // Retrieving Organisation service context object
      IOrganizationServiceFactory serviceFactory =
      (IOrganizationServiceFactory)serviceProvider.GetService(
      typeof(IOrganizationServiceFactory));
      IOrganizationService service =
      serviceFactory.CreateOrganizationService(context.UserId);
      // Exception handling to make sure that
      // plugin target object is an entity
      if (context.InputParameters.Contains("Target") &&
          context.InputParameters["Target"] is Entity)
      {
        Entity entity =
        (Entity)context.InputParameters["Target"];
        // Checking if the logical name of target
```

```
            // entity is contact
            if (entity.LogicalName == "contact")
            {
              // Name of plugin trigger message as create or update
              if (context.MessageName.ToLower() == "create" ||
              context.MessageName.ToLower() == "update")
              {
                string city;
                string postCode;
                // Exception handling to make sure code
                // is only triggered if city and post
                // code are present.
                if (entity.Contains("address1_city") &&
                entity.Contains("address1_postofficebox"))
                {
                  // Reading city and post  office code value
                  city =
                  entity.Attributes["address1_city"].ToString();
                  postCode =
                  entity.Attributes[
                  "address1_postofficebox"].ToString();
                  EntityReference region =
                  this.RetrieveRegionID(city, postCode, service);
                  // Adding region attribute to the entity
                  if (region != null)
                  {
                    if (entity.Contains("new_regionid"))
                    {
                      entity["new_regionid"] = region;
                    }
                    else
                    {
                      entity.Attributes.Add("new_regionid", region);
                    }
                  }
                }
              }
            }
          }
          // As the function is only accessed from inside
          // the plugin class so the access modifier is Private
          private EntityReference RetrieveRegionID(
          string city, string postOfficeBox,
          IOrganizationService service)
          {
            // Query expression to retrieve Region based
            // upon city and post code
```

```
EntityReference region = new EntityReference();
ColumnSet columns = new ColumnSet("new_regionid");
QueryExpression regionQuery = new QueryExpression();
regionQuery.EntityName = "new_busregionroaster";
FilterExpression filterExpression = new FilterExpression();
filterExpression.FilterOperator = LogicalOperator.And;
ConditionExpression cityCondition =
new ConditionExpression();
cityCondition.AttributeName = "new_city";
cityCondition.EntityName = "new_busregionroaster";
cityCondition.Operator = ConditionOperator.Equal;
cityCondition.Values.Add(city);
filterExpression.Conditions.Add(cityCondition);
ConditionExpression postOfficeCondition =
new ConditionExpression();
postOfficeCondition.AttributeName = "new_name";
postOfficeCondition.EntityName = "new_busregionroaster";
postOfficeCondition.Operator = ConditionOperator.Equal;
postOfficeCondition.Values.Add(postOfficeBox);
filterExpression.Conditions.Add(postOfficeCondition);
regionQuery.Criteria = filterExpression;
regionQuery.ColumnSet = columns;
EntityCollection regions =
service.RetrieveMultiple(regionQuery);
if (regions != null)
{
  if (regions.Entities.Count > 0)
  {
    if (regions.Entities[0].Contains("new_regionid"))
    {
      region = (EntityReference)regions.Entities[0]
      ["new_regionid"];
    }
  }
}
return region;
}
}
}
```

3. The next step would be to build the project and make sure that it compiles without any compile-time errors:

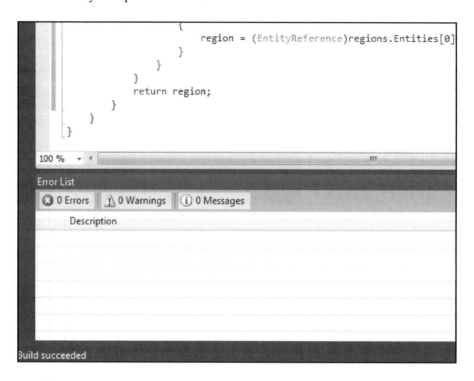

Finally, we will need to register the assembly just as described in the earlier sections. We will need to register the plugin class with two steps: create the contact and update the contact with filtering attributes, **Post Code** and **City**.

Scenario 2

This scenario deals with the usage of shared variables in a plugin. Using shared variables, Dynamics CRM provides a framework in which custom data values can be exchanged between registered plugins in the same execution context.

Shared variables are the most useful when we need to handle some complex scenarios involving plugins. Using shared variables, we can avoid creating unnecessary calls to the Dynamics CRM organization service as well as the creation of unnecessary fields. This scenario explains a very basic situation related to shared variables in which we will pass a value calculated during a pre-event to be used across a post event.

Note that the idea of discussing the following example is to just an overview of how shared variables can be used in a plugin. All the steps mentioned in the following example can be accommodated in one plugin also. However, in some cases that might not offer much flexibility. Therefore, in order to avoid any extra calls to the organization service and the creation of extra fields, we can utilize the concept of shared variables

- Here is the code base of a plugin written on the pre-event of a Contact entity. For creating and assigning a value in a shared variable, we can use the following code:

```
using System;
using System.Collections.Generic;
using System.Linq;
using System.Text;
using Microsoft.Xrm.Sdk;
using Microsoft.Crm.Sdk.Messages;
using Microsoft.Xrm.Sdk.Query;

namespace SamplePluginProject
{
  public class PreCreateUpdateStudent : IPlugin
  {
    public void Execute(IServiceProvider serviceProvider)
    {
      if (context.InputParameters.Contains("Target") &&
      context.InputParameters["Target"] is Entity)
      {
        Entity entity =
        (Entity)context.InputParameters["Target"];
        if (entity.LogicalName == "contact")
        {
          if (context.MessageName.ToLower() == "create" ||
          context.MessageName.ToLower() == "update")
          {
            // Setting value in Shared variable
            context.SharedVariables.Add("VariableName",
            (Object)"variablevalue");
          }
        }
      }
    }
  }
}
```

Note that whatever value is being passed must be serializable; otherwise, the plugin execution will fail. The following plugin code base can be written on the post update event of the **Contact** entity:

```
using System;
using System.Collections.Generic;
using System.Linq;
using System.Text;
using Microsoft.Xrm.Sdk;
using Microsoft.Crm.Sdk.Messages;
using Microsoft.Xrm.Sdk.Query;

namespace SamplePluginProject
{
  public class PostCreateUpdateStudent : IPlugin
  {
    public void Execute(IServiceProvider serviceProvider)
    {
      // Obtain the value from the execution
      // context shared variables.
      if (context.SharedVariables.Contains("VariableName"))
      {
        string variableValue =
        new (string)context.SharedVariables["VariableName "];

        // Do something with the value.
      }
    }
  }
}
```

Scenario 3

This scenario deals with how we can implement impersonation in a plugin. By default, when a plugin is executed, all the calls and actions made inside the plugin are done under the security context of the calling user. However, in many cases, inside a plugin, we may have to make certain calls that would require some elevated privileges.

For example, in the first scenario that we discussed in this chapter, we wrote code that reads regions and bus region roaster records present in the Dynamics CRM system. However, the user who is entering the student details in the system may not have access of these two entity records. Therefore, as per the code, if the user will try to enter the student details in the system, they will get a security exception while executing the retrieve command.

Due to this, we will need to impersonate the plugin calls whenever we encounter such scenarios. We can implement an impersonation in a plugin in two ways:

- **While registering the plugin step**: When we are registering the step itself, we can explicitly specify the plugin assembly to execute the plugin step in the context of an impersonated user:

    1. Right-click on the `plugin` class and select **Register New Step**:

2. Refer to the dropdown **Run in User's Context**. Click that dropdown and select the user in the context of which you want the plugin to be executed:

3. After selecting the user, click on the **Register New Step** button in the bottom-right corner.

- **While executing calls inside the plugin**: If we define the impersonated user in the plugin registration tool itself, it may give us some issues while moving the customizations from one CRM organization to another. Therefore, to avoid this, we can also define impersonation during runtime. We can achieve this by passing the userid property. Check out the following code snippet. As a matter of consistency, we will use the same plugin class that we used in *Scenario 1*:

```
using System;
using System.Collections.Generic;
using System.Linq;
using System.Text;
using Microsoft.Xrm.Sdk;
using Microsoft.Crm.Sdk.Messages;
using Microsoft.Xrm.Sdk.Query;

namespace SamplePluginProject
{
```

```
public class PreCreateUpdateStudent : IPlugin
{
  public void Execute(IServiceProvider serviceProvider)
  {
    // Plugin Context object
    Microsoft.Xrm.Sdk.IPluginExecutionContext context =
    (Microsoft.Xrm.Sdk.IPluginExecutionContext)
    serviceProvider.GetService(typeof
    (Microsoft.Xrm.Sdk.IPluginExecutionContext));
    // Retrieving Organisation service context object
    IOrganizationServiceFactory serviceFactory =
    (IOrganizationServiceFactory)serviceProvider.GetService
    (typeof(IOrganizationServiceFactory));
    IOrganizationService service =
    serviceFactory.CreateOrganizationService(new Guid
    ("8240cddf-fb54-4d96-90db-0ff926be0c14"));
  }
}
}
```

Now we can use this service object for executing all Dynamics CRM-side operations such as create, update, and so on.

Summary

As Microsoft Dynamics CRM continues to evolve, the focus of Microsoft is to try and make custom coding as less as possible. However, every now and then, there is bound to be some customer requirement that cannot be implemented without any custom coding. At that stage, plugins come to our rescue.

The main motive and skill that every Dynamics CRM consultant needs to enhance is to analyze the requirements correctly and categorize them categorically in terms of configurations and customizations. Other out-of-box configurations such as workflows and business rules should be explored before we accept the need to write a custom plugin to meet the desired needs of the customer.

In the next chapter, we will be going through Business Process Flows and Business Rules. You will learn how to create and use them for automation in Dynamics CRM.

11
Business Process Flows and Business Rules

In this chapter, we will go through various scenarios explaining business rules in detail. Business rules were first introduced in Microsoft Dynamics CRM 2013. Before that, developers had to use JavaScript for any client-side scripting or validation. Business rules provide a rich interface, using which people can configure most of the client-side scripting and validations, which previously required some sort of coding experience.

In this chapter, we will be covering the following topics:

- **Creating business rules**: We will see some scenarios related to creating business rules and how they can be useful.
- **Business Process Flows**: Business Process Flows in Dynamics CRM are a set of steps that help guide the users across the business processes in the system. We will see a realistic scenario for better understanding.

Key components

The following are some of the key components of a business rule:

- **Scope**: The scope of a business rule defines the execution context of a business rule. It can acquire the following values:
  - **Entity**: Business rules will be executed in all entity operations, including the server-side events happening on the entity

- **All forms**: Business rules will be executed on all the entity forms. However, the rules will not apply to server-side execution
- **Specific forms**: Business rules will only be executed on specific chosen forms while setting up a business rule

- **Condition**: Condition refers to the criteria or the requisite state evaluated before a business rule action is executed. The conditions basically refer to the state of the entity and its attributes. For example, you may write a business rule that refers to a condition that checks the values on a created field.
- **Action**: Action refers to the process that will be executed by the business rule once the condition governing it is met. The following actions can be executed by the business rule:
    - **Lock /Unlock field**: This action makes a field read-only or editable.
    - **Show error message**: This action shows an error message on the Dynamics CRM UI screen.
    - **Set Field Value**: This action sets a value in any field on the entity.
    - **Set default value**: This action sets a default value in any field during form load. The Set Field Value action is similar to Set Default Value and only differs in usage. Using a default value, we can set a value on form load. If we don't want the field to acquire a value during form load, we can use the *Set Field Value* action instead.
    - **Set business required**: This action changes the field requirement for any attribute. In Dynamics CRM, the requirement options are as follows:
        - Options
        - Business recommended
        - Business required

- **Set visibility**: The action basically hides and shows any field on the entity form.
- **Recommendation**: This is a new action that has been introduced in Microsoft Dynamics 365. We will explain the usage of the action in the coming scenarios.

Key changes

Business rules were first introduced in Microsoft Dynamics CRM 2013. Since then, Microsoft has made many enhancements in business rules. The following are some of the key changes that have been brought in:

- In Microsoft Dynamics CRM 2013, we could only write business rules on entity forms. We could not apply them on the server side. This was changed in Microsoft Dynamics CRM 2015, wherein we could write the scope of the business rule as an *entity*. This implies that the rule will be triggered during all the operations related to the entity.
- When business rules were first introduced, we could only write *if* statements. There was no provision to write rules concerning *Else If* and *Else*. This was rectified in Microsoft Dynamics CRM 2015.
- There were some issues in writing business rules and JavaScript events on the same entity field. This issue was also rectified in Microsoft Dynamics CRM 2015.
- With Microsoft Dynamics 365, Microsoft has introduced a more user-friendly interface to the business rule designer. It makes it more easy for people to write the business rules.
- A new *Recommendation* action was also introduced in Microsoft Dynamics 365.

 Note that, as Microsoft Dynamics 365 has introduced a new UI designer for business rules, all the following scenarios will showcase the business rules in the new UI designer. However, it's very similar to the designer that is present in Microsoft Dynamics CRM 2016.

Creating a business rule

Here's how you can create a business rule:

1. First, navigate to the solution and the entity for which the business rule is to be created:

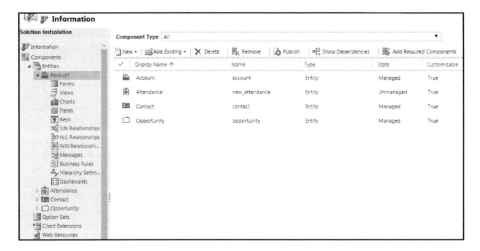

Solution

2. In the entity components, click on **Business Rules** to create/modify a business rule:

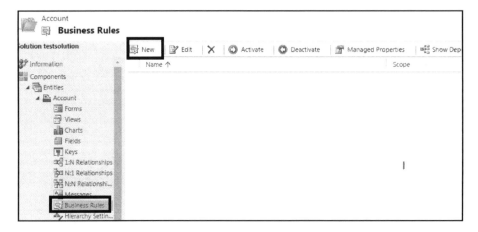

New Business Rule

3. Click on the **New** button to create the business rule:

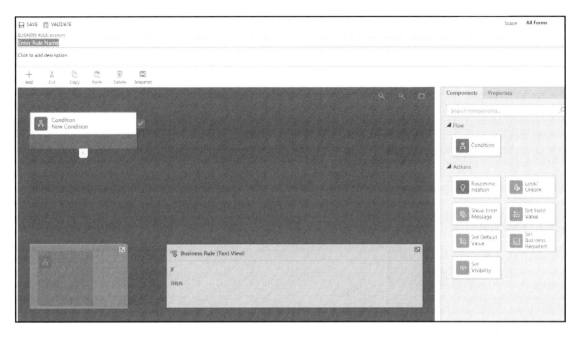

New Business Rule

4. To set the scope of the business rule, click on the scope drop-down menu. It will display the following options:

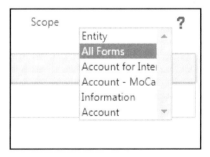

Business Rule Scope

As illustrated in the preceding screenshot, here are some options to set the execution context:

- If we need to set the execution context of a business rule as the entire entity, we can set it as **Entity**
- If we need to set the execution context to all the forms, we can select the **All Forms** option
- If we need to set the execution context to a form only, we can just select that particular form
- To set the condition governing the business rule, click on the condition box:

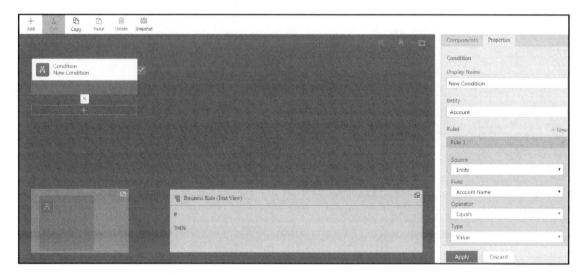

Adding Condition In Business Rule

On the right-hand side, we will get the options to set conditions against the values present in any field. For example, if we want to compare the current **Account Category**, we can set a condition, as shown in the following screenshot:

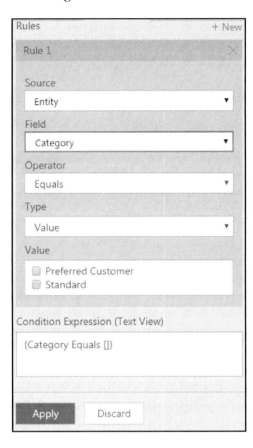

Adding Condition In Business Rule

The preceding example shows how a condition is specific to an option set attribute. Similarly, we can also configure a condition specific to attributes with other data types, such as date time, integer, and so on.

We can also configure multiple conditions in the same business rule. The conditions can both be in the same evaluation statement as well as in a different *Else If* block. The following steps show how both the features can be achieved in the rule:

1. **Adding multiple evaluation criteria in the same rule**: If we add multiple rules in the same condition expression, the conditions can be configured with both the *and* and *or* operators. Here's how we can add multiple rules in the same condition block:

   1. Firstly, set the value expression in the first rule in the condition expression. Then, click on the **+ New** button:

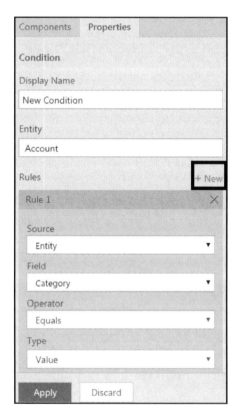

Adding New Condition In Business Rule

On clicking the **+ New** button, the system should automatically add a new rule for the same condition:

Adding New Condition In Business Rule

Based upon the requirement, we can also configure the two rules by either **AND** or **OR** condition.

2. We can also add multiple condition blocks in the same rule. The idea for doing so is to have multiple *Else If* conditions in the business rule. To do so, you can just click on the **+ Add** button. Doing this will add a new *Else If* condition in the business rule:

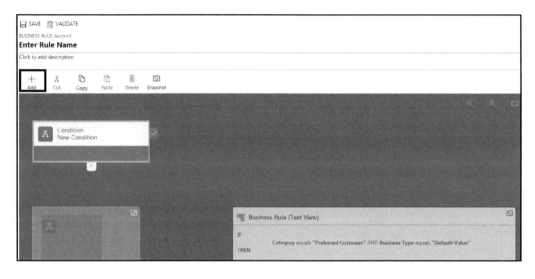

Adding additional condition in business rule

This will add a new condition block in the business rule:

Adding additional condition in business rule

2. **Adding action statements for the condition**: Each condition defined inside a business rule must have an action against it. Here's how you can configure the actions in a business rule:

   1. First, select the condition for which you want to configure the action. Then, click the **+ Add** button and select the action that you want to configure:

This is how you can add an additional condition to the business rule:

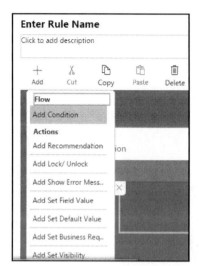

Adding additional condition in business rule

2. Now, select the action that needs to be configured. On doing so, the action will be added to the selected condition. You must then select the attribute on which you want the action to be applied to:

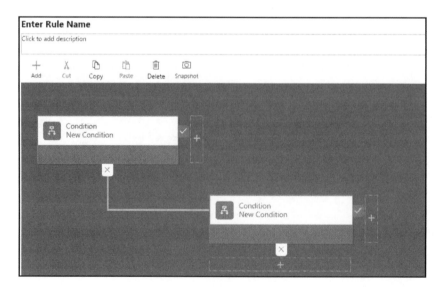

Adding additional condition in business rule

Now click on the + sign to add the action:

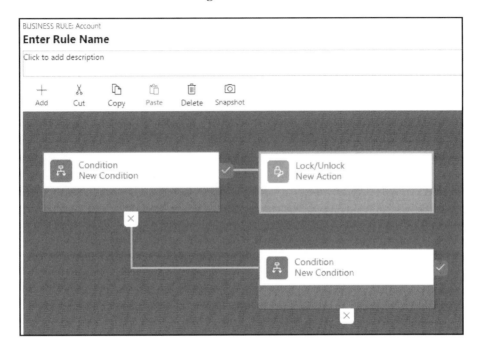

Adding conditional lock/Unlock action in business rule

Click on the action block to specify the attribute:

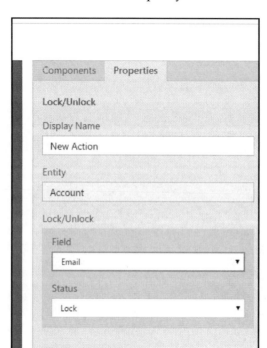

Adding lock/unlock action in business rule

Based on the action selected, different fields, such as value selector, will be visible.

3. After you are done with the addition of all the conditions and corresponding actions, you should click on the **VALIDATE** button to make sure that the rule has been set correctly. In case there is some issue in the business rule, an error message will appear on the screen:

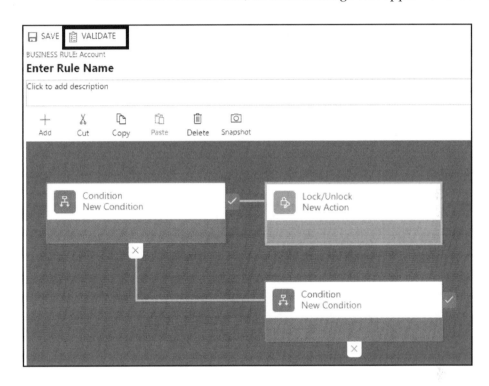

This is how you can validate the business rule:

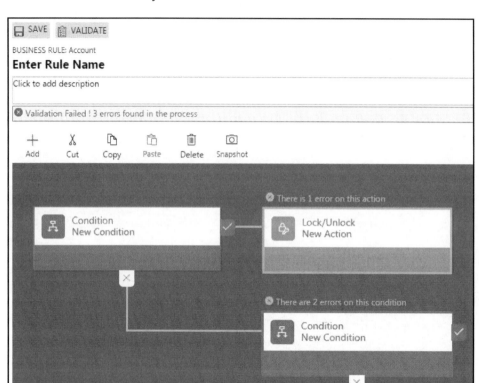

Validating business rule

Scenario walkthrough

The following scenario illustrates how business rules are managed in Dynamics CRM. For ease of understanding, we will continue with the same school management scenario that we had explored in Chapter 5, *Working with the XRM Framework*.

Scenario

The teacher of a class wishes to highlight some key student information to the school staff whenever they open a student's record. The following are the conditions and the corresponding messages the teacher wishes to be displayed:

- If the attendance of the student is less than 60 percent and the final year score is less than 50 percent, then the following message should be displayed:
  `Student attendance as well as marks are below expectation.`
- If only the final year score is less than 50 percent, then the following message should be displayed:
  `Student performance is below the expected level.`
- If only the attendance is below 50 percent, then the following message should be displayed:
  `Student attendance is below the expected level.`

The student navigates to the **Contact** entity and navigates to the **Business Rules** section:

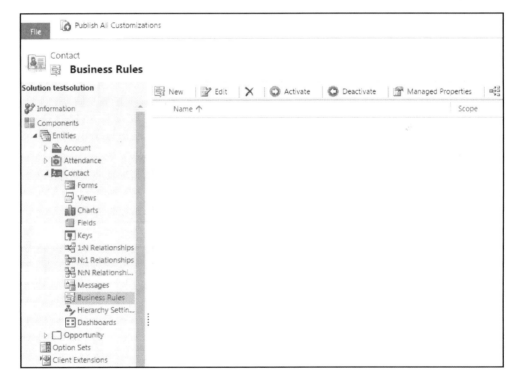

Dynamics Solution

Here are the steps that the teacher needs to follow to set the aforementioned rules:

1. Click the **+ Add** button to create a new business rule. The business rule designer should open. Now, fill **Field** with `Final year score`, **Operator** with `is less than`, and **Value** with `50` to set the required condition:

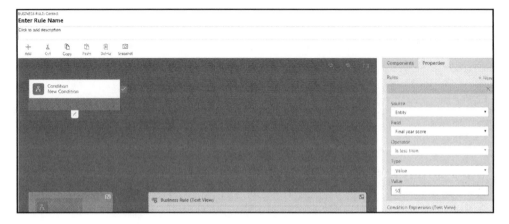

Business rule scenario 1

2. Click on the **Apply** button and, then, click on the **+New** button to add another rule to check the value of attendance:

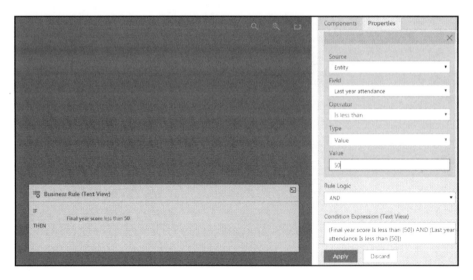

Business rule scenario 1

3. Note that as both the conditions need to be satisfied in this rule, **Rule logic** needs to be **AND**. After the rule is added, click on the **Apply** button. Then, click on the **+ Add** button again to add an action statement for the condition. Select the **Show Error Message** action statement:

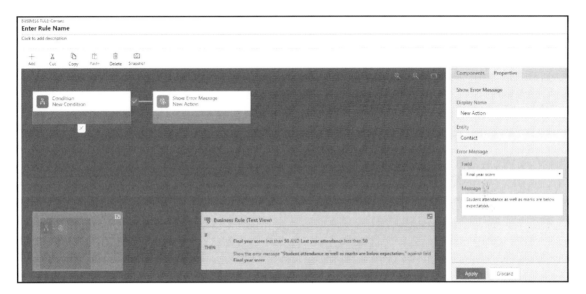

Business rule scenario 1

Now click on the **Apply** button. On doing so, the action should be added to the condition. In the preceding example, the message will appear on the **Final year score** field. If you desire to make the message appear on the attendance field as well, they can just add another action block in the same condition block.

4. Now, click on the **+ Add** button to add a new condition block. The new condition will act as an *Else If* condition to the condition that you added in the preceding steps and will only check for the **Final year score** field:

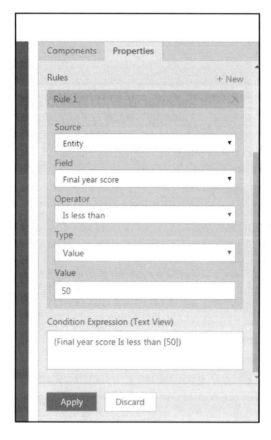

Business rule scenario 1

This is how it will look overall:

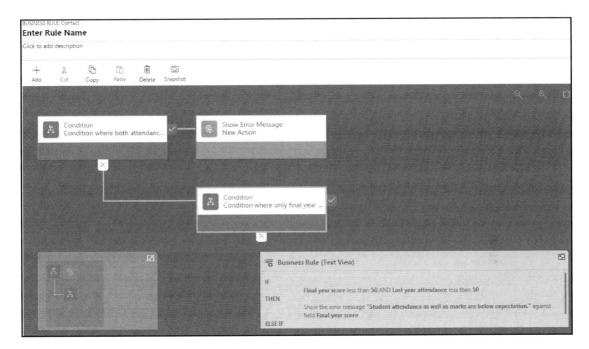

Business rule scenario 1

5. Again, add an action statement for the new condition block. The action should again be of the same type, **Show Error Message**, and the message to be displayed should be `Student performance is below the expected level`:

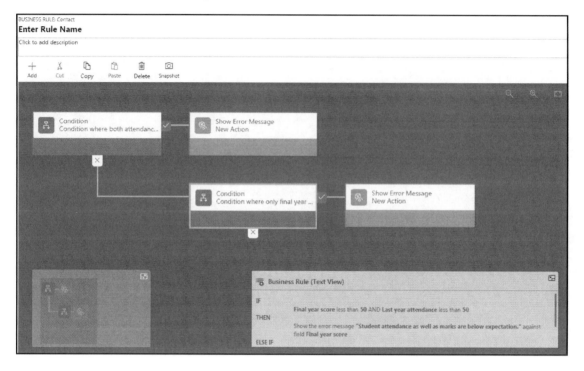

Business rule scenario 1

Similarly, we can add conditions for the last block.

Business Process Flows

Business Process Flows in Dynamics CRM are a set of steps that guide users across a business process in the system. A Business Process Flow is divided into various stages, with each stage containing a set of steps or fields. Based on the requirement, we can even make a step or a field, as required. Business Process Flows do not serve as an automatic process but as a guide for users, through which they can complete a task.

Out-of-box Dynamics CRM provides business process flows for standard entities such as **Account** or **Contact**. We can also configure them against custom entities. We can refer to the existing Business Process Flows by navigating to **Settings** | **Processes**:

Process Center

In the processes screen, the user can open the **Business Process Flows** view:

Business Process Flows

Attributes

Apart from the common attributes, the following are the two main attributes for any business process flow:

- **Primary entity**: All Business Process Flows, whether out-of-box or custom, need to be associated to an entity in Dynamics CRM. Primary entity defines the entity to which a Business Process Flow is associated with. It basically means that at each stage, the Business Process Flow will refer to one or more than one fields of that entity.

    We can create a Business Process Flow for any entity as long as the entity is configured for Business Process Flows. By default, when a new entity is created in Dynamics CRM, it is not configured for Business Process Flows. The user must check an option to enable the entity for Business Process Flows:

Business process flow configuration

It is not necessary to select this option while creating the entity. Therefore, even if a user forgets to check this option, he/she can always go back, select the option, and save the record. However, once selected and saved, this option cannot be undone by the user.

When an entity is configured for Business Process Flows, Dynamics CRM will automatically create two fields, **StageId** and **ProcessId**:

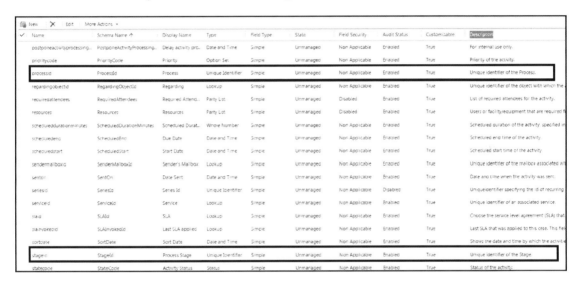

Business process flow configuration

- **Status**: A business process flow can acquire two possible states: **Activated** and **Draft**. If its status is **Activated**, it basically implies that users can use this process for their work. Otherwise, if it is **Draft**, it implies that users cannot use the process in its current state.

Creating a Business Process Flow

The following steps show how to create a new Business Process Flow for an entity:

1. Navigate to the solution section and open the solution where you want to create the Business Process Flow. After opening the solution, navigate to the section of processes:

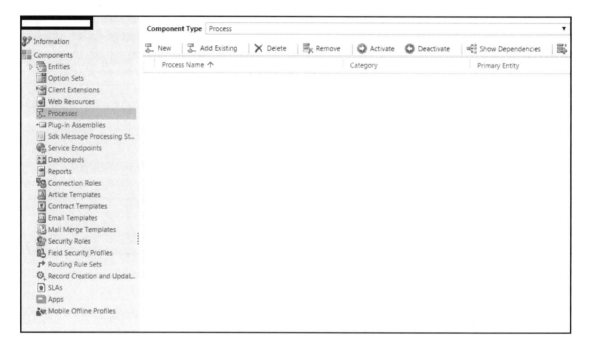

Business process flow creation

2. Click on the **New** button. It should open a new window for creating the basic details of the process. Note that, as we are discussing the implementation of a Business Process Flow, we will select **Category** of the process as **Business Process Flow**. You must select the entity for which the process flow needs to be configured. As discussed, it implies the main entity that the process flow will run against:

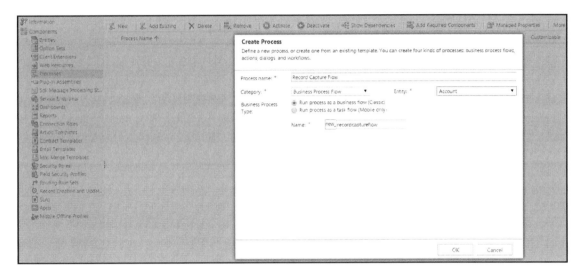

Business process flow creation

As shown in the screenshot, you can also decide the device on which the process flow should appear. After you enter all the information and click **OK**, a window should open up where you can enter the details about the Business Process Flow.

 Note that, as Microsoft Dynamics 365 has introduced a new UI designer for Business Process Flows, all the following scenarios will showcase the Business Process Flows in the new UI designer. However, functionality and feature-wise, it's very similar to the designer UI present in Microsoft Dynamics CRM 2016.

Check out the following screenshot:

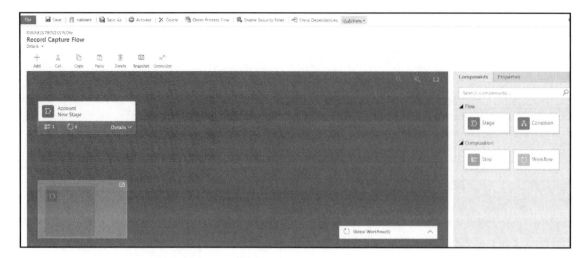

Business process flow creation

Once a stage is added to the business process flow, the user can add the attributes or steps that need to be captured in that stage:

Business process flow creation

As illustrated in the preceding screenshot, each step in the stage represents an attribute information to be filled. The following screenshot highlights how they are captured:

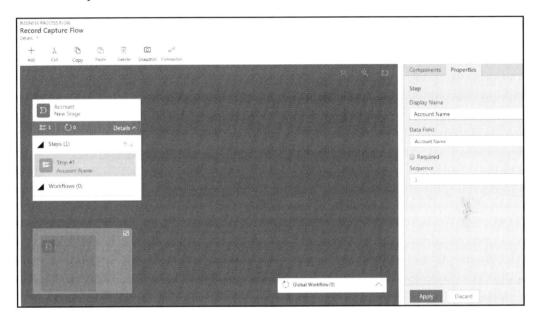

Business process flow creation

To add more steps to the stage, you can click on the **+ Add** button. This will add a new step to the stage:

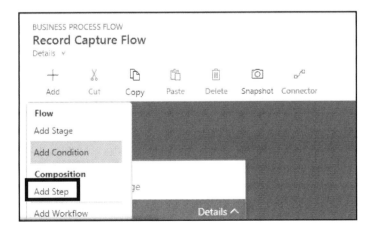

Business process flow creation

This will give you an option of a adding new step in the stage. You can also make it mandatory by clicking on the **Required** checkbox:

Business process flow creation

As illustrated in the following screenshot, multiple steps can be added to the same stage:

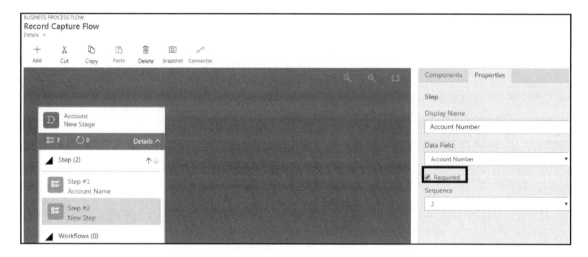

Business process flow creation

Once done, click on the **Apply** button.

To add a new stage to the Business Process Flow, you can click on the **Add Stage** button. It will give you an option of adding another stage to the Business Process Flow:

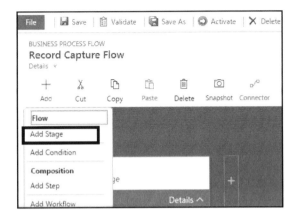

Business process flow creation

You can then click on the + button to add a new stage:

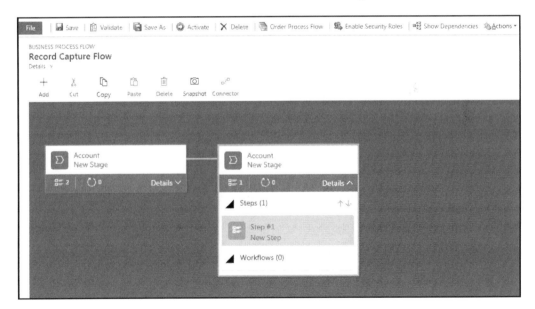

Business process flow creation

For adding steps, in the new stage, you can just follow the previous instructions related to the **+ Add** steps. In case you wish to capture the value of a related attribute, you can select the related entity in the entity dropdown and, then, select the required attribute:

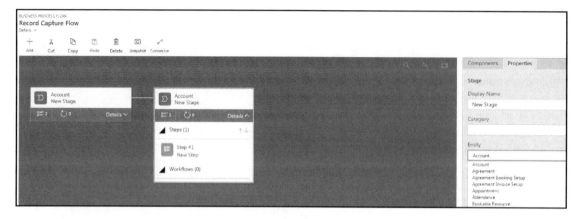

Business process flow creation

To add a conditional stage to the Business Process Flow, you can just click on the **+ Add** steps. The user can then select the **Add Condition** option:

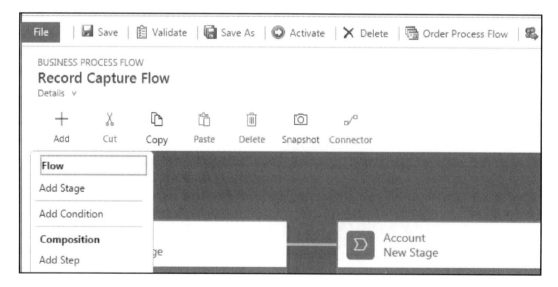

Business process flow creation

As illustrated in the following screenshot, multiple stages can be added to the Business Process Flow:

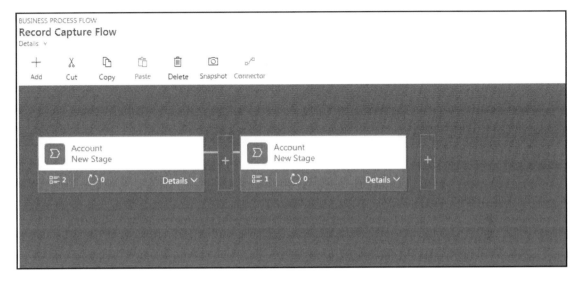

Business process flow creation

As illustrated in the following screenshot, you can also insert conditions to evaluate the next condition the Business Process Flow can be moved to:

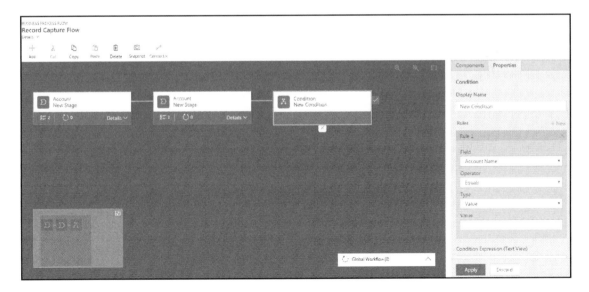

Business process flow creation

You can then enter the required condition in the statement:

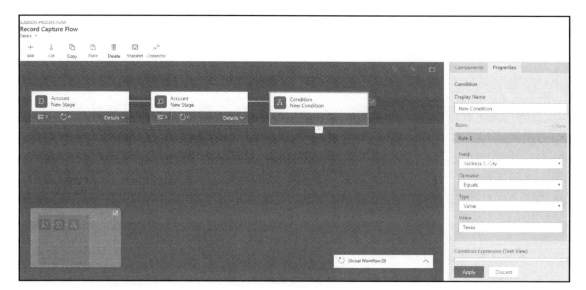

Business process flow creation

Scenario walkthrough

The following highlights how Business Process Flows are managed in Dynamics CRM. For ease of understanding, we will continue with the same school management scenario that we had explored in Chapter 5, *Working with the XRM Framework*.

Scenario

The teacher of a class wishes to capture some key information for any person registering in the management system. If the person is registering as a student, the teacher would wish to capture their performance in the final year exams that they attended in their previous school. Otherwise, if they are registering as a parent, the teacher would like to capture their current professional details.

Let's see how we can design the process.

As discussed earlier, we are using Dynamics CRM's out-of-box Contact entity to represent students, parents, and teachers. Therefore, the process being discussed will need to be set up on the **Contact** entity:

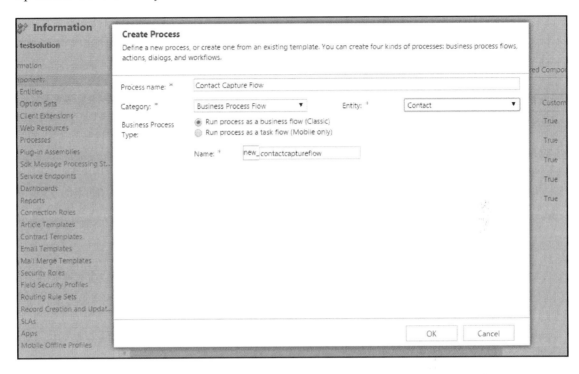

Business Process Flow scenario 1

Let's look at how we can achieve the requirements:

1. In the first stage, capture the value in the **Contact type** field. Note that, according to the school management system, the possible values in **Contact type** will be **Student**, **Teacher**, and **Parent**:

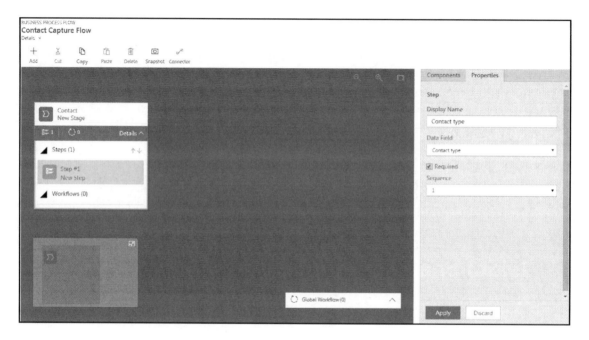

Business process flow scenario 1

2. In this stage, we will add a new condition statement for checking the value present in **Contact type**. Based on the value entered in this field, the next stage of the process flow will be decided:

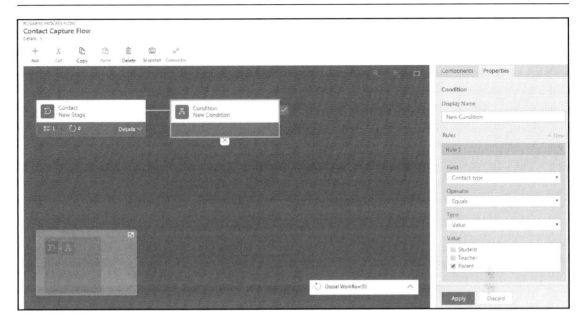

Business process flow scenario 1

3. In case the value is **Parent**, the next stage will be to capture the job title of the parent:

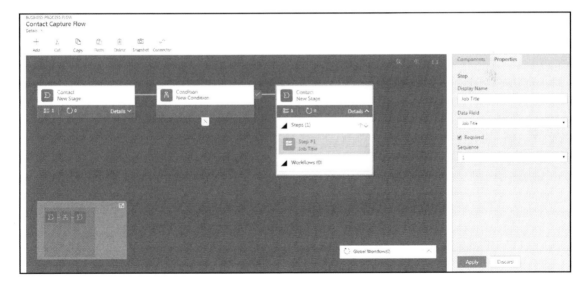

Business process flow scenario 1

4. In the *Else* statement, we can again check whether the contact being captured is **Student**:

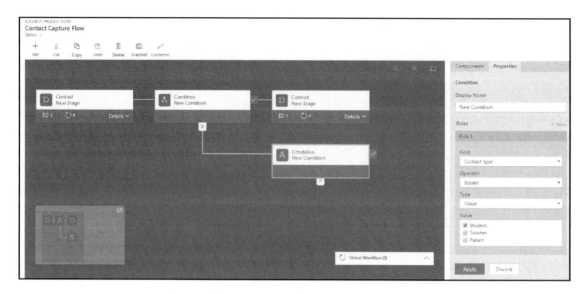

Business process flow scenario 1

If the value is **Student**, we will add a conditional stage for capturing the student's school:

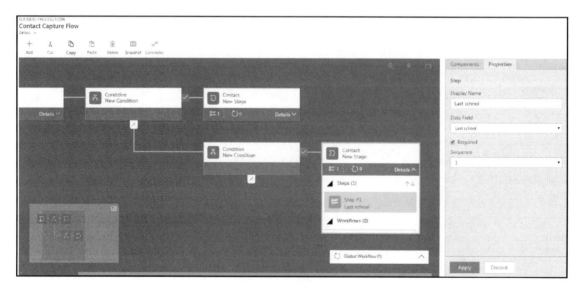

Business process flow scenario 1

5. Then, click on the **Validate** button on the Business Process Flow header:

Business process flow scenario 1

If the Business Process Flow is correct, it should display a **Validation Successful** message:

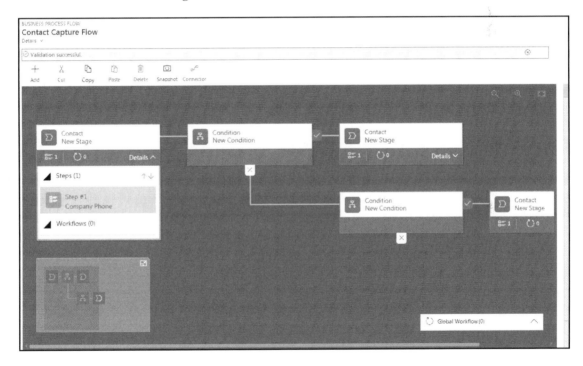

Business process flow scenario 1

You can now activate the Business Process Flow and publish the customizations.

6. To run the Business Process Flow, you can navigate to the contact record entity form and click on the **Switch Process** button:

Business process flow scenario 1

7. Once you do this, a popup window will open. On that window, you can then select the Business Process Flow you want to work on:

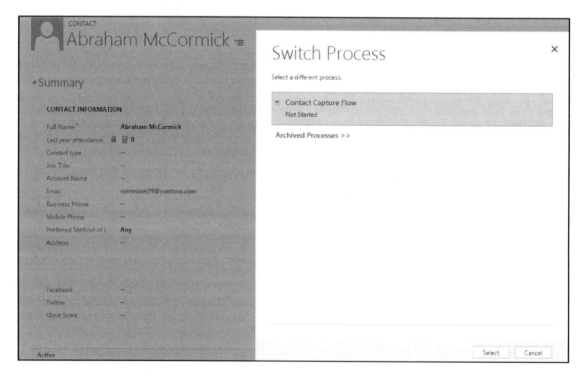

Business process flow scenario 1

After you select the process, review that the selected business process appears on the record:

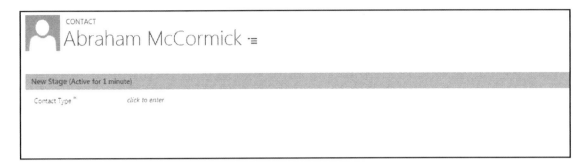

8. Now, once you enter the value in the **Contact Type** attribute, based on the value, you will be redirected to the next stage:

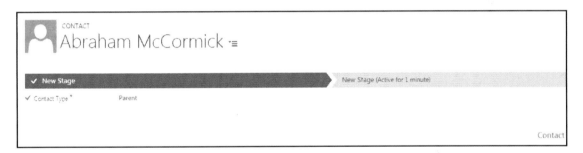

Review that, as per the condition, the Business Process Flow moves to the next stage:

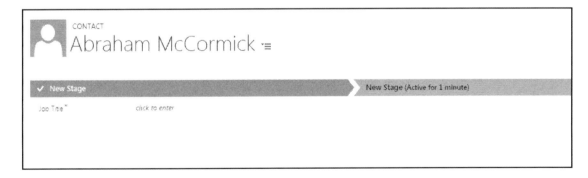

Summary

The preceding scenario may have provided an overview of how business process flows and business processes work and how they can be helpful for automations in Dynamics CRM. You learned how to use Business Process Flows to execute logical processes or steps in your business process. In addition, we looked through how business rules can easily define and set the rules for validating data, setting visibility, and disabling fields. You may also have noted that they are very simple to create without coding.

In the next chapter, we will be covering some features that we have not covered so far, in the previous chapters of this book. We will look at different features such as customer field type, solution improvements, feedback and rating functionality, and also the Relevance Search functionality.

12
New Features in CRM 2016

This chapter is focused on covering some small but awesome features that were left uncovered during the rest of the scenarios presented in this book and include some of the features again for a quick reference. Every such feature is explained by means of a business scenario. Relevant details to explain the feature have also been mentioned in the required steps.

Here's a quick list of the scenarios presented in this chapter:

- Customer field types
- Solution improvements for entity assets
- The feedback and rating functionalities
- The relevance search functionality

Scenario 1 – using customer field types

Lisa is a CRM Administrator at Acme Ltd and wishes to add a field for primary contact on the **Competitor** entity, as their company wishes to keep a track of the primary contacts for their competitors. This can either point to a contact or an account in their CRM system. Earlier, we had to create two different fields for contact and customer:

The following are the steps Lisa can perform to accomplish this requirement:

1. Navigate to **Settings** | **Customization** | **Customize the System**:

2. Expand **Competitor** | **Fields**:

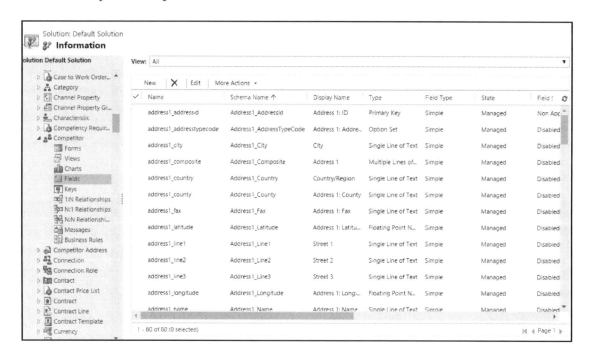

3. Click a new field and select **Data Type** as **Customer**. Click **Save and Close** once done. **Customer** is a new custom field type available in CRM 2016, which can point to both a contact as well as an account entity:

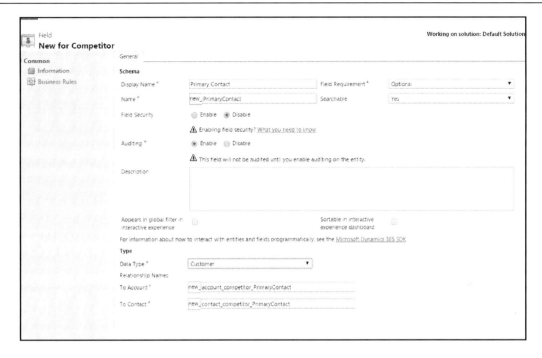

4. Navigate to **Competitor** | **Forms**, add the newly added **Primary Contact** field type, and drag it onto a suitable area in the form:

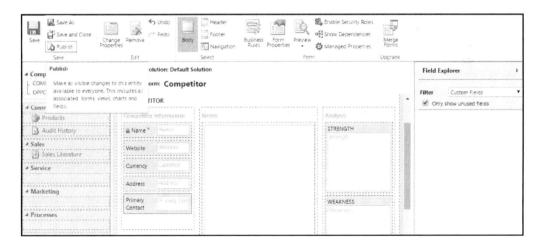

5. Click **Save** and then **Publish**.

Now, Acme Ltd can use a single field on a **Competitor** entity to select either a contact or an account to connect, as per their needs.

Scenario 2 – working with solutions

Lisa, who is the CRM Administrator at Acme Ltd, has another set of issues that she wishes to address with respect to managing different running projects to enhance the Dynamics CRM system at Acme Ltd.

She wants to segregate the fields and views into different CRM solutions based on the Project implementations for the **Account** entity. Till now, it is difficult to divide different components that belong to developers, customizers, or authors. With the help of the solution that we're going to discuss in this section, Lisa can easily create a different unit for each of them. Lisa can follow these steps to accomplish this requirement:

1. Navigate to **Settings** | **Solutions** and create a new solution by clicking **New**:

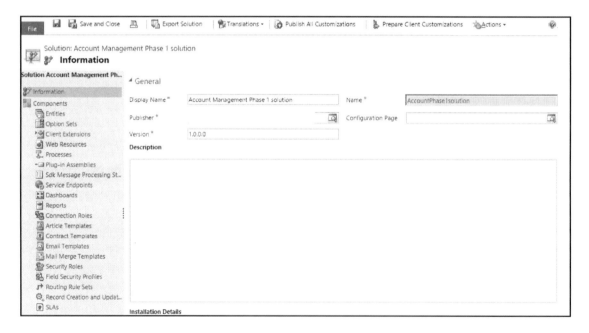

2. Navigate to **Entity.** Add the existing Entity and select **Account**:

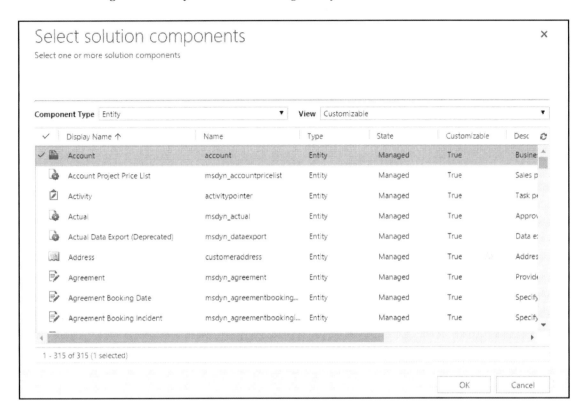

3. On Clicking **OK**, there is a selection available for different items under the **Account** entity, which needs to be included as follows:

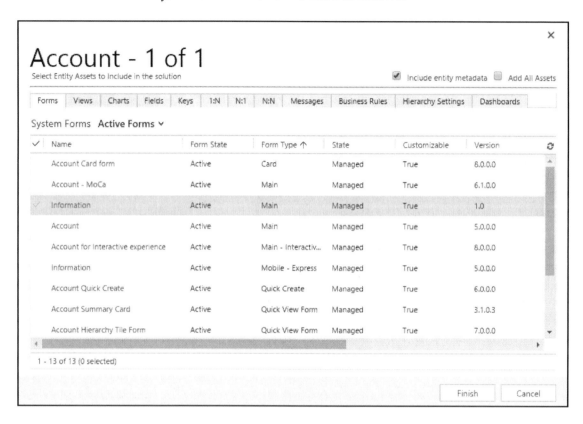

This component can now be selected one by one to include only the entity assets that need to be part of this solution.

Entity assets can be one of the following:

- Forms
- Views
- Charts
- Fields
- Keys
- 1:N Relationships
- N:1 Relationships

- N:N Relationships
- Messages
- Business Rules
- Hierarchy Settings
- Dashboards

Two other configuration options that can be set are:

- **Include entity metadata**: Entity metadata information such as **Audit settings** are included
- **Include all assets**: If checked, all entity assets are included

4. Navigate to **Fields** and include the required fields by ticking them:

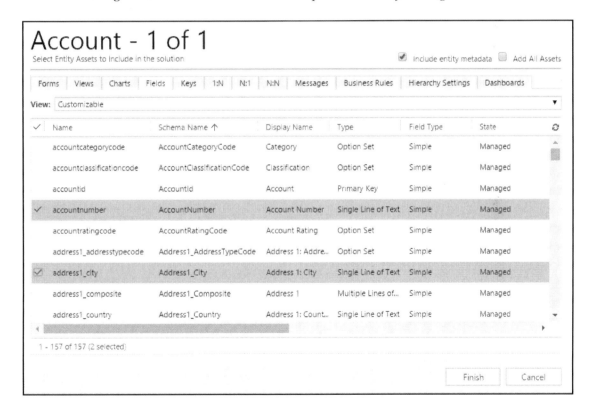

5. Next, navigate to **Views** to include the required entity views. After selecting the required Views, click **Finish**:

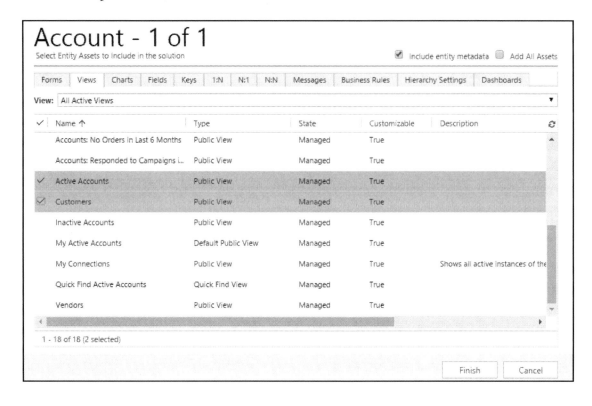

6. Look at the solution now. Expand **Entities** | **Account** | **Fields**. Only the selected attributes are added to the CRM solution:

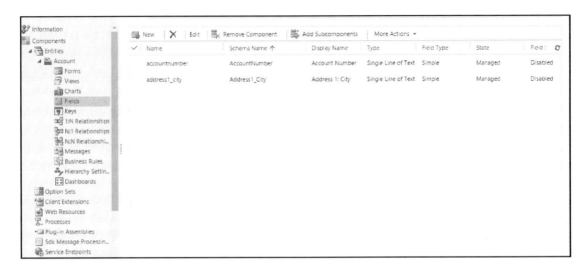

Lisa is now effectively able to manage the subcomponents and to only send the most relevant ones in a CRM solution.

Scenario 3 – feedback

Lisa, who is the CRM administrator at Acme Ltd, has been asked by the marketing manager to find some way to collect internal feedback from the marketing executives at Acme Ltd on the recent campaigns run by the company for their customers. **Feedback** can be used to provide a solution to this. It can store the responses received from the recent campaigns.

Lisa can follow these steps to fulfill this requirement:

1. Navigate to **Settings** | **Customizations** | **Customize the System**.
    Expand the **Entities** | **Campaign** entity. Select **Feedback** on the entity
    customizations:

2. Click **Save** and then **Publish**:

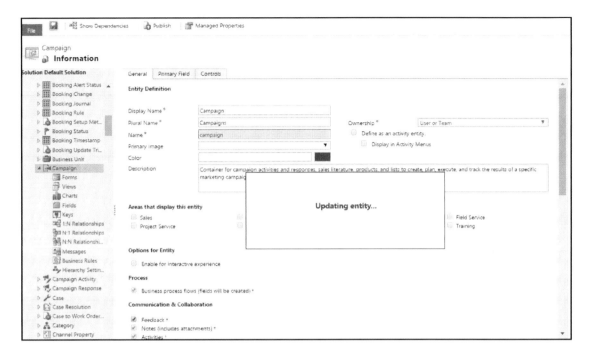

3. Next, navigate to **Campaign Entity** | **Forms** and select the **Campaign** main form:

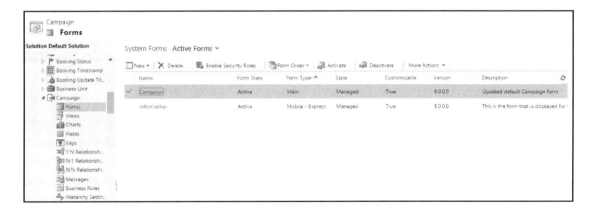

4. Select **Insert** and then the subgrid option. Give the name as `Feedback` and select the **Feedback** entity from the dropdown for a list of related entity records:

5. Click **OK**, save the Form Editor, and click **Publish**:

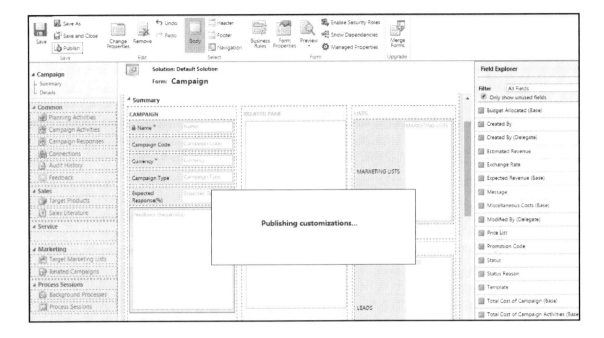

Note that to allow any **Security** role to give feedback, the **Security** role needs to have privilege on the **Feedback** entity available. For instance, here on the **Marketing Professional** security role, enabling the privileges for the **Feedback** entity is as follows:

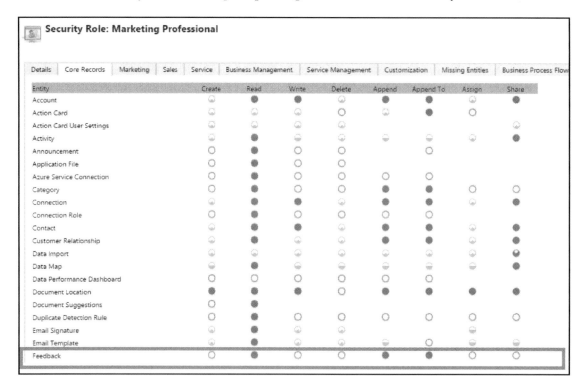

Now, let's see **Feedback** in action.

If you navigate to any of the campaign forms, you will be able to see the campaign form with a subgrid for **Feedback**, as follows:

Clicking the + button on the top right of the subgrid will open up a feedback form:

Click on **+ New** to add a new feedback:

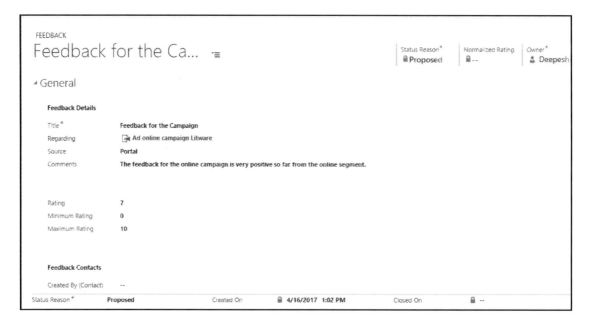

This feedback can later be collated to provide insights in the form of charts. Initially, the feedback is in a proposed state.

While reviewing the feedback, the marketing manager can come and set the final review status for the feedback to **Accepted** on the **Status Reason** option present on the header of the feedback and save the feedback:

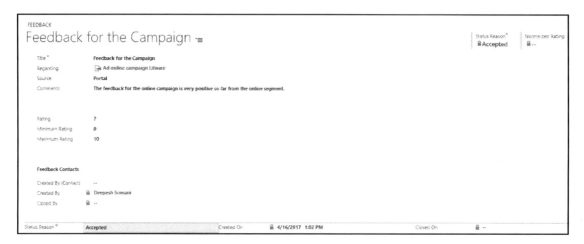

Optionally, the marketing manager may decide to close or reject the feedback by clicking **Deactivate** and then choosing the option, as follows:

The feedback functionality can be used for other CRM modules, such as **Sales**, **Service**, and so on. The business scenario we just discussed is only to showcase the functionality with respect to the **Marketing** module.

Scenario 4 – configuring relevance search

Lisa is right now consulting with Jim, the process improvement manager at Acme Ltd. Jim wishes to improve the way users in the organization can search CRM data for certain important entities, such as **Account**, **Contact**, and so on. Lisa starts researching on the options available in CRM 2016 online to improve the search functionality.

Right now, when users in the CRM system search for data, for example, by the `datum` keyword to locate a datum account, the search yields no result, as you can see in the following image:

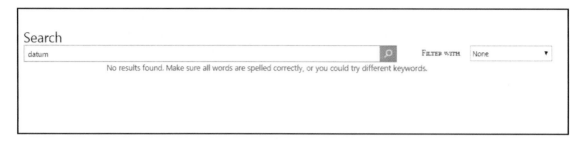

Lisa can perform the following steps to sort this out. Please note that **Relevance Search** is only applied to the Microsoft Dynamics CRM 2016 Online version. **Relevance Search** returns search results sorted by relevance, in a single list. Categorized search returns search results grouped by entity types, such as Accounts, Contacts, or Leads:

1. Navigate to **Settings** | **Administration** | **System Settings**:

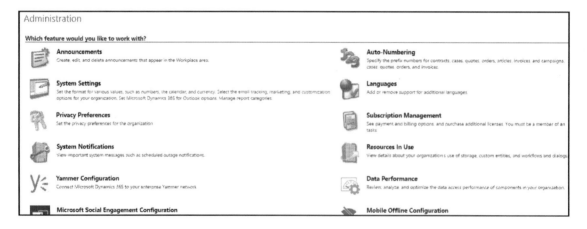

2. Under the **General** tab, select the checkbox for **Enable Relevance Search** and click **OK**:

3. Once you select **OK** and enable it, navigate back to the **Settings | Customize the System | Configure Relevance Search** button on the **Entities** component:

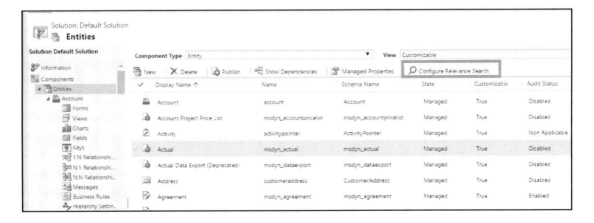

4. Select the entities including **Account** and click **OK**:

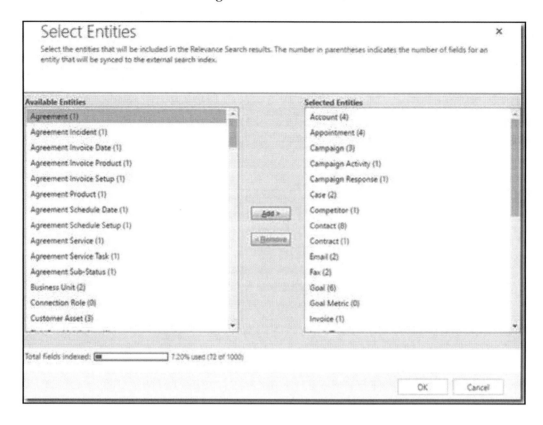

5. For configuring the fields that can be used in **Relevance Search** for the entity, the configuration needs to be done under the **Quick find** columns. For this, navigate to **Account | Views**, double-click on the **Quick Find Active Accounts** view, and select the **Add Find Columns** option:

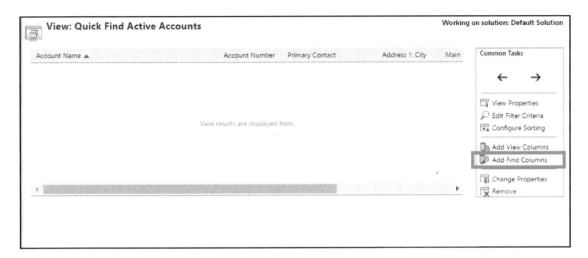

6. On the field selection window, select all the relevant fields available:

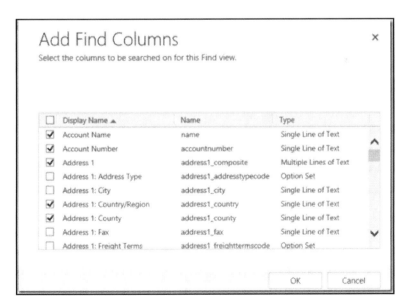

7. Save the entity customization and publish them.

Now to see relevance search in action, click the search icon available on the top of your CRM options:

This time around, searching for the keyword datum yields detailed results, improving the search functionality for Acme Ltd:

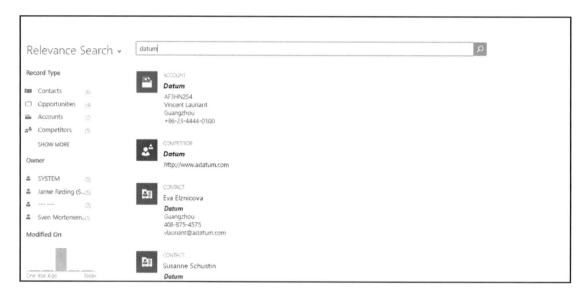

Optionally, users can navigate to **Personal Settings** by clicking the icon available in the top-right corner of the CRM screen and select **Options**:

Here, under **General** settings, the users can choose to change their search experience.

Summary

In this chapter, we discussed in detail about using a new customer field type, entity assets in solutions for better release management, feedback and rating functionalities, and the use of the Relevance Search functionality for Microsoft Dynamics CRM 2016 Online.

Index

execution mode 300
execution order 300

F

features, Microsoft Dynamics CRM 2016
  about 23
  customer field type 24
  entity assets, solution improvements 24
  feedback 24
  rating 24
  relevance search 24
feedback 24
feedback scenario 365, 368, 370, 371, 372, 373
filtering attributes 300
flip switch 258
form scripts
  for data, validating 20
  for enhancement 20
  for ribbon command 20
  for tasks, automating 20
form, in Dynamics CRM 2016 app
  look and feel, for mobile scenario 242, 244, 246, 248
  look and feel, for tablet scenario 242, 244, 246, 248

I

input mask 260
Interactive Service Hub
  about 58
  activities performed 70, 72
  Related tab 69
  requirements 59
  scenarios 73, 76, 78
  timeline tab 65, 68
  walkthrough 62

K

key components, business rule
  action 316
  conditions 316
  recommendation 316
  scope 315
  set visibility 316
Key Performance Indicators (KPIs) 15

keypress handler 218

L

lead response tracking scenario 107, 108, 109, 111, 113
linear gauge 260
linear slider 257

M

marketing list
  about 11, 84, 86
  campaign 12, 87
  cost 87
  creating 86
  dynamic marketing list 11, 86
  list type 87
  members 87
  quick campaign 87
  static marketing list 11, 86
  targeted at 87
Marketing module
  about 10, 83
  account 84
  campaign 84
  campaign activities 84
  campaign response 84
  contact 84
  contents 83
  lead 84
  lifecycle 10
  marketing list 84
  structure 85
message 299
metadata
  retrieving, with Web API 231, 234
Microsoft Dynamics CRM 2016
  about 7
  analytics 18
  campaigns 12
  campaigns, working 12
  client-side enhancements 20
  excel templates 18
  mobile enhancements 21
  overview 8
  quick campaigns 12

202, 206, 208, 209, 211, 213, 215
scope, business
  values 315
secondary entity 299
secure configuration 300
Service Hub
  configuration 60
service level agreements (SLAs) 15
service management
  examples 57
Service module
  about 13
  activities 14
  case 15
  contracts 16
  entities 57
  entitlements 15
  Knowledge Base 16
  lifecycle 14
  SLAs 15
solutions
  working with 360, 362, 363, 364, 365
stages, event pipeline execution 300
stages, plugin execution pipeline
  Main Operation 278
  Post-Operation 279
  Pre-Operation 278
  Pre-Validation 278
stages, sales process
  customer support 28
  demonstrate value 28
  lead generation 28
  qualify leads 28
  quote closing 28
star rating 262
static marketing list
  about 86
  members, adding 87
step name 300

T

tablet application
  requisites 240
tablet web browser
  combinations, supporting 241

support 241
template
  uploading, to Dynamics CRM 174
timeline control
  configuring 263, 266, 267, 269
timeline tab, Interactive Service Hub
  activities, filtering by date or type 66
  activities, searching 65

U

unsecure configuration 300

V

visual controls
  about 21
  arc knob 261
  autocomplete 261
  bullet graph 262
  calendar control 259
  corresponding field type 262
  flip switch 258
  in Dynamics CRM 2016 257
  input mask 260
  linear gauge 260
  linear slider 257
  multimedia control 261
  number input 260
  option set 257
  pen control 258
  pen control, configuring 270, 272, 274, 276
  radial knob 258
  scenario 263
  star rating 262
  supported modes 262
  timeline control, configuring 263, 266, 267, 269
  website preview 260

W

Web API
  about 225
  event handlers 229, 231
  need for 227, 229
  used, for authentication 225
  used, for retrieving metadata 231, 234
website preview 260